D1594809

Gift From

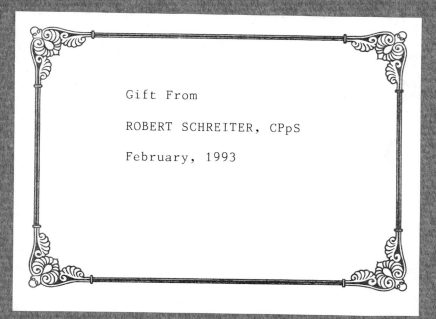

ROBERT SCHREITER, CPpS

February, 1993

Lifetime Beginner

WITHDRAWN
The Catholic
Theological Union
LIBRARY
Chicago, Ill.

LIF

TIME BEGINNER

AN AUTOBIOGRAPHY

by NIKKYO NIWANO

translated by Richard L. Gage

The Catholic
Theological Union
LIBRARY
Chicago, Ill.

KOSEI PUBLISHING CO. *Tokyo*

This book was originally published as two volumes, *Shoshin Isshō* and *Niwano Nikkyō Jiden*. Layout of illustrations by Nobu Miyazaki. Typography and book design by Rebecca M. Davis. The text of this book is set in monotype Perpetua with hand-set Perpetua and Perpetua Titling for display.

First English Edition, 1978

Published by Kōsei Publishing Co., Kōsei Building, 7-1 Wada 2-chome, Suginami-ku, Tokyo 166. Copyright © 1975, 1976, 1978 by Kōsei Publishing Co.; all rights reserved. Printed in Japan.

Contents

1. Jūzaemon's Place

At the time of my birth there were forty-two households in our village, Suganuma, Nakauonuma District, Tōkamachi, in the mountains of Niigata Prefecture; at the present there are only six. My family were farmers. We had about eighty ares, or roughly two acres, of paddy land for rice; about fifty ares, around one and a quarter acres, of dry fields for other crops; and about three hectares, nearly seven and a half acres, of mountain forest. This was enough to feed us all, though it did not make us wealthy. Under the one roof of our house lived two families, fourteen people, in a family composition complicated enough to warrant a word of explanation. My father, Jūkichi, his father's second son, had been adopted by his own elder brother, Shōtarō, who was ten years his senior. Shōtarō disliked the backbreaking work of the fields but was skillful at many other kinds of endeavor. For instance, he was a good carpenter and plasterer. He could make wooden pails and buckets as well as a professional. My father, on the other hand, had a personality that suited him to the farmer's steady, hard labor. When my grandfather Jūtarō retired from work, he made my father the head of the house and the guardian of the family's traditional inheritance; but my grandfather ensured balance in the family by having his elder son, Shōtarō, adopt my father.

My uncle Shōtarō and his wife had three children. My mother and father had six. Our grandmother died before we were born, but grandfather was still in good health and lived in the same house with us.

The system, though complicated, worked well. My uncle brought in cash with his work as a carpenter and plasterer, and my father raised food in the fields. Emotional involvements might have created situations that could threaten the stability of the arrangement. But in fact, we all got along well together, with no serious disturbances. Our family life was bright and peaceful. Indeed, whenever any of our relatives had domestic troubles, they would point to us as a model of the way a household ought to live.

Sometimes there were minor conflicts among the women. I do not know how old I was at the time, but I woke in the middle of the night once to hear my mother and father talking. (Their bedding was spread next to mine.) My father was saying, "You shouldn't take it that way. It could cause trouble for everybody." From time to time, my mother made sounds indicating that she understood and agreed.

That incident was my first glimpse of the world of adults, a world very different from the one we knew as children. I recall that it was a shock at the time. It must have made a deep impression on me, for even now, many decades later, the memory is fresh.

But as a child, I forgot the fantasy of the night the moment I awakened the following morning. The liveliness and happiness of our household made the forgetting easy. There was never a time that any of us sat alone for a meal. Mealtimes were always noisy and enlivened by all kinds of conversation. When we left for school, we took turns carrying four lunch boxes—there always seemed to be four children of school age.

People who praise me say that I am straightforward and cheerful. Others say that I am gullible and easygoing to a fault. Both assessments are accurate. But I can add another: I do not like to quarrel or fight. Later I learned peace and harmony as Buddhist ideals, but they were a part of my emotional makeup from childhood. My personality is the product of the character of my family. I suppose I am gullible and easygoing. Be that as it may, I am deeply grateful that my childhood family-life instilled in me a love of peace and harmony. Such love is enough for me.

In my childhood, my grandfather had already retired from all work except some straw weaving. He loved to joke and was so cheerful and so kind that he was popular both in our village and in neighboring villages. And it was not only his good nature that accounted for his popularity. He had a certain amount of medical knowledge and skill that enabled him to give first aid and perform minor surgery on swellings or boils. There was no doctor in our village. Though it falls within the administrative jurisdiction of Tōkamachi, the village is located in the mountains, six kilometers from the town. Even today rabbits and badgers run through the neighboring fields. In such a place, people were grateful for my grandfather's medical skills.

All the houses in the village had famous local home remedies on hand. Whenever anyone had a stomachache or caught a cold, these medicaments were called into use and generally found effective. But when people had boils that proved difficult to treat or when they were stung by poisonous insects or bitten by vipers, they invariably came to my grandfather for treatment. I have heard that he usually did his work well. Many people came to him for moxa therapy, for which he enjoyed a high reputation. He did not accept money.

He obtained his medical knowledge while still a young man. At the time, there was an epidemic of dysentery and typhus in the Tōkamachi region. A field hospital was set up in our village, and nursing help was solicited from the local people. Since the diseases were dangerous, most people hesitated to undertake the task; but for some reason, my grandfather served as a nurse. While doing this work, he observed what the doctors did and learned the basics of medical treatment and surgery. The length of his service is uncertain; but it must have been fairly long, since he was accorded a certain respect.

Much of his medical lore was Chinese in origin. I recall seeing him compound medicines from herbs by means of a grinding wheel and a stone mortar. Rhinoceros horn rubbed against shark skin to make a powder was considered excellent for colds. I was given this medicine at the first sign of a fever. When midwives were unavailable, my grandfather even delivered babies. Medical laws were still not firmly established at that time; and since he accepted no payment, there was no question of trouble with the government.

His medical work gave my grandfather joy and a purpose in life. He was in the habit of saying that human beings must do something for the sake of others. If they do nothing but eat and sleep, they are no better than insects.

When I was four or five years old, I loved to play in the snow. I would stay outdoors until icicles formed on the hem of my coat and until my hands were purple and my fingers nearly paralyzed with cold. When I came indoors, grandfather scolded me for being foolish enough to nearly freeze. Then he would strip me naked and put me next to his own skin beneath the cotton-padded upper garment he wore. His naked flesh warmed my body. I later learned that this is the best way to prevent frostbite. But for me, as a child, it was only an indescribably pleasant experience. I would soon be toasty warm. Then I would slip my still chilled hands into his armpits. Grandfather would shout with shock at the cold of my hands, and this too brought me immense pleasure. As he warmed me with his own body, grandfather always said, "Shika [my former name was Shikazō], be a good boy. Don't cause anyone any trouble. And grow up to be a man who does good for others."

Only an innocent child, I had no idea what he meant. His words made no impression on me. I only thought to myself, "Granddaddy's started talking that way again." Now, when I remember them, my grandfather's words seem very important. A child soon forgets things like this. There is no reason to expect him to take seriously advice like "be a good boy" and "grow up to be a man who does good for others." Nonetheless, grandfather's words must have engraved themselves deeply enough on my subconscious to burst into life again more than twenty years later. When I accepted religious faith, I remembered those words and understood their meaning afresh. My strength is small, but I have resolved to serve people by teaching them the way of the Buddha. One of the things that inspired me to take this step was my experience of the warmth of my grandfather's body and the meaning of the words he often said to me.

In rural villages it is not unusual to find many families with the same name. Niwanos were plentiful in our village, and our house was known by my great-grandfather's name, Jūzaemon's place, to distinguish it from the houses of other Niwanos. My grandfather, Jūtarō, was skillful at settling disputes and troubles not only for us, but also for people from other families. Indeed, whenever anybody had a problem, the advice given would be, "Take it to Jūzaemon's place."

One of the strongest recollections I have of him in this connection involves a young bride who had run away from the home into which she had married. Since she had been introduced to the family of her groom by my grandfather, she went to him first. Sobbing, she said, "I just can't live with that family."

"There, there. It's all right," said grandfather gently. "If that's the way it is, you stay here as long as you like." Then he added, "But it would be disgraceful for a runaway bride like you to be seen walking around the village. No matter what happens, you stay in the house."

Morning, noon, and night, she was served her meals. She had no work to do. She was treated like an important guest. And after three or four days, she said, "I guess I'd better go back . . ."

My grandfather sat her down in front of him and gave her a good lecture. He told her that she had not gotten along well with her in-laws because she had not tried to adjust herself to their way of living and thinking. Thanks to my grandfather's splendid handling of the situation, the bride returned to her husband's family; and there was no further disagreement.

My grandfather was the go-between for twenty-eight marriages, and it was a great source of pride for him that they were all successful. People today would be very surprised at the way weddings were arranged in those days. The arranged marriage is not uncommon in Japan even today, but now the two people generally meet and get to know each other first. In the past, often no such meetings took place. The bride might see her groom for the very first time at the wedding ceremony, as the two of them drank sakè from ceremonial lacquer cups. To more modern minds, such a wedding might seem the height of callousness, but miraculously the couples were usually quite happy.

Grandfather had a special way of matchmaking. When someone came to him and said, "Anybody'll do; find a bride for our boy," he would accept. He knew practically everything about the people in our village and the neighboring villages. Thinking, "The father of this house is a sound, strict man; his daughters are likely to be well brought up," he would select a bride. But when people came and specified the kind of person they wanted for their son or daughter, he would refuse, saying that such a task was beyond his abilities. Later he would tell us, "People say they want this or that kind of bride, but who knows what is going to happen throughout life? In marriage one side adjusts and changes to agree with the other side."

This philosophy—reflected in this remark and in the advice he gave the runaway bride—was one of the great pillars of my grandfather's life.

Another major pillar of his life is found in this sentiment: "No matter what a person does to you, don't hate the person. If you must hate something, hate the wickedness of his act." As a child, I did not understand; but I have come to see that the wickedness is the thing that causes the person to act in a bad way.

Although he never talked about it himself, I have heard that my grandfather, too, was gullible and that he once lost a chance to advance in the world because someone deceived him. I know that, at a labor conscription in 1867, he did not get all of the money that was promised him as per diem allowance.

During the disturbances that preceded the Meiji Restoration of 1868, orders went out to each village to send one laborer to help drag cannons and transport ammunition and provisions for the government troops in their battle against rebellious dissidents. Farmers living in the remote rural areas completely isolated from the centers of political upheaval and change did not care which group won. But, learning that transport for the government forces would be dangerous work, they all attempted to avoid the duty. The government demanded one person from each village. If a village failed to comply, the village man in charge would be forced to undertake the responsibility himself.

One day, as my grandfather was buying sakè in the village store, he was accosted by the district head, who urged grandfather to work for the government forces. The headman said that, in addition to the per diem the government promised, the village would pay another per diem. He was, he said, much too busy himself to go. As I have said, grandfather was gullible; and in this case he was possibly influenced by the desire for money. In any event, he agreed to go.

He managed to return home safe and sound and received the money the government promised. But the village never gave him so much as a sen. He used to grumble: "I suppose the district head thinks I'm lucky to have made it home alive and to have collected from the government. But a promise is a promise."

My father used to tell him to stop talking about it and not to complain any more; but my grandfather always replied, "No, a promise is a promise." Though he was optimistic and openhearted, this one thing preyed on his mind; and he continued to talk about it the rest of his life. But he never spoke ill of the district head. That was an instance of his hating only the wicked act and not the person who perpetrated it.

Grandfather lived to be eighty-three years old. Shortly after attaining that age, he received two bottles of sakè and a large sakè cup from the emperor Taishō, who made gifts of that kind to subjects who passed the age of eighty. My grandfather was extremely happy; but not long afterward, like an ancient tree, he died.

My father can be described succinctly: he was steadfast. He went silently about his farming. I have heard that once, when I was a child, the family was in financial straits until my father cleared fresh land to expand our cultivable area. Then things became much more comfortable. He said very little; he was strict; and I never remember his spoiling or fussing over us children. But we knew we could rely on him. When I was old enough to help in the fields, he clearly explained to me the way to use a hoe and how to weed. There is a trick in handling a hoe at the right angle. At first, I would either dig too deep with the blade or hold the handle so that the blade merely skimmed uselessly across the surface of the ground. Gently my father said, "This is the way." And like a machine, he made successful stroke after stroke with the hoe.

It seems only yesterday that I stood surprised at and respectful of the skill and accuracy with which he pulled weeds, not breaking the roots, and deftly shook the dirt from the clumps. Giving me the hoe, then gripping it himself—his hands over mine—he showed me how I ought to go about my work. I can still feel the rough, strong skin of his hands.

This unostentatious farmer, my father, inherited two traits from my grandfather: skill in medical treatment and talent for peacemaking. Medicine he learned from observing my grandfather at work.

Father left each morning early for the fields and returned late. After he had finished his supper, there were usually people waiting for treatment. Showing no displeasure at all, he would give them moxa therapy. Not infrequently, he was stopped by patients on his way to work. Our fields were located on the middle reaches of some slopes and in valleys remote both from each other and from our house, which was on the farthest edge of the village. In order to reach the fields for work, father had to pass through the entire village, leaving himself open to requests for help from all the inhabitants. Sometimes we children would leave for the fields early. After we had been working for some time, if father still did not arrive, we would laugh, saying that probably he had been buttonholed by someone on the way and was doctoring again.

At harvest time, when we were always eager for any kind of help, the patients still did not hesitate to call on my father. If any of us complained that we were too busy to spare him, he would say, "In a family of six or seven, one person can always be spared to help others. If we do not help when we can, nothing in the world will go right." He talked little, but when he said something, it was to the point and had considerable weight.

When I was about to leave to work in Tokyo, he said something to me that laid the cornerstone for my later life: "Look for a place of work where the salary is low, the hours long, and the work heavy." The impression produced by my father's words was intensified by their very paucity.

My own eldest son, Kōichi (now called Nichikō), tells a story about my father. When I decided later in life to spend ten years in religious training away from my family, my wife and children went to my father's house in the country. On the fifteenth day of the New Year holiday that year, they were sitting around the open hearth of the main room in the farmhouse. My son put his foot into the ashes of the hearth several times. Suddenly my father seized the steel chopsticks used for handling charcoal in the fire, swung them up high, and shouted in a rage, "Do that again, and I'll break your leg."

The fifteenth was a day sacred to Seishi-bosatsu, the Bodhisattva Mahāsthāmaprāpta, and it is forbidden to put the feet in the hearth on that day. Kōichi knew this and was merely testing to see whether he could get away with breaking the rule. But he shrank in fear at the threatening look on the face of the grandfather who usually did everything he could to please the children. Though I smiled at the story, I understood exactly how my son felt because I recalled many similar experiences that I had had when a child.

The second of grandfather's characteristics inherited by my father was the art of making peace. Many of the households in our village were linked by marital ties. When troubles arose—no matter whether simple squabbles or more serious matters—in my father's time, too, people always said, "Take it to Jūzaemon's place." He always worked out a solution satisfactory to all parties. Frequently, he went to help, even without being summoned. He could not stand to see people in trouble and do nothing to aid them.

If, on the way to the field, he happened to see gravel or soil that had tumbled from the hillside into the road or a spot on the roadway shoulder that was crumbling, on his way home he invariably repaired the damage. He knew that in an area like ours, where snowfall was heavy, even a slight defect of that kind could cause snowslides in winter.

He was robust and was always kind and generous. He readily gave away whatever we had in abundance. And he would select the best vegetables for gifts, leaving the damaged and worm-eaten ones for us to eat. He was a good cook, and at all village parties he was in charge of the food. I realize that I ought not to praise my own father, but that is the kind of person he was.

My mother's name was Mii. She was from a farming family named Hosaka in the village of Mizusawa, in the same district as the village in which I was born. A tender, hard-working, ordinary Japanese farm wife, she was for me something entirely absolute. She trained us strictly but never seemed severe. Her affection and care for us were given completely unconditionally, as was our love for her. In a household of fourteen people, she was constantly burdened with an immense load of work.

One of her tasks was patching our clothes. The only time of the year when we wore kimono made of the same piece of cloth from top to bottom was at New Year and the Bon festival in the summer. When the area around the knees wore thin, a sleeve from an old garment—sleeves seemed to damage less easily—would be used to cover the hole or tear. There were people who did patching for money. For instance, an old widow in our village would ply her needle industriously all day long for food and a small amount of money. But my mother, who was handy with a needle herself, never hired anyone for help with the mending.

At night, when we were all in our beds, spread on the floor around the open hearth, I would peep out and see her sewing quietly in the light of a lamp. At such times, she reminded me of Kannon, the Bodhisattva Regarder of the Cries of the World; and I was able to fall asleep with a sense of complete security and peace.

In addition to ordinary housework and such tasks as patching clothes, mother did a variety of other kinds of work. For instance, weaving in the winter and cultivation of silkworms in the spring and summer left her almost no time for rest. My mother's weaving entailed the entire process of cloth preparation. She purchased flax, split it, spun it into thread, and bleached it to a brilliant white by spreading it on the snow in the sun. After the first snows of winter, from morning to night, we heard the clattering of her loom. In a winter she was able to weave three *tan* of cloth—one *tan,* about twelve yards, is enough cloth to make a kimono for an adult. She sold her cloth for from three to four yen a *tan*. In today's currency, those three or four yen are equivalent to fifty thousand yen, or about two hundred American dollars. For a large country family, such a cash income was extremely important.

Though that work was strenuous, it was light compared to the labor of raising silkworms, the busiest part of which coincides with the hectic days in spring when the rice seedlings must be transplanted from their seedbeds to the flooded paddies. At that season, the whole house was filled with baskets of silkworms. At all hours of the day and night, the women of the house had to feed those voracious creatures the mulberry leaves they require to grow. Mother, who was most skillful at this work, raised more silkworms than anyone else in the village.

But physically she was never very well. She often suffered from a bad stomach and would bind her waist with cord to ease the pain. In those days, we talked of a "bad stomach." Thinking back on her situation now, I feel certain that mother had a stomach ulcer that grew progressively worse. Every year, when the silkworm work slacked off, she took to her bed. When she was pregnant, she never gave in to her sickness. At such times, sheer nervous strength saw her through. But after the baby was born, she would be unable to rise from bed for a long time. For two or three years before her death, she could not eat what the rest of us ate but prepared plain rice-gruel for herself in a separate pot.

She was the mother who worked tirelessly and without personal enjoyment to save money to buy new sashes so that her six children could be dressed in something special for festivals and New Year. She was the mother who died at the early age of forty-three. She was, for us, the embodiment of Hibo Kannon, the Bodhisattva of Maternal Compassion.

In the remote mountains, at a time when transportation was poor, our diet was so simple that many young people today might be hard put to understand how we survived. The amount of rice we raised was usually insufficient for the needs of the family and was never large enough to allow us to sell any. To eke out the supply, rice was always cooked with a mixture of filler foods, like sweet potatoes, millet, mountain herbs, and *daikon* radish. In winter, chopped leafy vegetables were added to a kind of rice gruel called *okayu*. Only in June, at the height of the seedling-transplanting season, did we eat our fill of plain white rice. To supplement our staple, we had only bean-paste soup and pickles. Bean curd was a special treat seen only on holidays of great importance. Seafood was available only in May, when traveling peddlers brought sardines for sale.

When I was in the fourth or fifth grade in primary school, a peddler came to the door with his basket of sardines. Mother told him we did not need any, but I wanted the fish badly and pleaded with her to buy some. She did not listen to my pleas. Nor is that surprising, since to give each member of the family one fish, she would have had to buy fourteen. And that would have meant a considerable outlay for a country family with virtually no monetary income. Still, I could almost taste the delicious fish. Unable to contain myself, I darted around my mother, pulled her sleeves, and pushed her toward the peddler in the frantic hope that she would give in. To an extent, she did. Fortunately, there was no one else in the house at the time; and she bought one sardine, for me. I was in seventh heaven. Rushing to a hill behind our house, in a place where no one could see, I built a fire, roasted the fish, and consumed it. I thought it was the most delicious thing I had ever tasted.

When I had finished and was starting gaily on my way home, I suddenly felt strangely sad. It was an unpleasant emotion that I cannot describe. I dispelled it by breaking into a run.

That was all there was to it then. But ever since, though I seem to forget it for long stretches of time, I occasionally recall that feeling, always with a sharp pain. That briefly experienced emotion must have been an awakening for me—the first pangs of conscience.

2.
Things Learned Early

OUR SCHOOL was located on the shore of Ōike Pond, which, fed by mountain springs, was a wonderful spot for fishing and for swimming —my special interest. The faculty of the school consisted of the principal and one assistant teacher. The assistant taught one class, in which the first, second, and third grades were combined. The principal taught the other class, consisting of the fourth, fifth, and sixth grades.

I was tall, even as a small child. When I entered the first grade of primary school, I was already taller than all the second-grade pupils. I always stood in the back row when we lined up, but I was the leader in many activities. For example, I was always first in wrestling and races. Gradually, I came to be the class big shot. At first, I was only a little better than average in my studies, but I steadily improved; and by the fourth grade I was number two in the class.

Number one was my good friend Sōtarō Takahashi, who came from the village of Ōike. His family placed a great deal of emphasis on study, and his two older brothers before him had been scholastically on top and the leaders of their classes. My family was devoted solely to farming. The minute we children came home from school we had either to look after the younger children or to work in the fields, and we thought that was perfectly natural and never dreamed of studying at home. It seemed right that Sōtarō should be better at schoolwork than I. We were good friends, and I entertained not the slightest wish to compete with him for first place.

Ever since the fourth grade, Sōtarō had been class leader; then in the second term of the sixth grade, the class did a strange thing and elected me in his place. Sōtarō was a small, quiet boy. I suspect the other members of the class hoped it would be fun to see what a high-powered brat like me would do as class leader.

I was confused, but matters were much worse with Sōtarō. His whole family was upset. All the other boys in the family had been class leaders. Sōtarō's fall from the top position caused a storm in his household. The entire responsibility fell on him. Despondent over his predicament, Sōtarō became what today is called neurotic. I felt sorry and worried about my best friend. There was nothing I could do about the second term of that year. I served out my period as class leader. But at the beginning of the third term, I threatened each member of the class: "If you elect me class leader again, you may regret it."

In this way, we put things back on the old footing. Sōtarō was class leader, and I was number-two man. The experience I had of watching the effect of family pressure on Sōtarō has stood me in good stead with my own children. I have never forced them to strive for better grades than they can achieve through conscientious effort and have always been upset to hear of other people's punishing their children for the sake of school performance.

Later Sōtarō was adopted by the Konishi family, who owned a lumber company. He inherited the business and—under his own name, the Takahashi Lumber Company—made it prosper. After World War II, educational reforms called for the establishment of a system of six years in primary school, three years in middle school, and three years in high school. At that time, a middle school was built next to the old Ōike primary school. Sōtarō's company handled the contract and provided the lumber. I made a contribution, too, but I have heard that out of his own funds Sōtarō made up the money that was lacking to complete the building. Until his death, in 1975, he was a dedicated member of the Echigo Kawaguchi Chapter of the Niigata Branch of Risshō Kōsei-kai. Four of my classmates are still alive and in good health. When I have a chance to visit Suganuma, we get together and have a good time talking over old days.

As I have said, I was a high-powered brat; but I had very few fights. I was on good terms with all my classmates. And the only time fighting was called for was when I wanted to use my superior strength to prevent a young child's being bullied by an older one. I never hesitated in such instances, and on several occasions I was made to stand in the corner as punishment for fights of this kind. But we children always made up quickly after our squabbles. None of us held grudges.

At this point, I should pause to mention the two fights I have had since reaching adulthood. Neither was glorious.

Once when I was operating a pickles dealership, the wagon I was pulling through a street in the Nakano district of Tokyo collided with a night-soil wagon. The puller of that wagon charged into me, and I downed him at once with a judo *ōsoto-gari* technique.

The second fight occurred under more complicated circumstances. When I was in naval training in Maizuru in 1927, there were several judo experts in our class. Two of them, Shirō Abè and Shimazō Itō, were to become east-west fleet champions. Later, Abè and I were assigned to the same battleship, the Nagato. I was on the judo team, too, and whenever we were in port we would go to the local judo hall for training. Once when we were at Kure, four of us decided to get in some judo work. Abè and I from the Nagato and Shimazō Itō and one other man from another ship went ashore and traveled to the local training hall.

It turned out that Abè, who was a poor drinker, had been hitting the bottle that day. The minute we walked into the Kure training hall, he shouted, "What do you call that? Not a one of you knows anything about judo!"

In the hall at the time, about twenty men were seriously engaged in training. They did not respond well to Abè's remark. We were just four sailors in uniform. Among the twenty men in the room were a number of petty officers; and as might be expected, Abè's loud jeer rubbed them the wrong way. With shouts and threats, they charged us. But we were too much for them. Before long, the four of us had downed them to a man. Deciding that we had better not hang around long, we made tracks for the ships.

When we got there, Abè and I learned that word of the incident had preceded us. The senior petty officer called us to his cabin and raked us over the coals. We had been in the wrong, certainly. And, to make things worse, we had laid hands on our superiors. We were beginning to be very worried when, after he had said his fill, the senior petty officer told us to get out and go to bed.

It was with a deep sense of relief that I crawled into my hammock, only to be startled shortly thereafter by the senior petty officer, standing at my elbow with a bottle of sakè. "Drink it," he said and left. I rushed to Abè's hammock to see if anything similar had happened to him. He had a bottle too. We woke up all the other men in the cabin and had a party. I am not exactly proud of this story; but I must say that I recall the fight with a certain feeling of exhilaration and satisfaction, maybe because everything worked out all right in the end.

I always considered it part of daily life to look after younger children and to fight for them against older bullies if necessary. I often had to baby-sit with my younger brothers and sister. When farm work was heavy, in the summer, we had either to look after the small ones or to work in the fields. Working in the fields meant that we could not go to school at all. I was not an especially studious boy, but I genuinely disliked missing classes. I usually volunteered to look after the babies because I could strap them on my back and take them to school with me. In general, this system worked well. I did not mind wiping their noses, helping them in the toilet, or cleaning their bottoms when it had to be done. There was only one part of the duty that got me down. When the babies would start crying and no amount of coddling or tickling would make them stop, I felt like bursting into tears myself.

My experience with my little brothers and sister made me less susceptible to the repugnance most people feel about excrement. I recall, for instance, something that happened when I was in the first grade. One of our classmates dirtied his pants. The other children began to titter and whisper among themselves: "Something smells bad." The guilty boy stood in an awkward way and started sniveling. The teacher was not in the classroom at the time. All the others began to roar with laughter and to tease the boy, who was by then on the verge of a flood of tears. At that point, I went to the boy, pulled down his pants, and cleaned him thoroughly.

One year an epidemic of typhus struck our village. One house after another was affected. In those days, rural people knew very little about hygiene. Even after the patient had been removed to the nearby emergency hospital, the villagers would not go near the infected house. If they had to pass it, they would run, in spite of the health authorities' insistence that it was perfectly safe.

The typhus in that particular year infected someone in the house of a schoolmate, Sōkichi Ikeda. The person soon recovered, and the authorities gave the whole house a clean bill of health. One evening it turned out that the next day was the Ikeda family's turn to make a track to school by getting up early, putting on snowshoes, and walking back and forth to pack down the snow that had fallen the night before. But no one had told them of their responsibility, and no one would go to the house, out of fear of contagion. All the people I knew said how bold I was to go to the Ikeda house to carry the word. I thought they were silly for talking that way. After all, the patient had recovered; and the house was declared safe.

Our first-grade teacher, Miss Jitsu Ōta, was a tall, bright-eyed beauty who wore her hair in a Western style and was the subject of the love poems of all the boys in the village. She had studied very hard to become an assistant teacher and was so attractive and kind that we all considered it a great joy to be her pupils.

By the time I was in the upper classes, Miss Ōta had moved to my mother's village; and little Miss Shige Onozuka had taken her place in the first, second, and third grades. I did not have her for a teacher but I enjoyed joking with her because she would joke back. Though not as beautiful as Miss Ōta, she was very charming and kind. I teased her for being small, and she teased me for being tall. When I was in the sixth grade, she taught the first three grades during regular school hours and instructed the upper-grade girls in sewing until evening.

As the oldest group in school, we sixth-graders were responsible for locking up the building. Usually, however, I closed only the transom over the sewing-room door and left the rest to the girls. One day, after I put away the hooked pole used to lock the transom, I noticed that Miss Onozuka had gotten out of her seat for a moment to explain something to someone. Without her seeing it, I slipped a pincushion into the seat of her chair and quickly stepped out of the room. I heard her shout of pain as she sat down. And then the thrilling chase began. Miss Onozuka and all the girls in the class, armed with brooms and yardsticks, came dashing out after me. It was wonderful.

One day after I had finished school and Miss Onozuka had moved to Tōkamachi, some friends and I were carrying firewood to sell in her town. By then a young man, I was engaging in the sole occupation that was a source of additional cash income for us. Whenever it was necessary to pay taxes or whenever I wanted to buy a book that I thought I must have, we went to the mountains, gathered firewood, and took it to Tōkamachi to sell.

On this occasion, as we set our loads down at the edge of town, Miss Onozuka approached. "Well, it has been a long time, hasn't it? You certainly have grown."

Bashful and awkward, I scratched my head and bowed. She asked if I would sell her my load of wood. When I said yes, she requested that I carry it to her house for her. She started ahead of me, and I followed.

I was at the age when a young man begins to be self-conscious and aware of women. It made me shy to walk with her. Besides, I was afraid that she would start talking about the times I had teased and kidded her in school. All the long way to her house, which was located on the opposite side of town, I felt uneasy. But when we reached her house, she kindly invited me in. Seating me beside the hearth, she offered me tea and cakes and talked about our days together at school. "I suppose I remember you best because you were mischievous. A teacher always remembers the mischievous ones." She laughed, putting me at ease. After an enjoyable chat, I finished my tea and cakes, accepted the money for the firewood, and went home.

Twelve or thirteen years ago, after a lecture in my home village, I heard that an elderly lady named Shige Onozuka had come with another lady, named Yone Shigeno, and had asked to see me. Realizing that this must be our teacher and suspecting that she might have something important on her mind, I searched throughout the meeting room but without success. She had already gone. Later, I had people check and found out that she had been married, that her name was now Ishiguro, and that she was living in good health in the city of Niigata. Some time later she came to help me celebrate my sixtieth birthday. I met her two times after that. She always had something cheerful and bright to say: "You were so tall that I had to look up to you when you were a fifth-grader." I had hoped to see her again; but, sadly, on May 12, 1976, while the Japanese-language edition of this book was in proof, she died.

The third of the three teachers I want to mention is Denkichi Daikai, a warm, kind man and the principal of our school for twenty years. I tried to abide by everything he said and especially remember two of his admonitions: be kind to people; worship the gods and the buddhas. I took what he said about kindness a little too far in my eagerness to follow his advice, since I would go around constantly wondering if any one of my friends had not hurt himself, lost a book, or fallen into a stream so that I could show kindness in helping the person in trouble.

From the first time I heard it, I carried out his injunction to worship the gods and the buddhas. My family were members of the Sōtō Zen sect. Both my grandfather and my parents, who were pious, conducted devotionals morning and evening. Though we belonged to a Buddhist sect, we had—as do a great many Japanese families—a small Shinto shrine in the house.

After hearing the principal urge us to worship, for a while my brothers and sister bowed before the Shinto shrine and rang the bell of the Buddhist altar regularly, but they soon tired and gave it up. I was the only one who continued. Even when the others were dashing for school in the morning and it looked as if I might be late, I did not skip devotionals. If I had, I would have been uneasy the whole day.

People used to say that I was odd because I always bowed when passing Suwa Shrine (a tutelary shrine along our road to school) and the statues of Jizō (the Bodhisattva Kshitigarbha) and of the Koyasu Kannon (the painless-birth Kannon). At one place, our path was dangerous because it passed between a steep cliff and a deep cleft. In the spring, snowslides occurred at this point. For the sake of protection, the name of the buddha Dainichi Nyorai (the Tathāgata Mahāvairocana) had been carved on a natural stone there. I bowed reverently to that too in passing. As I reflect now, I see that these formal acts of reverence, even in childhood, helped stimulate natural reliance on the absolute that controls all human life and the force that seeks to guide human beings in the right way. In providing me with two important guides—kindness to others and reverence for the gods and buddhas—the simple country-school principal became my lifelong benefactor. The things he taught me continue to direct my daily life today.

No one in the world seems as interested in love affairs as journalists. Whenever I am interviewed by the press, someone invariably asks whether I had a childhood sweetheart in my village. I was no saint as a boy; but disappointingly for the journalists, I had nothing that could be called a love affair. Recently, however, something interesting turned up in connection with me and Yone Shigeno, whom I mentioned earlier.

She was a close relative and, until her marriage, was a Niwano. The same age as I, she was a clever girl with more spirit than many boys. From early childhood, we played together. Good at everything, she always gave me stiff competition in games. After finishing school she went to work in a weaving shop in the nearby city. When she returned to the village, she was a full-grown, attractive young lady. I took her with me to festivals and Bon festival dances. As usual, we were on the best terms; but we were relatives. I regarded her as a sister.

A few years ago, a reporter went to our village to gather information about me. He met Mrs. Shigeno and came back with this story. Once when Yone was a little girl, my grandfather, who was, as I have said, an amusing and interesting man, jokingly remarked to her, "You're tall. Just right for our Shika. How about marrying him?" She snapped back at my grandfather: "What do you mean. I don't like him!" Yone told the reporter that, at the time, she was secretly fond of me but that she was too embarrassed to come out in front of a group of people and say she would marry me. The journalist reported all this triumphantly, but I could not repress a laugh. Though I am afraid it will not satisfy the romantic, this is the tale of my first love.

Almost all my memories of childhood are pleasant. In early April, the snow that had covered the mountains and the fields throughout the winter began to melt. Here and there, the white blanket on the rice paddies broke. Rivulets appeared; and along embankments, purple willows put forth silvery buds. As wild parsley and chives sent out fresh greenery, the dark earth began to appear in places where sunlight was strongest and lasted longest. All winter the hard icy sheet on all the roads seemed permanently impermeable. In early April, we would make cuts in it; and within a week, the sun above and ground heat below would have removed it entirely.

By late April, the only snow that remained would be in the valleys and on shady parts of the slopes. The trees shot forth green buds, and a variety of bracken and wild herbs pushed through the earth crust. For country families in Japan, these herbs, eaten with soy sauce or with a delicious paste of soy sauce, sugar, and ground sesame seeds, are great delicacies looked forward to eagerly each spring. In bamboo groves, shoots rose slowly from the ground. For my brothers, sister, and me, going to the woods to gather baskets of these delicious shoots was work made fun.

Seed rice was planted in seedbeds in the beginning of May; and in the middle of June, each household entered the period of frantic activity and hard work associated with transplanting the seedlings to the paddies. At those times, all hands were needed. Children were given time off from school to help by pulling up seedlings and carrying them in baskets to the fields for planting. At eleven or twelve, I already considered such childish tasks beneath me and helped the neighbors level the paddies. A horse was used in this work. Since the job was not usually entrusted to children of less than fifteen or sixteen, I was very proud to be allowed to lead the horse around by the bridle.

We kept horses and cows on our farm. This meant that every morning we children had to cut fodder. In addition, my mother raised silkworms and eagerly awaited our return from school so that we could gather mulberry leaves to feed them. None of us considered our chores unpleasant or trying. They were no more than we expected to have to do. Besides, the work was light and fun; and I suspect it helped me to grow into a large, strong man.

Transplanting the rice seedlings was to an extent a community undertaking. Families that finished early went to help families who were running a little behind. Households who knew beforehand that they were short of labor would discuss the matter together and work out a mutual-assistance schedule. The work was hard, but when it ended there was a festival to celebrate. At that time, the farm families served all the delicious things that ordinarily were not part of our diet: lentil dumplings, broiled sardines and herring, and rice cookies and sweet beans cooked in leaves. We children played while we ate.

Of course, the harvest festivities in the autumn were even more elaborate. But winter, too, had many things to offer. We played on homemade skis and sleds. Sometimes we sat indoors around the warm glow of the hearth and listened to fairy stories. We toasted and ate glutinous rice cakes and amused ourselves as brothers and sisters will. The winters were long, but we were never bored. One of the pastimes that I remember with special fondness was the building of snow houses. Packing down snow firmly as we worked, we made a large, domed mound. Then we hollowed it out from the bottom of one side to make a cave about four meters wide. Our snow houses were so strong that several people could climb on top without crushing them. From the outside, they looked like small castles. We spread straw mats on the floors inside to make a sitting room. From home we brought bean husks to make fires to keep ourselves warm—almost unbelievably comfortable when there were a number of children inside. We heated sweet sakè and toasted rice cakes. Sometimes we played in our snow houses until as late as midnight. When I think back on these things, I realize how fortunate I was to have been raised in the country.

I graduated from our local school in March, 1919, at the age of twelve. The financial circumstances of our family would have permitted me to go on to a higher school, but geography would not. The school I would have attended was six kilometers away, at the foot of the mountain, in Tōkamachi. Of course, this distance is not significant in a warm climate; but it prohibits commuting to school in a region like ours, where snow covers the ground for six months of the year. People unaccustomed to life in such a climate are surprised to learn that we had a summer route to Tōkamachi and a winter one. The summer route was direct and permitted vehicular traffic. The winter one led over the mountain ridge and was usable only by pedestrians.

To go to a higher school, I would have had to live in the town.

And when I finished that school, to continue studying, I would have been forced to go as far as the city of Ojiya, about twenty kilometers north of Tōkamachi. Renting a room and eating in the town would have imposed too great a financial burden on our family. Only the richest farm families could go so far as that for the sake of education. Furthermore, everyone in our village entertained the firm conviction that nothing good would come of sending children to the city.

Nor was our village alone in this. All the people in the mountain villages in our district felt that graduation from our small local school was sufficient. It is not that I did not want to go on to a higher school. Later I learned that my father too would have liked to have sent me, but no one else in our family had been given such an advantage. It would have seemed strange for me alone to continue my education. For this reason, my father followed the accepted local custom.

I was not disappointed or dissatisfied. It was my wish to grow up as fast as possible so that I could go out to have a look at the wide world. In those days, there was no electricity in our village. Often, as I cleaned the chimneys of the kerosene lamps, I would gaze at the evening sky and dream of a world that was hidden from my eyes.

But dreams are dreams, and reality is reality. My family expected me to be a member of the working team—even if an inexperienced one—as soon as school was over. Immediately after graduation ceremonies, we went to the forests, where there was still snow on the ground, to gather firewood for the next winter. There was no more time for playing.

After the firewood gathering came communal road clearing. Then there was planting of rice seed, preparation of the paddies, transplanting of the seedlings, and repeated weedings. In between these tasks, we had to prepare the dry fields, fertilize, and plant, and fertilize again.

Though I was still not considered a full-grown man, I was to all intents and purposes a farmer. Once again, geography made life harder for us than for other people. What little flat land we had for cultivation had been wrested from the slopes by leveling and by building retaining walls. The land was all terraced. Going to work and coming home again meant constant climbing and descending of hills. Even transporting night soil for fertilizer was different in the mountains. On flat land, the buckets can be slung on carrying poles and transported two at a time. In the mountains, a person must strap a bucket to his back. He can hear the contents sloshing just behind his ears as he walks along.

I like to work, but sometimes I thought farming labor in our village was more than I could handle. Nevertheless, maybe because of my optimism or my carefree nature, I managed and never really felt that I had been made to suffer. It never entered my head to run away. But I still cherished the hope of someday having a chance to see the great world outside.

In my youth, it was a local custom to join a young-men's association at the age of fifteen, which was considered none too early for a boy to start working like a man. Our village young-men's group held its first meeting each year on February 11 (the holiday to celebrate the founding of the Japanese nation). The first part of the meeting was devoted to business. New members were introduced, and plans were made for the coming year. At the conclusion of this business, sakè—perhaps fifteen was too young for this aspect of adulthood—and good things to eat were brought out. Each person contributed his own share to the fare, and we spent the rest of the day in singing, dancing, and making merry.

When I was admitted to the association, though still a child, I felt like a grown man and made a resolution to do everything I undertook with all my strength and to perform without complaining even tasks that other people disliked.

About one year later, I made a silent vow to the gods and the buddhas never to lie. During the warm days of spring that year, I had been troubled by severe headaches. Miraculously, after I made the vow, the headaches ceased; and I have never had another.

Our young-men's association was especially close-knit because it consisted of people from the no more than two hundred households in the seven villages in our district. Almost all the members were members of the fire brigade as well. I was admitted into the fire brigade when I was sixteen.

Of course, the association did a great deal of productive and constructive work like road and snow clearance; but the part of its activities that I recall most vividly and with the greatest pleasure was the music and dancing for festivals.

Suganuma celebrated many festivals. We were able to do this because we worked hard and because we were somewhat better off than the other villages in the region. For instance, not a single household in Suganuma paid tribute rice to anyone, though there were several houses in other villages that paid such tribute to houses in Suganuma.

The tutelary deity of Suganuma, whose festival we celebrated on July 11, was enshrined at Suwa Shrine. In Tōkamachi, the same festival was celebrated on August 27. Both days were holidays for which we pounded steamed glutinous rice into a favorite treat called *mochi* and prepared *sekihan,* glutinous rice steamed with small red beans.

But on the fifteenth night of the eighth month according to the old Japanese lunar calendar, we celebrated a far more important festival—that of the Koyasu Kannon. One of the several manifestations of Kannon, the Bodhisattva Regarder of the Cries of the World, the Koyasu Kannon is believed to ease the pains of childbirth. For that festival the young people put on a full musical program, including dances calling for lion masks and the mask of the long-nosed goblin called a *tengu*. All the songs we used were traditional and different from the versions familiar to young people today. Since the village had no electricity, we performed our rustic dances by the light of candles and kerosene lamps.

I loved the bustle and color of festivals. While still a boy, I imitated the dances. When people told me that I seemed to have talent, I started taking it more seriously. At the age of sixteen, I was practicing regularly. Then I was included in a group in which all the other members were twenty-one or twenty-two. Our dancing group enjoyed a high reputation not only in Suganuma, but in neighboring villages as well. We were often invited to other places to perform.

At about the time that I started taking festival dancing seriously, I undertook to learn to play the Japanese wind instrument called the *shakuhachi*. Winters were long; and, though there was indoor work—making various articles of straw and weaving on the loom—

young boys wanted something entertaining to do. A group of four or five of us decided that it would be fun to learn to play the *shakuhachi*. In the evening, when work was finished, without a teacher and certainly without any idea of the several schools of performance, we sat around tooting merrily.

But the *shakuhachi* is a difficult instrument. It is said that attaining a modicum of skill requires three years. Among our group, I was by far the worst player and seemed to be unable to learn to do better. But this only stimulated me to try harder. At night, when everyone was asleep, I would cover my head with my quilt and practice. Before very long I was maybe a little bit better than average.

I continued to play the *shakuhachi* during my service in the navy and for a while after I moved to Tokyo. But ultimately I became so busy that I had to give it up. About ten years ago, when I was cleaning a closet in Myōkō Memorial Hall, I found three of my old *shakuhachi*. I played a few notes on one and made a fairly good sound. The people in the room expressed surprise at my hidden talent. I thought to myself, "If you'd let me dance for you, I'd really give you something to be surprised at." But I suppose my dancing days are over. Still, I enjoy watching Japanese folk dancing and love the liveliness and brilliance of festivals. They seem to make me young again.

A young man of sixteen or seventeen wants to see everything, do everything, and go everywhere. As a youth, I did most things that adults did in terms of both work and play. I read more than most of my friends. I remember being especially moved by some works on the West by Japanese writers. With the help of notes and commentaries, I studied the Chinese classics on my own. A few of the books I read were old ones borrowed from friends, but I bought most of them with money earned by selling firewood in Tōkamachi.

In terms of work, from the winter of my fifteenth year to the spring of my sixteenth year, I went to the home of my maternal grandparents to help them with the spinning of thread, an occupation they pursued in spare time left when their farm work was done. They produced the kind of strong flax and ramie threads required for the famous cloth known as Echigo *jōfu*, produced in our region and considered among the finest of its kind.

An especially important event in my fifteenth year was climbing Mount Hakkai. In our part of the country, there are many famous mountain peaks. Among them, Mount Hakkai has long been noted for its association with religious faith. At its peak (some seventeen hundred meters above sea level) is located Hakkai Shrine; and on its slopes are the eight ponds that give the mountain the name *hakkai,* literally, "eight seas." All the young men in our prefecture considered it an unwritten law that one must climb Mount Hakkai before the age of twenty. Every year someone from our young-men's association made the trip, and I was eager to go too.

It was the first time I had climbed a mountain worthy of the name. I went with a young man five years my senior. We left the village early in the morning and, after crossing thirty passes, at last arrived at the foot of Mount Hakkai. When my companion said, "Now you're going to be in for it," I thought trouble must be ahead. In spite of shortness of breath and abundant sweat, however, I made it. And when I stood on the top of the mountain, I experienced an indescribably exhilarating feeling. Before me lay the broad expanse of Echigo (as our area is called) and the misty blue Sea of Japan in the distance. As I took in this panorama, I felt courage welling up in my breast. I said to myself, "I can do it." I did not know precisely what it was that I could do, but I felt determined to do something on a big scale.

Even now I can recall an emotion apparently urging me to fly into the sky. It was good to be young. That kind of stirring in the blood occurs rarely in life.

Taking advantage of the slack time winter inevitably brings to farm life, many of the people in our village worked on construction projects to make money during the cold months. In my fifteenth year, I worked helping my grandparents with their spinning. In my sixteenth year, I decided to test myself by undertaking backbreaking work of a kind considered too much for a boy my age. The Tokyo Electric Power Company was building a hydroelectric generator station at the confluence of two rivers not far from our village, and it was to that project that I applied for work.

The task to which I was assigned required a two-man team. Gravel was heaped in large straw baskets. A basket was slung from a thick log. Each of the men put one end of the log on his shoulder, and the pair carried the gravel to the place where it was needed. My partner was an almost frighteningly powerful young man three or four years older than I.

This was heavier labor than anything I had known on the farm. To make matters worse, my shoulders swelled and turned red. Then the skin peeled from them, making carrying the log hellish torture. Of course, our wages were very good. An ordinary unskilled laborer in those times earned about one yen and seventy sen a day; we were earning four yen a day.

Still, no matter how good the wages and no matter how stubbornly I persisted, I could not go on long carrying a heavy load on a log resting on bleeding, skinless shoulders. Just as I was trying to keep up my courage while realizing that though yesterday had been bad today was likely to be worse, heaven sent help in the form of snow. For the first snow of the year, the snowfall was heavy. One of the men working in the hauling shop had to go home because the snow fences were not finished on his farm. The foreman, who seems to have been observing the way I worked, surprised me by assigning me to the man's place in the hauling plant. My new task, transporting gravel, sand, and cement in wheelbarrows, made no demands on my shoulders, though the pay was the same. From that time on, my work went well; and I safely completed one and a half months on the job. During that time, I slept in the workers' shack. Subtracting the cost of my food and the little spending money I required, I still had one hundred and fifty yen when I returned to the village.

The year was drawing to a close when I reached home and handed all the money to my father. Before they could be happy, my parents were overcome with surprise. Although the yen had already begun to depreciate, in those days one hundred and fifty yen was still equivalent to about five or six hundred thousand nowadays. And for a farming family with very little cash income, it was worth twice that much. In the same year, my elder brother had gone to work for the winter at a hydroelectric power project in Gifu Prefecture. When he came home, he brought with him a total of twenty yen. My earnings were unprecedented.

My father was pleased, of course. But my mother's happiness knew no bounds. First she could not stop crying. Then she put the money in the household Buddhist altar and knelt in front of it, hands together in prayer, for a long time. I could tell that, though she was happy about the money, she was happier that I had grown to be man enough to earn it.

After the New Year holidays, I went to my grandparents' spinning plant in Tōkamachi, where I worked till the spring.

3. Two Trips to Tokyo

WHEN I returned home in the spring, the usual round of work—gathering firewood, preparing the fields, planting the seedlings, transplanting, weeding the paddies—began; but my desire to go out to work in the wide, unknown world grew stronger. The idea behind the desire was certainly not unusual. In those days, people in Niigata Prefecture often left their villages to find work. In my case, I was merely approaching the age when the itch became strongest. One day, I came straight out with a request to my parents for permission to go.

My father thought a while. My brothers were growing up and could handle their share of the work. Since I was the second son, inevitably, I would have to begin a branch family and make my own way in the world while my elder brother carried our family line on. My father understood my feelings and agreed: "All right, how about going to Tokyo to find a job?"

As I said earlier, my mother was suffering from a steadily worsening stomach ulcer. Her spirits were low. She was worried and did not want me to leave her side. Still, instead of disapproving my request, she encouraged me and urged me to work hard and stay in good health.

Ordinarily, people in our part of the country went to other districts to make money after the harvest was in. But since there were plenty of hands to help at our house and since my being away would make little difference, I decided to leave on August 27. That happened to be the day when both Tōkamachi and our village celebrated the festival of the Suwa Shrine deity. From early morning, the booming of the drums floated on the air. Listening to it, I began to wonder whether leaving home was as it is described in the song: "When you leave Echigo, it's with tears in your eyes. . . ."

No. Not for me. My heart was filled with courage and with expectation of all the things that lay ahead. I was even impatient with my elder brother for the time he took making preparations to go with me as far as Tōkamachi.

No tears for me. But my mother wept. Over and over again, she begged me to take care of my health and to write at once when I reached the city. "Yes, yes," I answered shortly. But now I see that it was her love and concern that made her speak the way she did.

Parting with my brother and filling my lungs with the invigorating morning air, I started along the road down the Shinano River toward the town of Ojiya. The thought that I was on my way to Tokyo drove everything else from my mind. In those days, the convenient train lines that now connect Niigata with the capital did not exist. To make the trip, it was necessary to walk to Ojiya and then take a toylike, lightweight train to the small town of Raikōji, where it was possible to make connections with the Shin'etsu Main Line for Tokyo.

I recall that morning as vividly as if it were only yesterday. I had on a striped undershirt beneath an indigo single kimono tied at the waist with a short black cotton sash. At my hip hung a packet containing the rice-and-bean balls my mother had prepared for me as a special treat. Tucked inside the front of my kimono was a wallet with my travel expenses. The wallet was secured to my sash by means of a string. I had on a broad-brimmed straw hat and carried a cloth-wrapped bundle containing clothing.

By the mountain road, the distance to Ojiya was about thirty-one kilometers. Along the way, I sat down once by a river to eat the rice balls. But, without other rest, I steadily continued on. It took about five hours to cover the distance.

Changing at Raikōji to the train bound for the Ueno district of Tokyo, I soon became lost in the constantly changing scenery flashing by the window. The vast expanse of the Sea of Japan that burst on my sight as we passed Kashiwazaki completely enthralled me. But as might be expected, when the sun set, I became tired and fell asleep, though I woke at each station.

At about two o'clock in the morning, I became fully awake to find that the train had stopped at the famous mountain resort of Karuizawa. I stepped out on the platform and rinsed my mouth with cold water from a fountain. This cleared my head. When I returned to my seat and tried to fall asleep again, I found that my eyes were wide open. I attempted to force them to stay closed as the train pulled out of the station. But at that instant, the thought that I was actually on my way to Tokyo and anticipation of what I would do when I got there sobered me physically and mentally.

What kind of work should I find? Of course, the first thing to do was settle down; but after that, all was fog and darkness. I was prepared to do anything; I was convinced I could do whatever I had to. Still, Tokyo, a vast city where millions of people struggled in competition to stay alive, was a very different place from Suganuma or Tōkamachi in the remote mountains. I kept repeating silently that I would have to keep a firm grip on myself.

But to do that I would have to make sound guidance rules. When I had joined the village youth association, I had made and abided by three vows: never to lie; to work with all my strength; and to undertake tasks that others find disagreeable. But as I drew closer to the great, unknown city, I began to suspect that these vows alone were insufficient and that there must be something much more important. I racked my brain without definite results. Then, I dozed. As I drifted back and forth in the dim zone between waking and sleeping, the following three rules came into my head.

Never to struggle with others: no matter how severe my experiences, to hold the firm belief that they are all according to the wishes of the gods and buddhas.

To work steadily and hard no matter whether others are observing me.

No matter how unpleasant the task, to see it through once I have undertaken it.

I felt certain that if I abided faithfully by these six rules I would be able to make my way even in the rough and tumble of Tokyo life and that I would grow into a man and find recognition. I repeated these rules over and over. I made an indelible mental note of them. And after I had done so, I fell into a sound sleep.

It was six in the morning when I arrived at Ueno Station, one of the major terminals in Tokyo. After having been pushed and shoved by crowds of people at the ticket gate, I went to the lavatory and washed my face. Later I ate the remaining rice-and-bean balls in the waiting room and went outside. August 28, 1923. The street, lined with bustling shops, was already packed with people, streetcars, jinrikishas, automobiles, and trucks.

I proceeded to what was then called Nihombashi Ward (present-day Chūō Ward), where a distant relative lived and worked as a manufacturer of pastry shells for a filled confection called *monaka*. A friend of mine worked in the shop, and I had written ahead to say that I was coming. Everyone there greeted me warmly, urging me to stay on and work with them if I had no other place to go. But I was eager to work hard, not to live the sweet life of a pastry maker. Learning this, my friends took me to an old-fashioned employment office—in those days, there was no such thing as today's government Employment Stabilization Bureau. The old-style employment offices may have had their drawbacks, but they were convenient for both employer and employee. The office we visited, Fujiya by name, introduced me to a retail rice shop called Isetoyo, in nearby Hatchōbori. From that day, I was hired as a general, live-in errand boy. There were three other male employees at the shop. All of them had been there for some time, a sign that the boss was a good man to work for. The senior employee, from Saitama Prefecture, had been with Isetoyo for seven years. The second man, from Shizuoka Prefecture, had been there for four years; and the youngest, from Chiba Prefecture, for three years. All of this looked promising and determined me to work as hard as I could.

In comparison with work in the fields and at the dam-construction site, what I had to do at the rice shop was easy. The rice was polished by machine, and the only heavy work was lifting and stacking bales and pulling the delivery cart. In those days, rice was not a government-controlled commodity, as it was until quite recently. Trade was free; and when the market price was high, it was possible to make very good money selling rice. Although it is impossible to know for certain, I might have spent the rest of my life as a rice dealer, if something had not happened to change everything.

Though not yet seventeen, I was big, strong, and always willing and eager to carry out orders. The owner of the shop and the senior employees seemed to like me. Not far away from our shop was a busy thoroughfare where various stalls were set up each evening and where there were both motion pictures and theaters where comic storytellers entertained. But more exciting still, only about five hundred meters away was the Ginza, the most famous street in all Japan. The older men promised to take me there some day. But this was not to be.

From early in the morning, September 1, 1923, was hot, leaden, and somehow ominous. I recall that it was eleven fifty-eight in the morning when the master of the shop turned to us and said, "Let's break for lunch." Then the whole earth groaned.

The house trembled; dust from the crumbling clay of the walls billowed everywhere. Things fell from shelves, and bales of rice began rolling about. Without thinking, I dashed outdoors to see tiles tumbling from the roof and the shop sign whirling from the wall. I was certain that the world was coming to an end, but I was only experiencing the first stage of what has come to be known as the Great Kanto Earthquake of 1923.

When the initial tremor subsided, everyone dashed into the street, where the streetcar used to run. But it sat, derailed, across the road. Dangerous electrical cables dangled from overhead. Suddenly a fire broke out in nearby Kakigara-chō. Black smoke rose in great clouds; flames licked the buildings. On all sides, people were shouting and screaming. I must have made part of the din. After all, I was only a country hick come to the big city five days earlier. For a while, I was at a loss to know what to think or do. Then I remembered something my father had told me just before I left home. "In Tokyo, they are always having fires and big earthquakes. If you act surprised and shocked when these things happen, people will laugh and call you a country bumpkin. Just drink some water and calm down."

Returning to the house and crossing the now floorless kitchen, I went to the sink and drank several deep gulps of cold water and came to myself. "I've got to do something fast! This place will burn down too!"

Then I ran into the street, where I found the master of the shop wandering about aimlessly. "Come on. We've got to get out of here!" I urged as I pulled him by the arm. I began loading whatever valuable possessions I could find into two big carts. I wanted the others to help me, but they were nowhere to be seen. True to old-fashioned business morality, they were running here and there, trying to find out what had happened to the shop's good customers.

But as the master and I were tying things down on the carts, they came back, one by one. When we were all together—the master, his wife, daughter, and son; the four of us male employees; and one maid—I started pulling one of the big carts. We could not afford to waste a moment, because the streets were already jammed with other people, all frantically trying to get away. We decided to go to the open compound of the large temple Tsukiji Hongan-ji. Of course, not knowing the way, I could only pull and follow the directions the owner of the shop gave me. When we arrived in the vicinity of the temple, we saw billows of sooty smoke, brightened by crimson tongues of flame, rising from the great roof. "This is no good! Too dangerous! We'll have to go somewhere else."

We did not know where to go; but after wandering around, we finally came to rest in the plaza in front of the bridge Nijūbashi at the Imperial Palace, in the center of the city. I was deeply touched by my first sight of the palace, especially since it was unexpected and had occurred under such extraordinary circumstances.

As the sun set, an unbroken stream of refugees flowed into the plaza. Before long the huge space was packed with people and their luggage. All around the open park roared a sea of flame that dyed the sky scarlet.

Fear aroused by rumors of tidal waves and other disasters kept all of us awake that night. On the following morning, the senior employees went to Hatchōbori and returned with the report that the Isetoyo rice shop had burned to the ground. Even so, the master and some of his valuable property had been saved. I felt that my father's advice to me had produced impressive results. Of course, many causes had enabled us to save the family and some of their goods. But I was certain that my ability to think calmly because I followed my father's counsel was one of those causes. This proved the power of good advice and became an important part of my future.

For two days and two nights we were jostled and pushed about by the crowds in the palace plaza. We had no place to go until, on September 3, we all moved to a house in Kagurazaka, Ushigome, where the married younger sister of our boss lived. The house was small, but on the second floor there was room for the four of us men.

Soon we became concerned about being a burden to the shop master. Although a part of his valuables had been salvaged, he had paid out most of his cash to wholesale dealers on the night before the earthquake. It was no time to go collecting money from customers who had in all likelihood suffered great losses. As we lay talking, we discussed the issue. The oldest of our group, who was twenty-six at the time, suggested that we run away during the night. The other two agreed and told me that I should follow suit. But I objected: "We haven't done anything bad. We have nothing to run away from. If we want time off, we ought to go straight to the boss tomorrow and ask for it."

I slept closest to the wall; there was no reason that the three senior employees could not have sneaked away in the night without my knowledge. But they did not. On the following morning, when we heard signs that the boss was awake and up, I suggested that the oldest tell the shop master what we proposed. But he refused: "It would look as if we were leaving him in the lurch."

I tried to convince him that we were asking to be allowed to leave, not for ourselves, but because we did not want to continue being a burden. Still, he and the other two could not work up the courage; and it fell on me, the junior and errand boy, to act as the employees' representative.

Downstairs, I knelt in front of the boss, as is the custom in Japan, put my hands on the floor in front of me in sign of respect, and said, "We have discussed this, and we think that we are a burden to you, especially now, since you are forced to live with relatives. We would like you to let us go. When you are on your feet and in business again, please get in touch with us. We'll come back at once."

There were tears in the eyes of this good man as he replied, "Actually, I've wanted to ask you to do this, but I paid everything to the wholesalers and don't have any money to give you. I couldn't bring myself to ask you to go without offering you something. But when I recover from this, I'll write to you. I hope you'll all come back."

From the small amount of money left in his wallet, he gave us each two and a half yen. "I know this isn't much. But believe me, it is the best I can do now. Maybe you can use it to buy something sturdy to wear on your feet for your long walk home."

Receiving a little dry bread in place of the usual box lunch, we all bade our master and his family farewell and went out into the destroyed city.

I never heard from the owner of the Isetoyo rice shop again. Someone investigated for me after World War II and learned that he and his family rebuilt the shop on the old site. Both the husband and wife died during the war, and the son perished on the battlefield. Their daughter married and moved to Setagaya Ward in Tokyo. Though I should like to know more, this was the most detailed information I was able to obtain.

Two and a half yen. Even under ordinary circumstances in a time of cheap prices, that was not enough to pay my expenses home. But in order to enable victims of the earthquake to escape from the city and return to their hometowns, train travel had been made free temporarily. In addition, I still had all the money given me as a parting present when I left home. As far as funds were concerned, I was all right.

Because Ueno Station had burned, train service to my part of the country had recently been initiated from the next station on the line, Nippori. I proceeded there and got into a long line of people waiting to board. I got on the train late at night. It was the evening of the fifth of September before I returned, exhausted, to our village.

Having heard that hundreds of thousands of people had been killed and wounded in Tokyo during the disaster, my whole family was worried. My father went to the temple Daikei-in, where he learned from the oracle that no matter what might befall other young people from our village I was absolutely safe. Most of the members of our family are innately optimistic. My father believed the oracle and was calmed, but not my mother. "Why did we send him to Tokyo to die? If we had kept him here until the harvest, he would not have been in the city when the earthquake struck." She seemed to have been convinced that I was already dead.

Then I walked in the door. Seeing me safe and sound, my mother immediately burst into tears. All the family and the neighbors rushed to see me and to rejoice that I was safe. But I was embarrassed that my first big trip to the city had lasted less than ten days.

My family warned me not to tell disturbing stories about the disaster. Soon I became very busy calming villagers who inquired about relatives and friends still in Tokyo. I told them to be calm and patient and to wait. In a few days, their relatives would certainly either come home or send word. I was always relieved when my predictions proved accurate.

I had not been home long when I began talking about going away again to find work. But my parents dissuaded me. They insisted that I should not hurry to leave in such a bad year and that I ought to help with the harvest and then spend the winter working in the spinning mill in Tōkamachi, as I had done before.

When winter had passed, I learned that the rapid reconstruction taking place in Tokyo offered all the work young country people could want. My blood boiled to be off again. But the speedy worsening of my mother's physical condition prevented my going away. My elder brother had gone to Korea as a soldier, which meant that my father and I had our hands full in the fields. In the daytime, my sister-in-law looked after mother. My father and I took her place at night. But none of our efforts to bring her relief had any effect; my mother died on June 22, 1924, at the age of forty-three. I was in the paddies transplanting rice seedlings and was not at her side at the last.

Though, like the rest of our family, usually given to looking on the bright side of things, I found that my mother's death made the world a dreary place. I was angry that our remote mountain village could not call on the medical assistance that might have saved her life if it had come in time. Even today, when I think of the way she worked all her life without ever having known the meaning of true enjoyment, I cannot restrain my tears.

In the country in the past, old people looked forward to a peaceful life in their late years. They could sun themselves on the verandas of the farmhouses and perhaps do a little mending. Grandmothers and grandfathers could sometimes take trips to hot-spring resorts for curative treatments. I was unable to provide even these modest pleasures for my mother. My only consolation was the knowledge that I had controlled my desire to go to Tokyo that spring. If I had left her alone at that time, I should have suffered profound regrets for the rest of my life.

The following year, with my father's permission, I returned to Tokyo to find work. The downtown areas had been rebuilt, but much remained to be done. Hearing that the outlying districts would probably develop faster than the heart of the city, I decided to try to find a job in the western suburbs. With an introduction from an acquaintance, I went to a lumber dealer called Katsumata, located in the Nakano district behind what had once been the Nakano Communications Battalion. Unfortunately, the owner of the company said he could not use me, as a new man had been hired only the day before. Seeing that I was disappointed, the neighboring charcoal dealer suggested that I try the gardener's establishment near Kitano Shrine in Nakano Tenjin-chō. He said gardeners could always use extra hands.

Arriving at the gardener's, which was called Uegin, I saw that the company operated on a large scale. They employed twenty men who lived out. Since I had no place to stay, I requested that I be employed on a live-in basis. In those days, a gardener earned two and a half yen a day. The company boss took twenty sen, leaving the worker with a daily wage of two yen and thirty sen. As a rank beginner, I received only two yen and ten sen. But I was not concerned about the wages.

When I left our village the second time, my father advised me to look for a job where the work was backbreaking, the hours long, and the pay low. His theory was that, working under such conditions, I would have neither the time nor the money to go wrong. I followed his counsel and worked as hard as I could. Before long, the boss of the gardening company was paying me a full wage.

At about this time, something happened that, though I soon forgot it, was to be of great significance in connection with my later life. On the night of December 8, a day associated with the buddha Yakushi Nyorai, I visited Arai Yakushi temple in Nakano. As happens on festival days, the temple grounds were crowded with people eating snacks and buying trinkets at the many stalls put up at such times.

As I strolled about looking at the things for sale, I noticed a group of people intently listening to someone. I walked in their direction to see what was happening.

Approaching the group, I saw that they were listening to a man from the Takashima Ekidan fortunetelling society, who was eloquently discoursing on the futures of some of the members of his audience. It sounded interesting, and I stood in the back of the circle, listening. Suddenly, he pointed to me and called out, "You there, the tall guy in the back. Come here a minute."

Shyly I did as he asked. For a while he examined me and my hands. Then he said, "You show good signs. You're a second son, aren't you? You must be. But you have the kind of characteristics that first sons usually have. I'm sure your brothers and sisters will put a lot of faith and trust in you. Judging from your palm [he raised my hand so that the others could see], I'd say you're unable to hold on to money. See, when you bring your fingers together, there's still space between them.

"Now, about the future. If you become a religious leader, you'll be a big success. But things are not going to be easy. When you're thirty-two or -three, you're going to hit bottom. But, if you don't give in, by the time that you're thirty-seven or -eight, you'll have decided what you want for the future. And your life will have settled down. You'll be at the height of your fortunes when you're forty-five or -six. If you make it safely through that period, you'll be on the highway to great services for society. How's that. Do you see what I mean?"

I thought to myself, "Fortunetelling charlatan, running off at the mouth! What's he talking about?" and forgot the whole thing.

Today, I can only stand in wonder at the accuracy of his predictions. Or perhaps it was not that they were accurate, but that, without my being consciously aware of it, they took deep root in my mind and inspired me to want to become a man of religion. Of course, whether I have been a success or not may remain to be seen until I am in my coffin.

As long as I am on the subject, I might mention a prediction made to me some while later. When I was almost nineteen and the time to take a physical examination for induction into the military was approaching, Matsue Niwano, a cousin, and I made a trip to Yahiko

Shrine, near the city of Niigata, and then went on to consult a shaman living in a nearby temple. It was customary for the people of Suganuma to consult this man in time of sickness, calamity, or other serious trouble. Both Matsue and I asked him to tell our fortunes. In a sympathetic voice, he said to my cousin, "No matter how you work, you will not escape hardships." To me he said, "As a man of faith, you will establish a school of religion." The shaman was a believer in the Hokke, or Lotus, sect of Buddhism.

Now I must return to my early days as a worker in the big city. Until the end of December, gardeners in Japan are frantically busy. But work drops sharply after the New Year holiday and throughout the month of January. About one hundred meters away from the gardener's where I worked, a man named Yoshitarō Ishihara, the son of my boss's wife, operated a charcoal shop. He had observed me and learned that I was a hard worker. One day he approached me. "There's no work in gardening in January and February, and you'll never get ahead. Why don't you come to my place and learn the charcoal business?"

I had been sitting around idle for days, and this sounded like a good idea. Explaining the situation to the owner of the Uegin, I got his permission and went to work at the Ishihara charcoal shop.

Mr. Ishihara had the reputation of being such an energetic worker that none of his employees could keep up with him. But acting on my policy of backbreaking work at low wages, I outdid even him. In the evening when he would be ready to stop, I would insist that we go on a little longer. Soon he came to put such trust in me that he asked my opinion on everything from stock purchase to loans and treated me very much as if I were his own brother.

Working hard and long was a principle with me. I did not rest even on holidays. I realize that people today might consider my attitude odd. Nor do I recommend that it be followed eagerly by everyone. Nonetheless, I was gaining in an important respect.

Occasionally friends who had come to Tokyo to work visited me and told me of their high wages—thirty or forty yen a month—and their two days off monthly. I had just one day off and was earning only fifteen yen. Still, whenever I began to think that it was unfair, I at once dispelled my doubts by recalling my father's parting injunction. The people who received high wages were only exchanging their labor for money and were always no more than employees. Later in life, I hired one of my friends who had been among this well-paid group and learned that he was sadly lacking in positive, aggressive spirit. He was, in other words, no more than an ordinary hired man. In my case, I received little monetary reward; but my employer took me into his confidence with the result that, in a short time, I was able to learn a great deal about managing a business. The value of this experience cannot be measured in terms of the difference between fifteen and forty yen.

Mr. Ishihara was a member of a society called the Organization of National Faith and Virtue (Wagakuni Shintoku-sha), which delved into the study of fortunetelling on the basis of the *rokuyō* and *shichishin* systems, both borrowed from ancient China. The *rokuyō* system is based on the idea of a six-day cycle that begins on the first day of the new year, according to the old lunar calendar, and continues unbroken throughout the year. Each of the days in the cycle is considered auspicious or inauspicious for various activities. The *shichishin* are seven deities believed to control all human actions. According to the beliefs of the organization, everything has a proper location and a proper time and direction for movement. If these places, directions, and times are not observed, the deities will be angry and will punish offenders. Rules governing these things extend to all aspects of life; consequently, one must be always on guard. For example, a man who buys a water ladle on a day that, in the cycle, is designated *Tomobiki* will keep a mistress. If this is true, then conversely, a person who wants to keep a mistress must purchase a water ladle on the day designated *Tomobiki*.

Because he was firmly convinced of the validity of the system, Mr. Ishihara was in the habit of writing down the measurements of all the things he purchased—even things as apparently trivial as a teacup—and making written application to the deities for permission to use them. But since he did not like to write, he entrusted the preparation of the applications to me. This was a heavy duty. The applications were important: without them, Mr. Ishihara would be unable to use anything. To enable me to perform the task, it became necessary to have me registered as an associate member of the Organization of National Faith and Virtue.

According to an old tradition, the end of winter and the beginning of spring are marked by a holiday called *Setsubun*. It was at this time that preparations for a new year were made. And in Mr. Ishihara's faith, this meant petitioning the deities for fresh permission to use everything in the house. For ten days before the holiday, I was kept constantly busy writing down definitions and dimensions of all of his possessions. "Request permission to use for one year a paulownia chest, so high, so wide, so deep, located so far from the end of the west wall in a six-tatami-mat room facing north. . . ." And so on. About half a sheet of paper was required for each application. Bound together, all of them made a ponderous tome. When everything was written down, the book was taken to the headquarters of the Organization of National Faith and Virtue, located in Ōkubo, where a seal was stamped on it, signifying permission granted by the deities. After this was accomplished, even if mistakes should be made in the use of the various objects, the deities would not take offense.

All this seemed ridiculous to me. I was willing to accept the possibility of misfortune following violations of rules about the proper uses and locations of things. But I considered it absurd to believe that the rules could be nullified by a seal on some applications to the headquarters of an organization.

In my task of writing the applications, without making a conscious effort, I soon memorized all the rules and, with natural curiosity, decided to try them out. For instance, once when making a delivery for the shop, I talked with a customer who said that his son had moved from home in the hope of curing a case of tuberculosis that he had recently contracted. I then asked if, in such and such a year, the family had moved a toilet or garbage bin in a westward direction. "Why, yes. We did, as a matter of fact," was the reply. I had remembered the rule that moving a dirty thing to the west in the year with the cyclic designation of *Butsumetsu* is supposed to bring about illness of the lungs.

To my surprise and to that of the people I talked with, I was right in about eighty-five percent of all cases. I did not believe in the teachings of the organization and attributed no spiritual abilities to myself; all the same, I was correct on many occasions. Why? I had a feeling that it would be wrong to brand all these rules categorically as nonsense. But this does not mean that I suddenly began demonstrating interest in religious faith or the laws of heaven and earth. What I was doing represented no more than curiosity and mild playing of the kind young men engage in when they offer to read a young lady's palm.

Now that I look back on it, this experience was not vain. Even the foolish things of the world often have serious value.

4. No Regrets

In spite of his enthusiasm and hard work, Mr. Ishihara was capricious. When May came, I went home to help with the planting. This was all right with my employer, since the charcoal business was slack in the spring and summer. But while I was gone, giving excessive credit transactions as the reason, Mr. Ishihara sold the charcoal business and set himself up in the pickles trade, with which he had no previous experience. On my return to Tokyo in September, I found Mr. Shōji Sugiyama in possession of the charcoal shop. He had purchased the capital investment, stock, and equipment plus the custom; but as of yet, he was unknown.

For this reason, I stayed on and helped for a while. By the spring, Mr. Sugiyama was well enough known among the customers to handle things himself. I returned to the village to work during the planting and then came back to assist in the charcoal business in the autumn and winter. I alternated this way for two years, occasionally helping Mr. Ishihara with his pickles trade.

On December 1, 1926, I passed the physical examination for entry into the navy and went to the Maizuru Training Corps of the Yokosuka Naval Station. Training was conducted at Maizuru because facilities at Yokosuka had been burned in the Great Kanto Earthquake of 1923.

In those days, many people volunteered for the navy—more than for the army. Volunteers and conscripts alike underwent six months' basic training and then received the rank of seaman fourth class, a rank that was later abolished to conform with the army system of grades. Our divisional commander was Lieutenant Kiyoshi Tomonari, an intelligent and warmhearted man. Our trainer was Petty

Officer Second Class Kōsaku Kikuchi. Both of them were very good to me.

When our group was assembled one morning shortly after I had been drafted, Kikuchi asked me whether it was true that I had gone no further than primary school. I said yes. Nodding and saying only, "I see," he dropped the subject. On the following morning, he asked if I were sure that I had gone no further than primary school. When I said yes again, he replied, "I see."

This kind of questioning continued for a week. At first, I had thought nothing of it. Then I began to wonder if he was trying to embarrass me in front of all the others. But at the end of the week, he said, "Niwano, you are now group leader. I want you to do a good job."

Possibly I let go because of the emotions I had been suppressing for a week. Suddenly I shouted, "No, I can't do it!"

In the old Japanese military, talking back to a superior was a serious affair. Disobeying an order was counted among the blackest of crimes and was accompanied by one of two punishments: a severe beating or a trip to the guardhouse. I knew that, but I could not help myself. Why did he suddenly tell me to be group leader after having embarrassed me in front of the entire group for a full week. For an instant, I had the idea that he was planning some new shame for me.

"What do you mean you can't do it?"

"I just can't!"

Although he looked exasperated, he said nothing more. Later I was called before the division commander. Lieutenant Tomonari asked me, "Why have you refused to serve as group leader?"

"I just can't do it," I answered.

"Why?" he barked. Even the lieutenant was beginning to run out of patience with my stubbornness. "This could get you into serious trouble, you know!" When, after a moment, his usual warmth and calm returned, he went on, "Niwano, you must have some reason. Tell me about it."

I told him frankly what was on my mind, and he laughed.

"So that's it. Well, you'll have to forgive us. The truth is that your record's been so good since you came here that we couldn't believe you had no more than a primary-school education. We just wanted to make sure. Some guys think the others will tease them if they've been to higher schools, so they hide their educations. You see what I mean? Now, how about accepting the job of group leader?"

I surrendered unconditionally and gladly accepted the job.

Everyone in our group except a man named Nobuyoshi Ōno and I had gone to some higher school. As group leader, I could not afford to be slack or I would call down real disgrace on my head. The first thing I resolved to do was to assume all the hardest tasks myself.

It was winter. The cold winds from Siberia and the Sea of Japan pounded the shores of Maizuru. Snow fell often. To me, born in cold Niigata Prefecture, this was nothing. But the people in our group who came from warmer climates suffered. I did all their work for them. Sometimes I had to do the labor of two or three people.

Latrine-cleaning detail was assigned on a rotating basis. We were training-group number three. When our turn came, the stone trough of the urinal was stained dark. I had considered it filthy for a long time. With determination to remedy the situation, I took off my shoes and socks and, hopping into the urinal, started giving it a good scrubbing with a stiff brush. The other men in the group pitched in, and we got the stone so clean that the urinal looked like new.

When the adjutant came around on inspection, he suddenly called out, "What's happened to the urinal?"

"We cleaned it, sir," I replied.

"But the color's different!"

"Yes, sir. That's the real color of the stone."

With a laugh, the adjutant said, "Is that so? Well, group three doesn't have to clean the latrine for the next six months."

Of course, we were happy about this. Though we pitied groups one, two, and four, who continued to get latrine detail, we considered ourselves fortunate.

At first some of the men looked down on me for my lack of education and envied me. But they soon came to see that I meant well. The whole group cooperated, and our record was the best in the division. I kept myself very busy. I did more than my share of the work. As leader, I had to look after the needs of the group. I practiced judo regularly. And so as not to fall behind the people who had more schooling, I studied like a demon, even in my spare time. It was a hard grind, but somehow I made it.

The training course lasted six months, but there was an achievement examination at the three-month mark. With an average of eighty-five points in all subjects, group three had the highest score in the division. At graduation, I was number-one man in the division and earned special praise for excellence. I must admit that I was very glad.

Throughout school in our village, I had never exerted any effort to do better and was always number-two man in a class of fifteen people. But in basic training, after making an effort, I was both number one and ahead of others with better educations. But it was not first place itself that caused me the greatest pleasure; it was discovering how to develop my own potential and learning that I could do well if I tried. I wrote a letter to my father at once, and the news made him very happy.

After graduating from the Maizuru training course and receiving a promotion to the rank of seaman third class, I returned to the Yokosuka Naval Station, where I was assigned to the battleship Nagato. Launched in 1920, this ship was the pride of the Japanese navy. She was the largest battleship in the world at the time: 201 meters long and 29 meters broad, with a nominal displacement of 33,800 tons (she was said to have an actual displacement of 41,000 tons).

Although the job usually went to a seaman first class who had finished gunnery-training school, on assignment to the Nagato, I was made third gunner in the number two turret of the second gun crew. I imagine that my excellent grades in training school influenced the people making this selection.

Head of the second gun crew and chief gunner was Jin'ichi Kusaka. Under him was Chief Warrant Officer Hidetaka Nakano, who liked me and gave me much valuable guidance. The Nagato was armed with 8 40-centimeter guns, 20 14-centimeter secondary guns, and a total of 15 high-angle guns, machine guns, and torpedoes. The second turret, to which I had been assigned, housed one of the main guns; and my appointment caused a great deal of talk among my seniors.

When our superiors came to inspect the turret, they often left everyone else alone and concentrated on asking me questions, as if they were testing me. I am sure that it was curiosity and not maliciousness that made them do this, but it was hard on me. After all, it was the first time I had ever been assigned to a battleship. In a job that was of utmost importance in time of actual combat, I had to use my head to an extent much greater than in basic training.

Once again, I was studying like mad, borrowing and reading all the reference books I could get my hands on. Mathematics is more important than almost anything else in gunnery. Fortunately, I am good at mathematics. In primary school, my overall grades had never been as good as those of Sōtarō Takahashi, but I far outdid him in arithmetic. In fact, when I was in the fifth grade I used to help the leader of the sixth grade, who sat next to me, with his arithmetic.

But the mathematics needed in gunnery is far more complicated than arithmetic and involves algebra, geometry, and trigonometry. At first, I was nearly swamped. Though I did my best in class, it was all very difficult; I deeply regretted not having studied these subjects earlier. In school, I never really liked studying and aside from arithmetic, for which I had a natural talent, and subjects like calligraphy, for which no preparation is needed, I did not care much for schoolwork.

In the navy, however, I gradually mastered the basics of mathematics. Then, continuing to work hard, I slowly reached the stage where, as had been true in primary school, it was my favorite subject. What I learned at that time has often come in handy in later life. For instance, when we are designing and erecting buildings for Risshō Kōsei-kai, in bed in the morning, I work out some of the pertinent problems in my head. Once when we were working on a school that was to have a circular floor plan, I figured out that if the diameter of the circle was thirteen meters we could get four classrooms on a floor; but if the diameter was increased to seventeen meters, we would be able to get six. I later discussed the matter with the architect, who, surprised at my ability, agreed with me. I have even discovered mistakes in architectural blueprints. Once again, lying in bed in the morning and recalling a blueprint I had seen the day before, I made mental calculations about something that had struck me as odd. When I brought the point to the attention of the designer, he scratched his head and admitted his error.

Talking about nothing but studies and grades, I must give the impression that I was overly serious as a young man. Serious I certainly was, but not overly. For one thing, I kept up my judo. One of the great pleasures of coming into port was the chance to practice judo in a real training hall, or *dōjō*. It was a great treat to have a chance to pit our skills against—and try to get the best of—judo men from other ships and from the naval station. I have already described the mishap that resulted from our overeagerness in this kind of competition.

I started practicing judo when I came to Tokyo the second time and found a job at Mr. Ishihara's charcoal shop. I worked hard and had a certain amount of confidence about my job; but as a hick fresh from the sticks, I thought city people all knew more than I and were able to get around better and do more things. I was convinced that I was behind them in everything. I told myself that I was just as good as they because I worked hard, but mental assurance of this kind is not enough to eliminate a feeling of inferiority.

At about that time, I learned that there was a judo training hall nearby and decided to give training there a try. This decision gave me a chance to experience a good taste of a feeling of inferiority.

I was tall, but thin (weighing only fifty-five kilograms). I had inherited my mother's weak stomach, and the kind of work I did made my body tight and stiff. Time and time again in judo training younger and smaller people threw me. I began to wonder if there was any hope and on several occasions came very close to giving the whole thing up.

But I did not. I continued training every evening after work. It was physically exhausting, but I never missed a day. After a while, I stopped losing as shamefully as I had at first. And before long, I came to the conclusion that I was not totally worthless. From that stage, I developed self-confidence in other things and finally lost my feeling of being inferior to city people. It may seem that my way of overcoming the feeling was not the best. Since the problem was mental, it might be argued that I should have solved it in a mental way. This would appear to be the basic approach. But it is not always necessary to use only the basic approach. It is possible to develop the body first and the mind and spirit later, for in the final analysis, the body and the spirit are inseparable. The idea expressed in the words "the form determines the content" is the reason for the salutary effect of sports on mental development.

One of the sources of fun for us on the ship was amateur entertainment. I had become what could be called a judo athlete, but in that field I was only a seaman recruit. In the amateur entertainment field, however, I was an admiral. Whenever we had an evening of songs and dances, I would get excited. Someone would invariably drag me out to go through my repertory, which consisted of the dances I used to perform at shrine festivals at home plus some currently popular songs and dances. Each year, for the big autumn show, I was selected entertainment chairman. Working with some friends who were interested in the same kind of thing, I wrote and directed the skits and comic scenes that we used to fill out the program of songs and dances. Sometimes I even acted in the skits. If I do say so myself, I was the entertainment star of the ship.

A full naval review was scheduled to be held in Tokyo Bay in November, 1928, and the battle cruiser Haruna had been selected as the imperial flagship. In preparation for the review, outstanding seamen were selected from the rest of the fleet for service on the Haruna. I was one of fifteen selected for that duty from the crew of the Nagato. I felt very fortunate, but the news greatly upset Chief Warrant Officer Nakano. He said to me, "Niwano, as long as you're here, you're popular with everybody. You can lead an easy life with us. Now, I'm happy too that you've been given the honor of being chosen for duty on the flagship. But remember, in a new place of duty you're going to have to face some hardships. Why don't you just say no and stay here? How about it?"

He called me to his cabin a number of times to ask me the same thing. Each time he met me, he inquired whether I had decided to stay. Of course, it made me happy to know that he wanted me to remain behind that badly. But I was still young. And his affection and trust in me could not match the attraction of serving on the imperial flagship. I continued to request his approval for the transfer, and finally he granted it.

On the day of my departure from the Nagato, with my sea bag on my shoulder, I had just started to the gangplank when I met Chief

Warrant Officer Nakano. I saluted him and was about to bid him farewell when he said, "So you're really leaving!" There were tears in his eyes. There were tears in my eyes too when I replied, "Mr. Nakano, please don't hold this against me." Giving me a firm handshake, he replied, "I guess there's nothing I can do about it. Take care of yourself." All the way down the gangplank and throughout the trip on the ferry, I never stopped crying.

It has been forty-odd years since I saw those two fine men, Chief Warrant Officer Nakano and Lieutenant Tomonari. Even now, though the Imperial Navy no longer exists, their humanity and kindness are deeply fixed in my heart. Later I learned that both of them were killed in the fighting in Asia during World War II. I gave them posthumous Buddhist names and have held daily services in their memories. As if to demonstrate how miraculous are the connections among human beings, to my surprise, Tomonari's widow has become a member of the Chūō Branch of Risshō Kōsei-kai.

One of the greatest harvests from my military experience was the reinforcement of my philosophy of nonviolence. I applied this philosophy to everything I did in the navy. In those days corporal punishment was permitted in the Japanese navy. People thought they were lucky to get off with a slap in the face because they knew the effects of the so-called spirit-stick, which was about the size of a baseball bat. One blow with it knocked a man's wind out; a serious beating with it left him half-dead, half-alive. Corporal punishment was an everyday affair, but in my entire military career I never struck anyone subordinate to me.

Once, I was ordered to conduct a training course. Many of my twenty-three students were slow to learn or stupid. I was as patient as possible. I repeated lessons, called on as many illustrations and models as I could, and demonstrated how to do things; but I never struck anyone. On the other hand, when one of the new men trained by me made a small mistake, deck officers smacked me in the face and said that the trainees were ignorant because I would not beat sense into them. Secretly I was proud that I never resorted to violence and put up with the blows dealt to me in the place of twenty-three other men. I continued to persevere in my private policy of nonviolence.

Another important result of my military training was learning thrift, not only for myself, but for everyone concerned. The water, food, and fuel on a ship are limited and must be made to last until the next port. Waste is forbidden. Water rationing was especially strict. We were allowed approximately nine-tenths of a liter for washing, gargling, and tooth-brushing in the morning. All our laundry had to be done in very small amounts of water. Most of our clothing was white, and it is a wonder to me today that we were able to keep it white on such a meager water ration. From my navy days to the present, I have cherished the habit of wasting nothing.

In the navy, I became enlightened to the universal worth of human sentiment, even under conditions in which discipline and order have the last word. At all times and in all places, the beauty of sentiment is a treasure of the highest worth. I have already mentioned the relations between me and Lieutenant Tomonari and Chief Warrant Officer Nakano (my superiors on the Nagato) and the way our friendships cut across rank. Another important emotional experience for me was my relationship with the housemother at a dormitory where many sailors stayed when we were granted shore leave at Yokosuka.

On the Nagato there were about fifteen hundred men, all busy with strictly disciplined military training and duties. In their spare time, these men sewed, embroidered, and knitted; I was pretty good at knitting myself and made several stomach warmers and pairs of socks. This plain, monotonous way of life continued for dozens of days or even months. When we returned to land, it was to Yokosuka (our home port), Kure (in the west), or Sasebo (on Kyushu). Few of us lived close to any of these cities. Even when we were granted shore leave, we could not go to our homes. Customarily, a number of us would pool our funds and rent rooms in private homes. In these places there was always a housemother who was kind and who rushed out to greet us on our return, welcomed us, and immediately heated the bath. After three months or so on water rationing, to relax in a tub overflowing with pure, hot water, then to smack our lips over lovingly cooked food, and to lie carelessly about on the tatami floor talking at random gave us all the feeling of being at home.

Chiyomi Suzuki, the housemother at the place where I usually stayed in Yokosuka, was more than kind and considerate. There was something truly wonderful about her. She had graduated from a women's higher school in Fukushima Prefecture. After her marriage, she had come to live in Yokosuka, where she had taken a license as a midwife. When I first met her, she was thirty, tall, fair, and beautiful in an unmistakably intelligent way. Nor was her intelligence confined to her countenance: she read books, magazines, and newspapers constantly and explained much of the recent news to us. She was especially well-informed on political matters; thanks to talks with her, I always made one hundred on the current-events tests we were given in class on the ship.

Although, as I later learned, she was constantly worried and unhappy because she and her husband did not get along well, she never let us see her troubles and was always warm and cheerful. Many sailors were fond of her, and some who had already taken lodgings elsewhere would gather at our place. I brought several who finally joined us on a regular basis. I came to regard her place as more or less my own. As soon as I would come to this home away from home on leave, I would change clothes and begin such chores as cleaning the garden or preparing the bath. I played with her children and carved wooden spinning tops for them. I was proud of the way I could carve a top with nothing but a single knife and make the center absolutely true.

I had grown up always wanting an elder sister. My mother had died when I was still comparatively young. Chiyomi Suzuki filled both these roles for me. But she did more: she became a symbol of purity. I felt for her something that I might have felt for the Virgin Mary or Kannon, the Bodhisattva Regarder of the Cries of the World. For an emotional young man just slightly over twenty, this gave me a sense of fullness. The beauty of that feeling will never fade, but will remain to nourish and enrich my life. I believe myself extremely fortunate to have had two virtually holy women in my life: my teacher Miss Ōta, when I was in primary school, and Mrs. Suzuki, when I was a young sailor.

After I was married and had started a pickles business, Mrs. Suzuki visited us. We talked over old times late into the night while my wife and I made preparations for the next day. We were too poor at the time to own an extra set of bedding. My wife and Mrs. Suzuki slept in our only set, and I sat on the floor and nodded until dawn.

They were still asleep when I pulled the pickles wagon away for the day's work.

Immediately after the formation of Risshō Kōsei-kai, in March, 1938, I called on Mrs. Suzuki to tell her about it. I gave her a blue-bound copy of excerpts from the Lotus Sutra and said, "I want you to be the first person to have one of these." Overjoyed, she looked at me with a wondering expression as she thanked me.

For a long while, we lost contact with each other. Then, once when I visited the Ōfuna Branch of Risshō Kōsei-kai, I asked Mr. Itō, head of the branch, to look for her. He found the place in Yokosuka where she lived at the time. I immediately wrote to her, and she visited our home in Asagaya two or three times. She even spent the night with us. She died a few years ago, and I still feel her loss.

I was assigned as fourth gunner in the second turret of the cruiser and imperial flagship Haruna, which, though roughly the same size, had a displacement of about five thousand tons less than the Nagato. Her main guns were thirty-six centimeters in diameter. As soon as I reached my post, I saw that the words of warning given me by Chief Warrant Officer Nakano had been correct. I was a greenhorn, and the officers gave me a very hard time. I could only interpret this as retribution for my having refused to listen to good counsel.

I am a congenital optimist. I had experience in putting up with trying situations and was confident of my ability to do so again. Silently, I went about my work, doing not only my own tasks but also those that other people did not want to do. Gradually, the officers stopped harassing me, and my subordinates put their trust in me. Before too long, I was able to work in the same mood of good will that I had enjoyed on the Nagato.

Because the Haruna had just been put back on the line after refitting, I joined the crew just at the right moment to have a rare experience. In those days, cannon shells were very expensive—one shot cost about ¥100,000 in today's money. Consequently, each big cannon fired only nine live shots a year. Just after I boarded her, the Haruna fired the big guns for the first time since refitting—each gun firing all nine shells in one series.

At that time, Prince Takamatsu, a brother of the present

emperor, was serving as an ensign in the eighth division aboard the Haruna. Shirō Abè, a friend and a fellow judo trainee, was also in the eighth division, with whom my division shared quarters. It seems that the prince heard about me from Abè. At any rate, he often spoke to me, instructed me, and asked me questions. Rumors were all over the ship about his imminent marriage. But to us, he was always simply a gallant young officer.

Twenty-five years later, on September 8, 1953, I had an opportunity to meet the prince again. On an inspection of social work, he visited Kōsei Nursery School, in Suginami Ward, Tokyo. While he was resting in a conference room, I recalled the times we had shared on the Haruna.

"Yes, yes! Seaman First Class Niwano. So you're that Niwano!"

He was surprised at the coincidence, but immediately we began reminiscing. I suspect he remembered me because, unlike all the other officers and seamen on board the ship, who were awed by his imperial station, I talked freely and openly with the prince, always maintaining proper respect for an officer, of course.

In about 1965, I had a chance to meet another old friend from the navy. I had flown to Osaka when a Risshō Kōsei-kai member, bearing a card from the head of the Shizuoka Branch, called at the headquarters, announced himself as Shūtarō Mochizuki (his surname had been Unno), and asked for me. He said that reading the earlier version of my autobiography, *Travel to Infinity*, had awakened so many old memories that he felt he had to see me. When I returned, I was delighted to hear that he had called but sorry that I had missed him. I wrote him a letter saying so and expressing my hope that we could meet again soon.

The chance came on January 28, 1968, when I visited Shizuoka. We had not met in forty years, but I could still see in this man traces of the Seaman Third Class Unno I had known.

Of the twenty-three new men assigned simultaneously to the Nagato, Unno was put in the ammunition depot, and I in the gunnery division. Our places of work were different, but we shared much in daily life. For instance, in the mess hall, where such things as table assignments are very important, we both sat at number twenty-two. As new crew members we were responsible for sterilizing the eating utensils, carrying food, and washing up. I cannot say how many times in one year he and I used cleaning powder to scour the lavatory and laundry basins of our superiors.

But we were both surprised to learn that we had been together at the training camp at Maizuru and on the Haruna, as well. We had no chance to become acquainted at Maizuru because he was in the twenty-third division and I was in the twenty-fifth. Later, on the Haruna, he was in the third division and I in the second. The third division was quartered aft, and we were forward. On a ship with a crew of fifteen hundred people, it is completely possible that we could go a long time without meeting. Nonetheless, the relation that had connected our lives throughout military service and then later as members of the same religious organization and that had led to a reunion after forty years amazed us both.

The full review of the fleet held in November, 1928, was a sight none of us will ever forget. There were two hundred large and small craft in Tokyo Bay, all with full crews and all in the finest trim. The present emperor, who was still a young man then, came aboard the Haruna for the review. As the band played the Navy March and as the imperial salute boomed, the Haruna sailed smoothly past the ships waiting in review. Setting aside all thought of militarism and war, I still enjoy the recollection of that magnificent pageant, the likes of which will never be seen in Japan again.

In 1929, shortly after the full review, I took part in a cruise around the Japanese islands, in fleet training, and in coast-guard duties. Then, on November 30, of that same year, I completed my naval service and was discharged. I like the sea and ships and had cherished the hope of making a voyage to distant places. But neither my fondness for the sea nor my desire for travel was sufficient to tempt me to a lifetime in the navy. And it was with no regrets that I returned to life on dry land.

5.
The Time Was Not Wasted

WHEN I was in the navy, we got ten days of leave a year. We were divided into two groups, one of which took leave at the end of the year and the other of which took it during the New Year holiday. Everyone but me wanted to be in the latter group. I always helped at the Ishihara pickles shop during leave and was happy to trade with someone when I was in the New Year group because I preferred free time at the end of the year, the busiest season for the shop.

After my discharge, I went back to work with Mr. Ishihara; but times were bad, and the shop was not doing well. To help out, I suggested to Mr. Ishihara that I pull a wagon about selling pickles from door to door. Of course, the work was much more exhausting than waiting on customers in the shop, but it increased our income. Somehow, the shop held on.

But beyond the work and the money, there was something about pulling the wagon that gave me a pleasure difficult to experience except under such circumstances: the chance to meet all kinds of people. As I drew my heavy load along the streets, people that I gradually came to know called out to encourage me. Just hearing them made my heart lighter.

Almost every day I went to a government-housing settlement where the guards from Nakano Prison and their families lived. Almost all the wives were engaged in some kind of cottage industry during the day. At noon, they all came out of their doors with buckets to draw water from a communal well. I often helped them. On rainy days, when I saw a wife putting up an umbrella and about to go to the well, I would quickly take her bucket and do her chore for her. She would thank me, and I would go on to the next housewife. This made me feel good. Lunch hour was my busiest time, but the exchange of good will that I experienced in helping these people was more important than business. Spiritual connections developing from this kind of relationship can happen anywhere and any time and are a source of indescribable pleasure.

To catch the attention of customers, while pulling my wagon I sang the songs I had learned as a child in our village and a number of currently popular tunes. My voice was loud, and gradually people came to call me the Singing Pickles Man.

At that time, Motoyuki Naganuma, who is now the chief director of Risshō Kōsei-kai, was a young boy working in the sweet-potato shop of his aunt Mrs. Masa Naganuma. I have heard from Naganuma that his aunt was a fan of the Singing Pickles Man.

Another of my fans was the wife of a guard living in the government-housing settlement. This group of buildings was arranged in a long line. It would have been time-consuming and tiring to pull my wagon from one door to another the whole length of it. Instead, I parked the wagon about half the way down the settlement and started singing. Soon, in reply to my voice, the housewives would begin coming out of their houses, carrying bowls for the pickles they wanted to buy. The louder I sang, the more ladies and bowls appeared.

One day, the housewife who was a special fan of the Singing Pickles Man stopped me in the street, complimented me on my singing, and asked me to sing at the prison wall for the prisoners. She said she had talked the matter over with her husband, a guard, who thought it was a good idea. I promised to do as she asked. When the time came, I stood at the base of the wall and sang as many songs as I could remember for the prisoners working in the fields on the other side. I later learned that they heard my singing and that it made them happy.

The affairs of the pickles shop began looking up to the extent that Ishihara proposed we expand and run the business together as a partnership. Since there were not enough hands to do all the work, I wrote to my home village and asked them to send my cousin Sai, whose name was later changed to Naoko, to come to help. I knew her well because we had worked in the fields and played at festivals together since childhood. Of course, inviting her to help us in the shop was tacitly asking for her hand in marriage. Both families, all our relatives, and Sai herself were in agreement with the proposal.

On January 7, 1930, after she had been assisting us in the shop for a year, we were married in a modest ceremony. Ishihara was the go-between. Sai's elder brother and mine came to Tokyo from the country. My cousin Takashi, who is now chief administrator of Kōsei Hospital, attended, but that was all. In our part of the country, it is traditional to give the eldest son a splendid wedding, with feasting and drinking lasting for about three days. Second sons, no matter whether they work at home or elsewhere, are required by unwritten law to contribute to the upkeep of the family until they are twenty-five. After that, they are more or less told to find themselves wives and set up on their own as best they can. Though our ceremony included only the inner circle of the family, I splurged to buy a formal kimono complete with an outer coat (*haori*), decorated with our family crest, and the traditional skirtlike outer garment called a *hakama*. Interestingly enough, those clothes stood me in good stead later.

As newlyweds, we did not enjoy much of a honeymoon. From morning to night, we worked in the same shop without a real salary because of the joint nature of the business. We lived in a small rented apartment with little more than a chest made of apple crates. Our most cherished hope was to have a house to ourselves as soon as possible. To this end, we worked very hard.

But in November of the following year, our oldest daughter, Tomoko, was born; and it became impossible for my wife to work any longer. Ishihara rented a small house to us; but as time passed, with one thing and another, it became hard to keep the accounts straight. Ishihara suddenly said he wanted to leave. I was annoyed by his arbitrary departure, but there was nothing to do but go into business on my own. Still, I regret that we parted on bad terms.

I set up a pickles shop on Hongo Street in Nakano. Removing the tatami and floorboards from one room of an ordinary family house, I made an earthen-floored room, where I stored the pickles. In addition to our main stock—pickled scallions and red ginger, salted plums, and a variety pickle called *Fukujin-zuke*—we sold sweet boiled beans and flavored and cooked sea tangle, both great favorites in Japan. I had about ten wooden barrels for the scallions, which my wife trimmed and cleaned while I was out pulling the pickles wagon. When I came home in the evening, I flavored the scallions and made other preparations. My selling route covered most of northwestern Tokyo.

Our products were homemade, and I handled all the sales, which meant that we could sell at a low price. Furthermore, the customers liked our goods. With the steady income gained through pickles sales, we stabilized our way of life and slowly began to save a little.

I wanted to become the biggest and best pickles dealer in all Japan. When, as a sailor, I had helped in Ishihara's shop, at the end of the day, we would sit down, have a small bottle of sakè each, and talk or sing. Ishihara often said to me, "Niwano, I want you to become the biggest pickles dealer in the country. You can do it if you try." After I became independent and the business began going fairly well, I cherished that dream all the more ardently. I even visited the factory of a large pickles company that supplied the army and navy. But at just about that time, I reached a turning point in my life.

A month after her birth, our daughter was stricken with a severe inflammation of the inner ear. An operation became necessary. Naturally, my wife and I were shocked that our firstborn should have to have a hole cut in her skull. We were further worried about her recovery.

Near our house was a friendly, good man named Yamagata, who ran a small shop selling a popular snack food called *oden*. One day, as he and I were discussing my daughter, he said, "Look, Niwano, doctors are all right, but why not give Tengu-fudō a try? They really do some wonderful things. If you don't believe me, go and have a look for yourself."

Not far from us a woman living in a row house worshiped Fudō Myō-ō (Acala), a Buddhist deity believed to protect people from all evils. She practiced faith healing and Shugen-dō, a Buddhist system that rejects study and doctrines and advocates rigorous physical training and discipline, often in the wilds of the mountains. A kind of shaman, this devout woman, whose name was Umeno Tsunaki, chanted incantations and prayed in her own house. I decided to follow Yamagata's advice and called on her.

After praying in front of the deity and conducting a ritual purification, she suddenly blurted out to me, "They will remove the bandages on the twenty-eighth of next month." She then instructed me on several things in daily life that I would have to observe and ordered me to come to religious services every evening without fail. Following her instructions, I visited every evening, prayed before the deity, and listened to her incantations. Whether this had anything to do with it I cannot say, but my daughter's postoperative condition progressed well. The doctor was not worried. But still he did not remove the bandages.

As I continued going to Mrs. Tsunaki's, I developed interest in the Shugen-dō system. After all, it was amazing that an uneducated woman should be able to diagnose the sicknesses of all kinds of different people and then to cure them. Though I could not explain it, I had seen proof that she could do these things. I had not reached the point where I deeply believed; still, I was convinced that this woman had something.

One evening she ordered me to go to the Narita Fudō of the temple Shinshō-ji on the following day, which was the memorial of Fudō. Rising early, I did as she told me. When I returned home, the bandages were gone from our daughter's head. When my wife had taken her to the doctor that day, he had said the bandages were no longer needed and had substituted a small patch of sticking plaster and gauze. It was the twenty-eighth; the uncanny woman had been absolutely right.

That evening, wrapping up a small amount of money to give her as a token of gratitude, I went to see Mrs. Tsunaki. Often people abandon religions that they adopt for a specific purpose as soon as that purpose has been achieved. But I had been interested in religious systems since the days when I had come into contact with the Organization of National Faith and Virtue. That night, I requested that Mrs. Tsunaki make me one of her students. Among her many disciples, who included her husband, some people often spoke of harsh training, like pouring buckets of cold water over their bodies outdoors during the coldest part of the winter. They claimed that such discipline induced a kind of trance and enabled them to have visions of the deity.

For a while, my training was limited to prayers and devotions. Nothing was said of the cold-water baths, until one day I brought the subject up myself. Mrs. Tsunaki said that she had already received word from the deity that I was to undergo this training but that the deity had been waiting until I should want to do so myself. Slightly surprised, I asked, "How many buckets full?"

"Thirty-five!"

Wearing nothing but a thin white kimono, I went into the garden; knelt by the well; drew water; and repeating the Esoteric Buddhist formulas I had been taught, poured the water over my head. The cold nearly made me jump. I trembled all over, but I drew more water and continued pouring. Losing myself in the operation, I continued until at last I had emptied thirty-five buckets. By that time, my back was as numb as if it had been frozen. But when the ordeal was over, I realized that I had been very serious and spiritually calm and unified. If this training is repeated daily, it becomes easier to enter the state of spiritual unification because conditioned reflexes, or autosuggestion, lead one into a realm that I think is the first step on the road to the state of concentration referred to as *samadhi* in Buddhist terminology.

While I was undergoing this training, the deity ordered that I abstain from the five cereals—including, of course, rice, the staple of the Japanese diet. I was allowed buckwheat flour, toasted and then kneaded with hot water, salt, and sugar. Though I had to remain on this fare for a week or even three weeks, it was easy for a person like me, raised on simple country food.

Giving up all things that have come into contact with fire was a little more difficult. Once again, the staple of my diet was buckwheat flour; but it was now mixed with cold, not hot, water. Further, since heat is used in their preparation, I could have neither salt nor sugar. Everything that I ate was raw. Still, I usually go through with something once I have made up my mind, and I went through with this. (I realize that many people find such abstentions foolish. I do not think they should be attempted by the average person. On the other hand, abstaining from such things as cigarettes, alcohol, and gambling is by no means a bad idea.) Shakyamuni, the historical Buddha, was enlightened to the futility of ascetic rigors.

But it must be remembered that before his enlightenment he subjected himself to superhuman hardships for six years, eating no more than one grain of rice and one sesame seed a day.

I feel that the religious disciplines I underwent before I came into contact with the true Buddhism had meaning for me. For the sake of the truth, the Law, and the happiness of others, a person must abandon himself, cut himself off from his desires, and bring life to its limit—that is, to the edge of death—at least once in his lifetime. I do not recommend that everyone make the attempt to do this. People who are born to a mission of this kind will find the chance and the motivation sooner or later.

In the system I was studying, ascetics have ranks. Although I was unaware of it, while I was undergoing this course of disciplines, I was raised one rank. Step by step, Mrs. Tsunaki announced to me that I had been given permission by the deity to hold the symbolic wand, then I was given the right to hold the ritual paper ornaments, and then I was allowed to wear the ritual *hakama*. This promotion raised me to the rank of an assistant master. None of her other students had advanced beyond the stage where they wore the simple white kimono. I felt pity for all of them, but especially for Mrs. Tsunaki's husband.

He did not seem to be a bad man, but for some reason the deity was extremely strict with him. One day, after he had finished the course of abstention from the five cereals and was praying in front of the divinity, he suddenly felt a great pain throughout his body. His face went bluish. When questioned, the deity announced that Mr. Tsunaki had grumbled to himself during his fast from the five cereals. This was so reprehensible that he was ordered to abstain for one month from things that had come into contact with fire. But as soon as he had managed to complete one course of abstention, there was always another for him. He was engaged in ascetic discipline the year round.

As an assistant master, I was empowered to perform incantations for the sake of faith healing, and I did so with great success. I cured people that doctors had given up. People who came to me limping, walked away sound after my incantations.

I had no idea why I could do these things. I had never gone into a trance. I had never seen or heard the deity. In my own eyes, I was nothing more than a perfectly ordinary human being, a seller of pickles. Nonetheless, miraculous things happened to me, one after the other.

For example, I became skillful at the fire ceremony, which involves placing lighted candles on the exposed affected parts of an ailing person's body and reciting Esoteric Buddhist formulas to effect a cure. A man with a back disorder lay on the floor, face down. He wore only a white kimono, which we pulled down to reveal his back. A bundle of from thirty to fifty candles—one and a half centimeters in diameter and fifteen centimeters in length—was placed on the exposed skin and lighted. As the candles burned, I chanted incantations. Before long, the flame from the bundle grew to as much as twenty centimeters in height. It was very hot, and the scalding wax dripped down on the man's skin. But by means of recitations of Esoteric Buddhist formulas and by mental concentration, I reduced the height of the flame to a normal two or three centimeters. This fire ceremony was especially impressive when used on a mentally ill patient. In such cases, as many as three hundred and seventy candles were placed on the person's head. This task was too much for me alone. Mrs. Tsunaki, her husband, and I exerted our best efforts; and when the red flame from the candles rose to thirty centimeters, we were able to reduce it again to two or three centimeters.

In school, I had always tried to follow our principal's advice to be kind to people. Nothing in the world is as pleasant to me as helping others. This is why I derived such profound joy from curing people who had been suffering.

Every day, without fail, after my work selling pickles, I went to Tengu-fudō, where I usually found from seven to fifteen people. Sitting around the hibachi brazier with those people who had already finished their incantations, I would share all kinds of ideas. When illnesses were discussed, I would apply the *rokuyō* system that I had learned while working for Ishihara in the years before my military service. I would ask whether the person in question had done such and such a thing at such and such a time. It was interesting to note how many times I was right. Gradually, the *rokuyō* discussions became so popular that people would jostle each other to get a place next to me beside the hibachi. But Mrs. Tsunaki was not jealous.

She was happy that the membership of Tengu-fudō was increasing and treated me respectfully as an assistant master. Though I had to get up early in the morning for work, surprisingly I was able to stay up at those sessions until as late as midnight. But none of this was working to my financial benefit.

Life was not easy for the Tsunaki family. Mr. Tsunaki was a day laborer; but in those times the unemployed were so numerous that it was almost impossible for him to find work. He ultimately came to rely on his wife for support. They had five or six children.

As might be expected of a shaman, Mrs. Tsunaki was completely uninterested in money. Her Tengu-fudō gradually gained in popularity until she had an income about the same as that of my pickles business. Still, the family was always in straits because, as soon as money came in, she would spend lavishly. They would eat and drink up all their funds. Then gas and light bills would accumulate unpaid. Often gas and electricity were turned off until I paid the bills. Mr. Tsunaki was concerned about the situation and asked me to say something to his wife. Of course, this could not be done until all the other members had gone home. Late at night, I would kneel on the tatami in front of her and urge her to be less of a spendthrift. Mr. Tsunaki would join in my pleas. Finally, with a glum face, she would nod agreement. But our words never had a lasting effect, for after only a little while she would be spending wildly again. But what could I say? It was her money.

Steadily increasing membership—as many as fifty or sixty people daily—made the small room where the Tengu-fudō meetings had been held impossibly cramped. A room was added to the house, but even that was insufficient. A rich female member of the group offered to lend a thousand yen—a very large sum in those days—for the construction of a new headquarters. With that much money, a small house could be erected. Mrs. Tsunaki was elated. I was frightened because I foresaw trouble. If she borrowed and did not alter her spendthrift ways, the situation might become very messy. My anticipation was aggravated by my own responsibility. Only a short while earlier, in order to stabilize the Tsunaki way of life, I had proposed that a membership organization, called the Fudō Lecture Group, be established. I assumed the task of managing the accounts of the organization, which meant that if the undertaking failed, I would be held responsible. I met the lady who offered the loan, to discuss the matter. Her conditions were comparatively easy; and feeling that there was no other road to take, I decided to counsel going ahead with the plan. I became the leader in leasing land from one of the members, negotiating with the carpenters, and seeing the construction of a small training hall through to completion.

Mrs. Tsunaki had become so taken with my way of working that she insisted I give up the pickles business and become a full-time ascetic in the Tengu-fudō organization. She promised to set me up as the head of a branch training hall.

But I did not like the idea. I had been able to help her and devote time to the organization as an amateur eager to be of assistance. But I reacted strongly against the idea that my whole livelihood would depend on this kind of work. I flatly refused, saying that I preferred the pickles business.

Still she insisted. With my spiritual talents, she claimed, I could become capable of curing any disease if I persevered. I would be able to devote my entire life to helping people. She said she had already received notification from the deity about my success in this work.

Helping people is one of my weaknesses; and when she began talking this way, I wavered. Business seemed a more sensible, stable way to make a living. But . . . I could not make up my mind. I had no one to discuss the problem with. Then I remembered hearing about a man named Seikō Kobayashi, who was a great expert at making predictions on the basis of people's names. He was said to be one hundred percent accurate in all cases. Thinking the matter over a while, I decided to consult him to determine which was correct, my judgment or the information received from the Tengu-fudō deity.

One day while on my selling rounds, I visited him and was amazed at what I heard. Upon no more than hearing my name, he related to me all kinds of absolutely accurate information not only about me, but also about my parents, brothers, sister, and other relatives for two or three generations back. Harboring a slight doubt, I gave him the names of some friends, and he analyzed them with equal accuracy. Then I got down to the problem I had come to talk over.

He at once said, "Don't get involved with that. It's all fake!" When I asked why, he replied that the apparently miraculous practices of the Shugen-dō system were no more than trickery. Had I been only an outsider, I might have accepted what he said unquestioningly. But I knew that what I felt and my own experiences were not fake. I told him what I could do, including the shortening of flames by means of no more than mental concentration. He rejected what I said. The argument grew heated. In spite of the other visitors waiting to see him and in spite of my pickles wagon standing at the door, we continued talking for four hours. At last he said, "Anyway, it's sad to see a young man of your caliber sucked into Shugen-dō. Why don't you learn name interpretation instead? I'll teach you everything I know."

The orderly name-interpretation system, founded on rules, was more attractive to me than mysterious spiritual abilities; and I was on the verge of asking to be made a student. Then I learned that Ishihara, from whom I had parted on unpleasant terms, had given up the Organization of National Faith and Virtue and had become a member of Kōyū-kai, the name-interpretation organization. Because I knew it would be embarrassing for us both to come together under these circumstances, I abandoned the idea of joining. But since I was unwilling to give in entirely—after four hours of disputation—Mr. Kobayashi kindly sent me the monthly pamphlets of the group. I studied them and soon mastered the techniques of name interpretation, though once again, it was only a hobby. I had no intentions of putting my knowledge to practical use. Nonetheless, on my daily work rounds, whenever I met people who were troubled or suffering from sickness, I used the *rokuyō* method and name interpretation to analyze their problems and to advise them about possible solutions. Interestingly enough, I was right in many cases.

When I had refused to become a full-time ascetic in the Tengu-fudō organization, Mrs. Tsunaki had abruptly said, "All right, then don't come around here any more!" At just that time, my family and I moved to the Suginami district. This gave me a chance to leave the group gracefully. I had spent two years in training with them. As I said earlier, I do not consider that time wasted. I am still grateful to Mrs. Tsunaki today.

6.
Two Eye Openings

I CONTINUED working hard at the pickles business. In August, 1934, when my second daughter, Kyōko, was just nine months old, Mrs. Iizuka, a midwife who lived near us, called to ask if I would not join a religious organization known as Reiyū-kai. I said something to get rid of her. But she replied, "I have come to you as an emissary of the Buddha. If you do not listen to what I say, something may happen to you within the next week or ten days."

Going on preparing vegetables for pickles, I thought, "What's she gabbing about?"

Mrs. Iizuka added, "Well, I hope nothing happens. But if it does, go to see Mr. Sukenobu Arai, an outstanding teacher, who lives at number twenty-four Niiyama Street." She drew a map showing me how to get there. Paying little attention, I quickly forgot what she said.

Exactly one week later, my second daughter fell ill with a very high fever and lost consciousness. Nearby lived a pediatrician from Keiō University Hospital. When I consulted him, he diagnosed the infant's case as Japanese sleeping sickness and said she could be in grave trouble unless she was hospitalized at once.

But we could not afford to hospitalize her. After exhausting all other possibilities, I decided to call on Mr. Arai. I joined Reiyū-kai at once and began to offer reverence to the spirits of my ancestors. In practically no time my daughter's condition improved. To me, this was proof of the merit of Reiyū-kai. My second daughter was less bright than her older sister in primary school. But she made great strides forward in middle and high schools and graduated with good grades. She has been healthy ever since her infantile fever and shows no traces of having been seriously ill.

But the thing that impressed me about Reiyū-kai even more than this startling proof was the Lotus Sutra. Mr. Sukenobu Arai, one of the most outstanding teachers in the organization, was very learned in Chinese and Buddhist classics. He had conducted his own course of research on the Lotus Sutra. His merits were so great that he was honored even by Mrs. Kimi Kotani, then president of Reiyū-kai. Although his chapter was but a small part of Reiyū-kai, people from the entire organization came to hear Mr. Arai's lectures on the Lotus Sutra.

In my part of the country, Buddhist sects revering the Lotus Sutra were not as popular as Jōdo Shū, Jōdo Shinshū, and Zen. In fact, the Lotus Sutra was not held in high esteem. Naturally, because of my unfamiliarity with the great text, Mr. Arai's lectures on it overjoyed and elated me.

The *rokuyō* system and name interpretation were interesting but not entirely effective in relieving suffering. At best they were effective—though not always completely—in eighty-five percent of all instances. In other words, fifteen percent of the suffering people remained unaided by them. Nor had the Shugen-dō system proved perfectly effective. Some people were not cured by it. Some were cured physically while their deep suffering and spiritual wounds went unattended. Furthermore, I was never convinced about spiritual powers that could not be understood by the person exerting them. In my own vague way, I constantly sought a rule that would save everyone, a rule that was not mysterious, but was convincingly based on reason and was clearly regulated and systematic.

Listening to lectures on the Lotus Sutra, I realized that I had found what I had been looking for. The Lotus Sutra was the perfect net in which to save everyone in the world. Physically and spiritually it could help both the individual and all of society. I was profoundly shaken by what I had learned. The impression made on me was of astonishing, vibrant freshness. It has remained fresh for over forty years. During that time, I have not missed reading the Lotus Sutra a single day. And the text has lost none of its subtlety, none of its ability to reverberate in my heart and sink deeply into my spirit. On the contrary, the more I read the sutra, the more impressive and profound it seems. Is there another teaching with this power? Is there another book that can be read with amazement and growing emotional impact every day for forty years?

Since I feel more indebted to Sukenobu Arai than to any other person, I must devote some attention to the way I met him and the way I studied with him. On the day of our first meeting, it was pouring rain. In the morning, I made my rounds with the pickles wagon for about two hours. Then, returning home and asking my wife to take very good care of our ill daughter, I went to Mr. Arai's house. I was drenched from the waist down when I arrived.

Passing through the gate, I saw a small, elderly man washing his hands at a stone garden-basin by the veranda. After an exchange of greetings, I explained why I had come; and he invited me into the house. He led me to the bedside of his wife, who was ill with a cold. I was shy about going in as wet as I was. But he told me not to worry. Five or six sheets of newspaper were spread on the tatami for me to sit on, while Mrs. Arai raised herself in bed and helped me fill in the application forms for membership in Reiyū-kai and kindly explained the rules to me. I later learned that Mr. Arai spent almost the entire day every day reading the sutra and writing posthumous Buddhist names. He engaged in very little guidance work, and his wife handled most of the administrative tasks.

On that day, because she was ill, Mr. Arai himself conducted introductory prayers for me. I was accompanied by Mrs. Waki Ogawa, who later remarried and, as Mrs. Abè, is now an important member of the Nagasaki Branch of Risshō Kōsei-kai. Mr. Arai enthusiastically read the Lotus Sutra and recited the sacred protective mantra for us. From that time, my daughter Kyōko began to get better. In one week, the sickness that the doctor had pronounced dangerous was completely cured, leaving not the slightest trace. Obviously, I became a devout believer and attended meetings of the Arai Chapter regularly.

Training at those meetings consisted of readings of the Lotus Sutra and chantings of the sacred mantra by a person capable of these duties. Then Mr. Arai sat at a low table in front of the Buddhist altar and delivered lectures on the Lotus Sutra. Often his speech became so impassioned that he stood and walked about. His remarks were filled with the Truth and with a power to touch the heart. Nor is this surprising; Mr. Arai himself had been saved from a grave illness by the sutra.

At the age of fifty-one, he had been suddenly paralyzed. He lost the abilities to walk and to speak. In addition, he suffered from a bad liver and impaired eyesight. As he lay in bed one day, with trembling hand, he took a pencil and wrote to his wife, "Bring me my copy of the Lotus Sutra."

At a nearby temple he had been given a copy in Chinese, which was easier for a person with his eyesight to read than was a Japanese version with its mixture of Sino-Japanese ideograms and Japanese syllabary characters. It seems likely that, for a long time, he had realized that the Lotus Sutra is the paramount sutra, the one whose virtues are immense. Mr. Arai's wife was weak but, like the obedient, old-fashioned wife she was, held the sutra in front of him and turned page after page when he signaled to her that he had finished one and wanted to go on to the next. He persevered diligently this way until he had read the entire ten fascicles of the Threefold Lotus Sutra.

When he had finished, a miracle occurred. His illness literally vanished. He rose and was able to move about freely. He told us that at that time he realized the greatness of Shakyamuni Buddha and the boundless virtues of the Lotus Sutra.

Although Reiyū-kai almost totally ignored the Lotus Sutra, some of its top leaders attended Mr. Arai's lectures. But not all of the people who came to the meetings were interested. Many of them went home after the incantation of the sacred mantra and the devotional services. Only about fourteen or fifteen regularly remained for the lecture. At about the time that our course had gotten as far as the chapter entitled "Tactfulness," the president of Reiyū-kai remarked that any one engaged in such study was a fool; the high-ranking leaders stopped coming, and attendance dropped to four or five people.

I was the only person paying ardent attention to the lectures. I had the impression that Mr. Arai was talking directly to me all the time. Once he told me privately that he would think the lectures worthwhile if no one came but me. From that time on, I visited him every day, taking no time off for the summer Bon festival, the busy season at the end of the year, or even the first day of the New Year holiday. He was burningly eager to teach the sutra; I was burningly eager to be taught. We agreed with each other like lovers; we attracted each other like the north and south poles of two magnets. Famous for his taciturnity, he was willing to talk all day when I came. If I had questions, I did not hesitate to bring them up. He always seemed to have been waiting for them and launched sparkling arguments around them. Bringing us tea, his wife often looked at us with an expression that said, "I give up on both of you." Under these circumstances, I continued attending Mr. Arai's lectures for a full three years.

Three months after I began studying the Lotus Sutra, my eyes were open. Courage welled up from the bottom of my heart. Until then, I had tried to help as many people as possible, but my efforts had been half a kind of amusement. Now the time had come to be completely sincere.

Two of the teachings with which I came into contact during this period suited my personal feelings exactly: the way of compassion of the bodhisattva—helping others and serving everyone in the world—is the true meaning of Buddhism; and the ability of the lay believer both to save and to be saved. The spirit of valor that I felt welling up in me would no longer permit me to accept the halfway measure of devoting myself to business and giving only spare time to religious activities. On many days, I neglected my shop and ran about doing religious work. Soon what small savings I had were gone, and I had to resort to pawnshops. I caused my wife a great deal of worry. A very hard-working, ordinary housewife, she lacked my kind of religious faith. It is not surprising that she complained about the way I did things. In spite of the fact that the number of our children was growing and work was very pressing, I often dashed out on what I called missions of aid. Even when at home, I spent most of my time reading the sutra. In addition, other members of our religious group called frequently; and my wife had to talk to them and treat them kindly, even though I lacked time to sit down and have a quiet discussion with her. It is only to be expected that circumstances of this kind should have caused her to complain. In my heart, I understood. That is why I never fought or complained. Nonetheless, I did not give in, but adhered firmly to my mission as a man of faith. "You're perfectly right," I would tell her. "But I'm an emissary of the Buddha." And with a remark of this kind, I would immediately go out on religious work.

I was part of a small team of religious workers, including Waki Abè (whom I mentioned earlier), Mr. Arai's wife, and her daughter Masako. We often did guidance work and other tasks for the organization. Since they were happy to have a man who was well-versed in the Lotus Sutra and who could talk persuasively, they often asked me to accompany them in visiting the ill or in doing other work. This contributed to my wife's discontent.

Not long ago, I heard that Mrs. Abè had laughingly told people, "In those days, when I came to Tokyo and called at the Niwano house, Mrs. Niwano would say to me, 'If you want my husband all that badly, take him. I'll tie a ribbon on him for you.' " My wife is supposed to have admitted saying this, and Mrs. Abè is said to have replied, "I should have taken you up on the offer."

Of course, it is easy to laugh about it now. But in those days, I was a source of great irritation to my wife. And the same kind of thing continued steadily for twenty years. Even though it was in the name of service for others, I realize that I brought her unhappiness and am sorry.

My ability to analyze accurately the troubles of the ill and the poor by means of the *rokuyō* system, oriental astrology, and name interpretation heightened the effects of our guidance work. Since Mr. Arai was more a scholar than a specialist in guidance, he frequently told me to handle such duties. After about seven months of this kind of activity, I was selected as an assistant director of the Arai Chapter of Reiyū-kai. Serving with me as an assistant director was Mr. Kōda, who was my senior in the group by many years and was editor of the organization bulletin. Since Mr. Arai was old, he generally sent me on missions of liaison with the headquarters. Frequent contacts during the course of this kind of work enabled me to acquire a wide and deep knowledge of Reiyū-kai and its teachings in a relatively short time. But in my eagerness to become more familiar with the

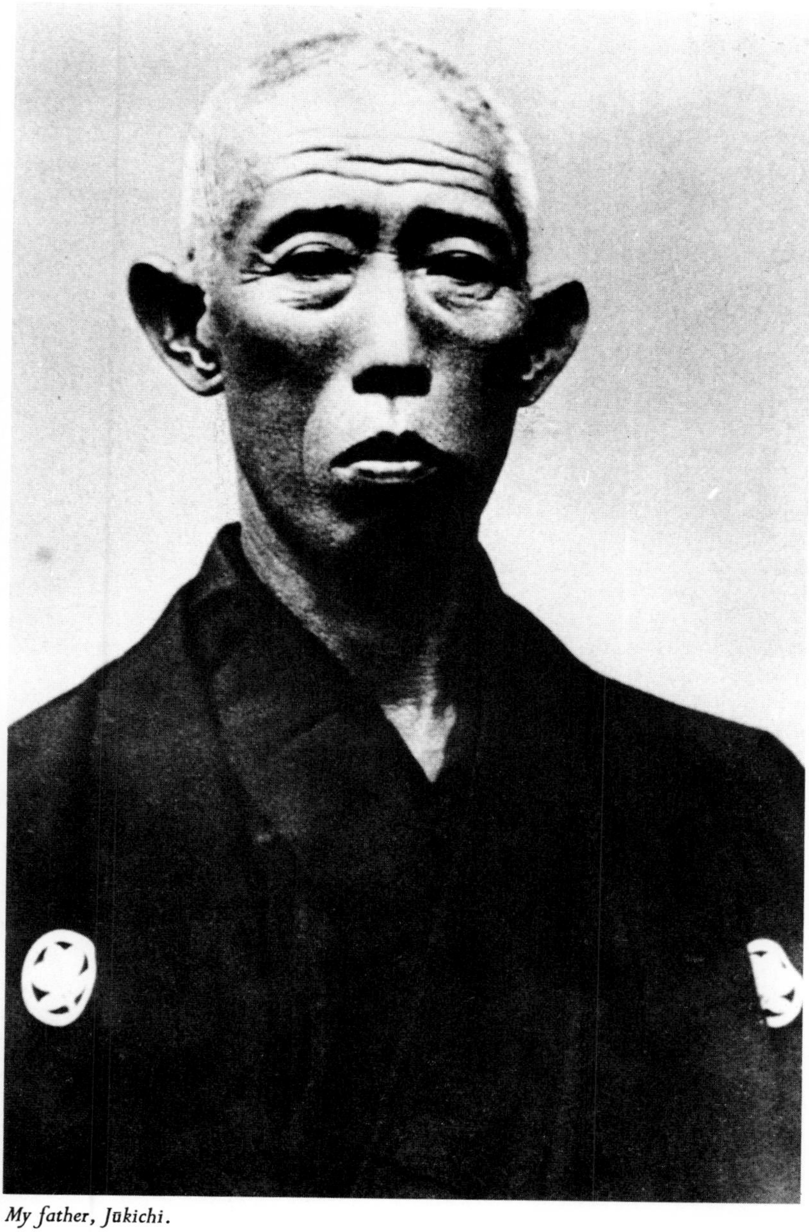

My father, Jūkichi.

Above, the village of Suganuma, where I grew up.

My boyhood home as it was when I was a child (below left), and as it is now (below right).

Below left, on the way to school we passed this stone with the name of the buddha Dainichi Nyorai carved on it.
Below right, Suwa Shrine, the tutelary shrine along our road to school.

Miss Jitsu Ōta, my first teacher. Mr. Denkichi Daikai, the principal of our school, who gave me two importa guides for living.

Ōike Primary School, which I attended for six years.

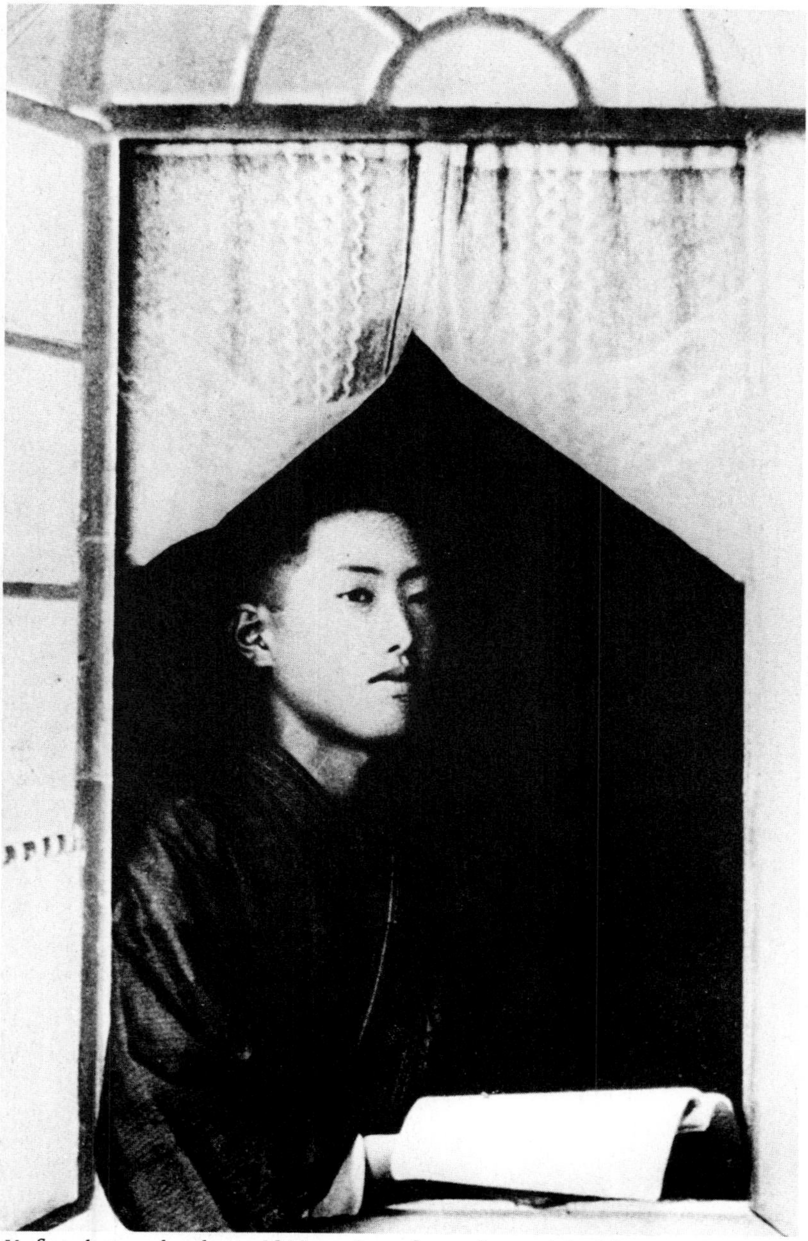

My first photograph, taken in 1920, not long after my fourteenth birthday.

My cousin Matsue Niwano and I had this picture taken on our way home after receiving predictions from a shaman near Yahiko Shrine when I was almost nineteen.

Seaman Recruit Niwano early in 1926, at the age of nineteen.

man Third Class Niwano, standing center, and turret mates on the Nagato.

Mrs. Umeno Tsunaki, head of Tengu-fudō, in 1932, seated with assistant master Tsunaki on her right and twenty-five-year-old assistant master Niwano on her left.

The Singing Pickles Man at twenty-seven with my wife, Sai (1), our daughters Tomoko (2) and Kyōko (3), Sai's elder sister Masu (4), my elder brother, Ishizō (5), and my younger brothers Nenozō (6) and Rinzō (7) after our visit to a local shrine during the New Year holidays in 1934.

The milkman's daughters, Tomoko, left, and Kyōko, right, in 1935.

Daughter Yoshiko and son Kōichi in 1943.

Sons Kōichi, left, and Kinjirō, right, in 1943.

Mr. and Mrs. Sukenobu Arai, who introduced me to the Lotus Sutra.

The thirty-one-year-old cofounder of Risshō Kōsei-kai on founding day, March 5, 1938.

Friends and family of the milkman and general manager of Risshō Kōsei-kai gathered to see me off in August, 1941, when I was recalled to the navy at the age of thirty-four. My wife, Sai (1), our daughters, Tomoko (2), Kyōko (3), and Yoshiko (4), our sons, Kōichi (5) and Kinjirō (6), my father (7), and Mrs. Myōkō Naganuma (8). I was home a few days later, physically disqualified from service.

The second pilgrimage of Risshō Kōsei-kai members to Mount Shichimen, made in October, 1941.

The pilgrims to Mount Shichimen wore short coats, like this one, on which I had written the Daimoku—Namu Myōhō Renge-kyō.

In November, 1941, on land next to Myōkō Naganuma's home, we began construction of our new headquarters.

teachings and to devote myself to guidance work, I neglected business. Though such negligence runs counter to what is expected of a Buddhist layman, I was unable to restrain my burning passion to seek the Truth and to serve others in the compassionate spirit of the bodhisattva. Then I came up with the idea of changing my business to one that would leave me plenty of free time, while giving me an opportunity to meet a great many people. After considering a number of proposals, I decided on a milk shop. Without further hesitation, I made the change and opened a milk shop in Fujimichō, Nakano Ward.

In the milk business, early-morning and evening deliveries took care of the pressing duties, and the rest of the day was free for religious work. By cutting down on meal time, I was able to hurry about on these tasks until as late as midnight. From the standpoint of a person who calculates nothing but his own personal profit, my course of action must seem very foolish. But I think that importance is frequently found in apparent folly. In ultimate terms my belief is that serving others is the fundamental qualification for true humanity and that allowing the maximum number of people to know the desire to serve is the way to produce a truly happy and peaceful human society.

If everyone pursued nothing but his own selfish ends, society would become a machine without lubricating oil. It would soon cease to function and would ultimately explode from overheating. The spirit of service is the lubricant needed to bring happiness and fulfillment to the individual and lasting peace to the whole world. This seems a remote ideal to some people. A dream for the future. But I do not agree. On the contrary, I think it is the image of a world that can be realized in the relatively near future.

The person who makes up his mind to devote himself to the service of others suddenly feels relieved and happy. He is no longer burdened with selfish desires. The daily things that cause grief cease to bother him. Bonds dissolve; he is free. This feeling alone is wonderful. I suspect this is the way a man who becomes a priest feels. But to experience it, one need not renounce the world. Resolving to serve others and to devote oneself to the interests of mankind produces the same effect and is infinitely more valuable.

The desire to serve—the meaning of the Buddhist spirit of the bodhisattva—is the kind of lubricant that can, even in small droplets, make the running of the great machine of society smooth and sure.

One of the good customers of my milk shop was the Saitamaya, a small store in Hatagaya Honchō, Shibuya Ward, that sold ice in the summer and baked sweet potatoes in the winter. The shop prospered, but the woman who ran it was always pale and sickly. She spent much of the time in bed in a room behind the shop and seemed to be getting worse. One day, as the time she spent in bed began increasing, I said to her, "You look very ill. What's the matter with you?"

"Oh, you're the milkman, aren't you? Well, I've got a weak heart and a bad stomach. I'm in generally bad shape."

"I'm sorry to hear that. Have you been sick a long time?"

"Pretty long. Ever since I was a young girl."

"Is that so? Tell me, do you have any religious belief?"

"I'm a member of Tenri-kyō."

"That's fine. But tell me something else. Do you pay reverence to your ancestors?"

"Actually, what with one thing and another, no. I don't."

"I thought you didn't. You ought to."

Then I started trying to convince her to become a member of Reiyū-kai. But she was stubborn and, stopping just short of telling me to shut up, refused to pay attention to what I had to say. Still, I did not give up. Each time I delivered milk, I brought the subject to her attention. Finally she said that, if I was all that serious about it, she might think of joining.

But that was as far as she went. Naturally, I took care of applications for her; but when I asked her to submit a list of her ancestors' posthumous names as is prescribed by Reiyū-kai, she hesitated, even though the names were recorded in a place where she could have obtained them all in a single day. After three days of waiting, I lost patience and wrote to her family for the names. In another three days, the list arrived; and I personally entered them in Reiyū-kai's register of the names of all the members and the names and death dates of their ancestors. On that day, the proprietor of the ice and sweet-potato shop felt much better than she could remember feeling and got out of bed. I was as happy as if her good fortune were my own. I remarked to her, "There, see how much better you feel. Now you must pay a call of gratitude." Then I took her to the Arai Chapter of Reiyū-kai.

In Reiyū-kai's system, the person introducing a new member acts as a spiritual godparent. After entering the group, the new member is obliged to pay a call of gratitude to the chapter and the godparent. In this case, I was the godparent; but thinking the whole thing silly, she would not visit me to express thanks. I did not take the matter too seriously and laughingly said, "All right. There's nothing to be done about it. I'll pay respects to the guardian deity for you."

According to the story, as I heard it later, on her return to her home, she found her nephew, whom she had invited to come from the country to work in her shop, writhing in agony on the floor with a pain in his stomach. She quickly brought him a doctor, who immediately diagnosed appendicitis and said that an operation was required at once or it would be too late. But operations, even for appendicitis, were serious in those days, since there was no penicillin. The proprietor of the shop said that she could not consent to surgery without the approval of the boy's parents. The doctor ordered her to get approval by the evening and, in the meantime, to apply ice packs to the boy's abdomen. If she did not abide by his instructions, her nephew's life would be in danger.

Then she suddenly remembered the brusque way she had reacted to her responsibilities as a new member of Reiyū-kai and hastened to send a boy for me. I heard the messenger out and decided to go. But there was one problem. Our third daughter had just been born, and there was no one to look after our second daughter, Kyōko, who was still very small. I resolved the difficulty by strapping Kyōko to my back and then hurried to the ice shop. When I learned the entire story, I spoke to the proprietor in a severe voice for the first time in our association. "You are getting only what you deserve. You were cured of your sickness. Still you refused to make a call of thanks to your spiritual godparent and to pay your respects to the guardian deity. Your ingratitude is being shown to you in the form of your suffering nephew."

She lowered her eyes. I continued, "Now make up for what you have done by joining me in reading the Sutra of Meditation on the

Bodhisattva Universal Virtue.'' She knelt behind me as I read the long sutra and recited the sacred mantra. As we did this, the pain in her nephew's stomach steadily decreased until it was gone and no operation was needed.

On the following day, the doctor was unable to locate the swelling that had been caused by the inflamed appendix. His pressing on the boy's stomach produced no pain. Shaking his head, the doctor said, ''This is the strangest thing I've ever seen. How can it have happened? The appendicitis seems to be gone now, but it can recur. Take good care of the boy.'' But the sickness never returned, and that boy, Hiroshi Naganuma, is now one of the directors of Risshō Kōsei-kai.

She thanked me. That was good, but what she said afterward was bad: ''How much do I owe you?''

For the second time, I spoke sharply to her. ''Do you think money is the only important thing? Believe me, that is no way to think. Money is beside the point. It's good to give, because acts of charity are part of our Buddhist practice. But giving must not be an exchange. I mean you must not offer money because a sickness has been cured or because you want a sickness to be cured. That is not charity. It is not giving. The best thing for you to do, the greatest donation you can make, is to give your selfish and stubborn person completely to the Buddha.''

At last my words had effect. Her eyes were open, and she was a different person thereafter. She went to the Arai Chapter of Reiyū-kai daily. She heard lectures on the Lotus Sutra and enthusiastically took part in the services. Even more surprising than her attendance at these meetings was the vigorous way she went about carrying the teachings to others. With a force and strength that seemed impossible in a woman who, until recently, had lain in bed, pale and wan, day in and day out, she devoted herself to guidance activities. On a single day, working together, she and I converted nearly fifty new members. Her industriousness and dedication astonished even Mr. Arai. The woman of whom I am speaking was, of course, Masa Naganuma, who was later to be known in Risshō Kōsei-kai as Myōkō Sensei.

7. Founding

Because of the cramped space of the single, small second-floor room in an ordinary dwelling in Akasaka that was its headquarters, Reiyū-kai was building a new, more spacious meeting place at Iikura Itchome to accommodate its rapidly increasing membership. In the mornings, after milk deliveries, I rode my bicycle to the construction site to help with the work. I returned home for evening deliveries and for night guidance work. The new building was completed at the end of 1937. On the thirtieth and thirty-first of December, grand ceremonies were held to celebrate the conclusion of construction; and on January seventh of the new year, a conference of chapter heads from all over the country was held. Everyone involved in the meeting was excited, since it was said that we were about to make Reiyū-kai the most outstanding religious organization in Japan. Though as an officer, I too was excited, in the back of my mind were shadows of doubt.

There were two reasons for this. First, I felt that the organization was going much too far in its efforts to increase membership. For example, it was tacitly assumed that each chapter that enrolled one hundred new members in a month would enroll two hundred the following month, four hundred the next, and so on in geometric progression. Each new member was required to purchase a sutra scroll for fifty sen and a roster for the names of his ancestors for one yen and thirty sen. Chapter chiefs who were very concerned to remain on the good side of the organization's executives went so far as to purchase these things themselves, even though they had no new members to take them off their hands. In time, some purchased more scrolls and rosters than they could store in their houses and were forced to build sheds for them. The head of our chapter, Mr. Arai, was a scholar. He had no intention of doing such a thing and often laughed at the excessive measures to which other chapter chiefs resorted.

My second reason for doubt was more serious and basic. I had heard that organizational headquarters was displeased about Mr. Arai's lectures on the Lotus Sutra. I could not imagine why this should be. What could be the objection to lectures on the sutra that was the basic scripture of Reiyū-kai? Reiyū-kai members read extracts from the Lotus Sutra in morning and evening worship services. Furthermore, Reiyū-kai's fundamental incantation was the *Daimoku, Namu Myōhō Renge-kyō,* which means "Hail to the Sutra of the Lotus Flower of the Wonderful Law." Nonetheless, since all of us younger members regarded Mrs. Kimi Kotani (then president) and our teacher and leader Kakutarō Kubo as virtual buddhas, we did not let our doubts about their stand on the matter take the form of action.

The nationwide meeting on January seventh had another purpose, apart from initiating a drive to make Reiyū-kai the strongest of all Japanese religious organizations. For about a year, rifts among the top echelons of the leadership had become frequent; and it was hoped that the conference would restore solidarity. In 1935, Shōdō Okano, a former director, and his wife broke away from the group to form their own organization, called Kōdō-kyōdan. In the following year, Kakutarō Takahashi and several hundred believers seceded and established Reishō-kai. Since Reiyū-kai was expanding rapidly, losses of this kind were unimportant; but they offended Mrs. Kotani. As if to increase the clouds of uncertainty already surrounding everything, for unknown reasons, at the time of the ceremonies to celebrate the completion of the new building, the heads of two chapters that had been extremely important in the development of Reiyū-kai were fired from their positions.

On the first day of the conference, which I attended with Mr. Arai, the chairman, Taira Ishida, addressed the group. "Ladies and gentlemen, our goal is to make Reiyū-kai the number-one religious organization in the country. In this, we shall be indebted to Mr. Kubo for his teaching and guidance. If anyone has anything to say on these subjects at this time, please speak up without hesitation."

For a while, one person after another asked questions and expressed opinions, until suddenly Mrs. Kotani, who was seated in the middle of the platform, arose abruptly, stalked to the speaker's desk, and shouted at the audience, "What the hell is all this about? You are supposed to be believers, but you act as if you were big shots. If anyone has a gripe, step up."

We were all astounded. A dark, unpleasant atmosphere enveloped the room, as, like water bursting through a dam, Mrs. Kotani gave full vent to her feelings. "Lectures on the Lotus Sutra are out of date. Anyone who tries anything like that around here must be inspired by the devil."

On hearing this, Mr. Arai, a strong-willed man, rose quickly and said to me, "I can't sit through any more of this. I'm going home. But you stay to the end and find out what they've got to say." I did as he ordered and remained in the conference room until nine o'clock at night.

Although I had the deepest respect for Mrs. Kotani and had no objection to Reiyū-kai's teachings of devotion to ancestors, I could not swallow the insistence that study of the Lotus Sutra be abandoned. For me this was the decisive issue. By the end of the meeting, I was ninety percent convinced that I could no longer remain in the organization.

On the following day, I visited Mrs. Naganuma to discuss the matter. She agreed that Reiyū-kai's stand was untenable and stated that she could no longer remain a member. With an attitude somewhat more positive than most Japanese women would take, she said, "Mr. Niwano, let's convince Mr. Arai to join us and set up a new organization of our own." I consented. The two of us immediately went to Mr. Arai's house, told him of what had transpired at the conference after his departure, and related our own ideas about a new organization.

"Yes, I agree that it's impossible to go on with Reiyū-kai. But I don't want to make an unpleasant scene by defying Mrs. Kotani, and I was the go-between at Mr. Kubo's wedding. Besides, I'm too old for revolutionary work. You two are younger. You take the lead in forming an independent group. As far as teaching and doctrine are concerned, I'm willing to help you as much as I can."

We all felt a debt of gratitude that made it difficult, even somehow reprehensible, to leave Reiyū-kai; but we could not allow feelings of fondness and attachment to interfere with our profound respect for the greatness of the Lotus Sutra. Mrs. Naganuma and I had another discussion and decided to form a new organization. We were young, and there were only two of us. The matter was settled easily and quickly.

We needed someone to head the group, but I was not the right choice. I had heard that my old boss Ishihara had joined Kokuchū-kai and had been studying the Lotus Sutra. I decided to get in touch with him, and he introduced us to Nichijō Murayama, a member of Kokuchū-kai. Mr. Murayama became our director general, and Ishihara our vice-director general. I was the general manager, and Mrs. Naganuma's husband the accountant. In addition, there were about thirty members whom Mr. Arai, Mrs. Naganuma, or I had taught in guidance sessions. We had no intention of forcing the growth of our membership. Some of the people who joined us then are still active members.

To solemnize the institution of the organization, we held ceremonies at Mrs. Naganuma's house and then made the headquarters a room on the second floor of my house. And this is the way the Dai-Nippon Risshō Kōsei-kai came into being, on March 5, 1938. The *Risshō* part of the name means "establishing the teaching of the true Law [that is, the Lotus Sutra] in the world." The *Kō* of *Kōsei* signifies mutual exchange of thought among people of faith, that is, the principle of spiritual unity among different human beings. *Sei* stands for the perfection of the personality and attainment of buddhahood. On the occasion of the founding of the organization, I changed my first name to Nikkyō, and Masa Naganuma changed hers to Myōkō. It was as Myōkō Sensei, or Teacher Myōkō, that she was to become familiar to thousands of people.

When doubts or problems concerning doctrine and faith arose, we went at once to Mr. Arai for instruction and help. We continued to do so until he passed away of old age in 1949; and ever since then, good relations have continued between Risshō Kōsei-kai and the surviving members of his family.

8.
Myōkō Naganuma

MYŌKŌ NAGANUMA was born as Masa, the sixth daughter of Asajirō Naganuma, in the village of Shidami, in northern Saitama Prefecture. One of her ancestors had been a samurai retainer of Ujinaga Narita, feudal lord of Oshi Castle, in the north of present-day Saitama Prefecture. After the fall of the castle in war, toward the end of the sixteenth century, this samurai, whose name was Sukerokurō Naganuma, settled in the village of Shidami. For several generations, the family managed to maintain samurai status; but Masa Naganuma's father was a good-natured man who was easily fooled. Ultimately he lost the family house and everything but a small plot of land. The family was forced to live on charity in a temple. These were the circumstances into which Masa Naganuma was born. To make matters worse, when she was six years old, her mother died. An uncle living in a nearby village took her in and made her work from morning to night in his domestic food-provision service. Innately, Masa was not the kind to give in easily. Her love of labor was probably instilled in her by her childhood experiences. In later life, she often spoke of the way people in the neighborhood used to praise her for being so industrious at such an early age.

She never lost her love of work. As a housewife and an owner of a small commercial undertaking she carried out all her duties eagerly and well. Even after she became the vice-president of Risshō Kōseikai and something like a living buddha in the eyes of its entire membership, she always seemed to be happier in the kitchen than in a teaching session. When there was cooking or washing up to be done, none of the other ladies could hold a candle to her for speed and skill.

At the age of sixteen, Masa was adopted by a much older sister. But eager to live an independent life, she soon left for Tokyo, where she first worked as a maid. Later she labored in an army munitions dump and arsenal, but the work had such a deleterious effect on her health that she left it and returned to her uncle's home in the country. At the age of twenty-six, she was introduced to a man from another old family in her native village. At the time, he was a barber. They married, but the husband proved to be a spendthrift and a wastrel. She submitted to him for years; but when it became clear that there was no hope of his reforming, she divorced him and moved back to Tokyo. In the tenth year of their marriage, this couple had had a daughter; but the child died of illness at the age of two.

In Tokyo, Masa married again, this time to the owner of an ice wholesale dealership. At the same time, she opened her own shop, where she did a thriving business in ice and baked sweet potatoes.

Constitutionally frail, after long years of hardship, she found herself suffering from a bad stomach, a weak heart, and uterine inflammation. Sometimes she hemorrhaged for as long as two months. The doctors announced that she probably did not have long to live. It was at about that time that I began giving her guidance. Convinced that she had been granted longer life because of the Buddha's grace, Masa Naganuma resolved to devote her whole self to the Buddha's Law.

Her second husband was incapable of keeping pace with her religious life. Immediately before the end of World War II, they were divorced. He later married a member of Risshō Kōsei-kai, and he and his wife became students of Myōkō Sensei.

When we founded the organization, she and I continued to operate our businesses. This meant that our work loads were murderously heavy. Of course, we had a director and vice-director general above us, but the major responsibility was ours. At the time I was in my thirties, and she was already well over forty.

We traveled everywhere together on our guidance work. Myōkō Sensei was a short woman; she came only to about my shoulders. Usually she wore traditional Japanese kimono and the wooden clogs called geta. I have a long stride, and when we walked together she had to trot to keep up with me. In doing this, she would swing her arms wide. One day, I commented on her way of waving her arms as she walked. She laughed but continued hurrying in order not to fall behind. Later I realized that I should have been courteous enough to adjust my walking pace to the convenience of a woman of short stature.

Nothing kept us from our guidance work. When the place we were to visit was far away, I would give her a ride on the luggage carrier of my bicycle. If the place was still farther, we would ride the packed buses and trains. In the blazing sun of summer and the cold winds of winter, we went on with our work without taking Sunday off to go to a play or a motion picture, without making shopping or pleasure excursions, and without so much as dreaming of the kind of trip to a hot-spring resort that all Japanese people love.

When I first offered her spiritual guidance, Myōkō Sensei was a weak, sickly person who had a strong will but who was introspective in nature. After she recovered from the illness that was afflicting her at the time, she became a different person. She brightened. She became richly emotional. And, although she was reticent, when she did speak, it was with fiery enthusiasm and passion. The people she spoke with were never left unmoved by what she had to say. But her personality had other outstanding characteristics. She was thoughtful and considerate in a womanly way, and she felt things more deeply than most people.

One night, the wind was piercingly cold as it rattled the branches of the leafless trees along the street. We had finished a day of visiting more than thirty houses and of offering spiritual guidance to some twenty-odd people. I was giving Myōkō Sensei a ride to Risshō Kōsei-kai's headquarters on my bicycle. As I pedaled with all my might against the biting head wind, she said to me, "I'm sorry to cause you this much trouble; you must be very tired."

I was tired and I was hungry. Finally, when our nighttime ride brought us to the doors of the headquarters building, I felt drained in both mind and body. I turned around to see how Myōkō Sensei was doing and found her crouching on the ground silently rubbing her knees. If a full day of walking and cycling in the cold wind had exhausted me, how much more tiring must it have been for a woman seventeen years my senior. Her legs were so chilled and numbed by the cold that for a short while she could neither stand nor walk. After a time had passed, she rose and, with a smile that a mother might give her child, said she was better and apologized for having detained me.

Inside the headquarters building it was almost as cold as it was outdoors. But soon we found comfort and warmth around a small heap of glowing charcoal in a hibachi brazier. First we rested for a brief while. Then Myōkō Sensei went out and came back with a tray on which were two small porcelain bottles of hot sakè.

"Drink this," she said. "It will warm you."

In those days, sakè was rationed. I do not know where Myōkō Sensei got it; I did not ask. But my first taste told me that it was exactly the right temperature. The sakè and the concern and consideration of the person who prepared it for me seemed to bring warmth to every part of my mind and body. Then, saying only, "I wonder if you'll like these," she put a plate with four or five grilled sardines in front of me. She knew precisely what I liked and what I wanted. She had offered it to me with perfect timing and without pretention or fuss of any kind. Though the food she offered was simple, her acts were of the kind that can be performed only by truly generous and gentle people. That evening, we sat until late at night listening to the wind in the trees and speaking warmly of the Law of the Buddha.

Myōkō Sensei and I were truly friends on the road of search for religious knowledge. She was to me a good teacher and a friend eager to refine my abilities and help me correct my faults. Before entrusting myself to the teachings of the Lotus Sutra, I had various experiences with faith. Other teachers praised me, but I cannot recall that any of them criticized me for or cautioned me about my religious attitude. After the founding of Risshō Kōsei-kai, Myōkō Sensei and I sometimes had sessions of religious training that virtually made sparks fly. She mercilessly pointed out all my faults—so many faults indeed that she seemed to be critical of such small things as the way I raised and lowered the chopsticks with which I ate. Whenever I objected to what she said, we had highly heated debates on the subject at hand. If a member of Risshō Kōsei-kai happened to need one of us during such a discussion, we would pause to take care of whatever business required attention and would then return to our argument with renewed fervor.

She often said, "No one can make happiness for you: you must make it for yourself." In this she closely followed the teachings of the Lotus Sutra, in chapter sixteen—"Revelation of the [Eternal] Life of the Tathāgata"—in which is related the story of a doctor who prepares medicine to cure his sons, who have mistakenly drunk poison. The doctor offers the medicine to his sons, saying, "This excellent medicine, with color, scent, and fine flavor altogether perfect, you may [now] take, and it will at once rid you of your distress so that you will have no more suffering." Some of the sons drink the medicine and are cured. Others, however, are too far lost in delirium to see the good sense of their father's offer and, refusing the medicine, remain uncured. This tale illustrates the plan of the Buddha whereby, in order to be saved, we must accept the salvation that he has prepared and offers. Even people who have become members of Risshō Kōsei-kai and have come into contact with the teachings of the Lotus Sutra cannot expect to attain the merits of virtue unless they attempt to live and grow in accordance with those teachings. To be happy, a person must correct his personality faults. He must reach out his hand and accept the medicine. This is what Myōkō Sensei meant when she said that one must make one's own happiness. This demonstrates her profound understanding of the Law of the Buddha. She was able to put that knowledge to excellent use in the ways in which she helped people.

In one instance, a young woman joined Risshō Kōsei-kai largely because she wanted to improve her health, which had deteriorated when she was in high school. An only daughter, she had been spoiled by her parents and had developed a stubborn streak. Myōkō Sensei was determined to guide the woman so that she could become a happy person of spiritual breadth. As part of her plan, Myōkō Sensei instructed the woman to clean the toilets in the headquarters building.

The young woman was perplexed to the point of illness by being compelled to perform a task that she would never undertake in her own home. But Myōkō Sensei remained silent; and the young woman, seeing no reason to refuse to do the work, went glumly about her job with a look of profound displeasure. One day, as Myōkō Sensei was watching the listless fashion in which the woman worked, she approached and said, "That is no way to get the job done. Here, let me show you. This is the way to clean." Myōkō Sensei thrust hand and cleaning rag into the toilet bowl and gave it a thorough scrubbing. The young woman stood by in amazement, watching Myōkō Sensei at work. As the woman did so, her body trembled slightly. From the following day, her entire attitude changed. There was a shining light in her eyes from that time forward, and she made steady spiritual progress. The young woman of whom I am speaking is Masae Okabe, who later became the head of the Nakano Branch of Risshō Kōsei-kai. There is no way of counting the people that Myōkō Sensei helped and guided to the kind of happiness this young woman found.

9.
The Practical Approach

IN ITS first period, Risshō Kōsei-kai (or simply Kōsei-kai, as we often call it) was purely a layman's organization: its leaders—Myōkō Sensei and I—ran ordinary businesses. Kōsei-kai membership dues were twenty sen a month. Sutra scrolls and registers for ancestors' names cost fifty sen, and a set of prayer beads cost one yen and thirty sen. Since we could not afford to make bulk purchases of prayer beads, we asked Shishin-kai, which had recently been formed by former members of Reiyū-kai, to sell them to us in the quantities we needed. The overwhelming majority of our new members were people who were seriously ill, who had mentally ill relatives, or who for economic or other reasons could not call on the services of doctors. In the eyes of the general public, we were no more than a milkman and a vendor of sweet potatoes conducting some mysterious religious rites in an upstairs room over a milk shop. Obviously, only desperate people at their wits' end came to us.

It was easy for us when people joined on their own initiative. Going out and winning new members, on the other hand, was hard work. My own approach was to convince by means of direct presentations of the truth of the Buddha's Law. Myōkō Sensei had her own, different system. Instead of teaching doctrine, she told people, "Unless you give it a try, you'll never know the happiness it can bring. The milkman has come bringing good news to you. Lend an ear to him. An illness like yours will be cured in no time." Her words were so convincing and her own faith so apparent that what she said always had a powerful effect. When she saw that the family she was dealing with lacked money to pay for sutra scrolls, name registers, and prayer beads, she tactfully slipped them the needed amount.

Mentally disturbed people recovered as a result of the religious faith we taught. Soon word about the effectiveness of our method got around. A person who had been helped would bring his friends and relatives; and before long, the number of members increased considerably. Of course, we still counted ourselves in hundreds; but we were well-known for the attention and care we gave our members. Indeed, we leaders were constantly called for assistance. The case of Mrs. Hoya illustrates the situation. Whenever she was in any kind of trouble, she immediately sent us a telegram. At once, Myōkō Sensei and I would be on our way to the fairly distant Kita Tama district, where she lived. Later, when Mrs. Hoya became the head of Kōsei-kai's Toshima Branch, she said with a repentant voice, "I was a graduate of a prestigious girls' school and thought nothing of abruptly summoning a milkman to help me. I see now how thoughtless it was of me."

Another early member who was associated with a renowned girls' school was Masae Okabe. When we first met her, she was still a charming girl wearing the student's middy blouse. She was very diligent in attending our meetings and was able to persevere in our strict training, as I had thought she would be. Not only did she persevere, but she went on to become the head of a Kōsei-kai branch.

I was called Mr. Niwano and Myōkō Sensei, Mrs. Naganuma by all the members of the organization except Matsuko Gotō. This young lady had long been buying sweet potatoes from Myōkō Sensei, to whom she referred as "Auntie." She continued this practice in training meetings and guidance programs until one day Myōkō Sensei remarked to her, "Don't you think it's about time you dropped that 'auntie'?"

Matsuko Gotō provided guidance for Yoshihisa Uematsu and his wife Fujiko, who lived in Yokosuka. Mrs. Uematsu was ill with pernicious anemia. About one month after the founding of Risshō Kōsei-kai, Mr. Uematsu joined us. One hot summer day about three months later, Myōkō Sensei and I went to visit his ill wife in Yokosuka. As we sat by her bed discussing respectful service to ancestors and the Buddha's Law, her husband brought us flavored crushed ice that he had purchased at a nearby shop. Myōkō Sensei said, "Give some of that to your wife." Handing the ice to the woman herself, in an utterly confident voice, Myōkō Sensei went on, "If you eat that, next month, you'll be able to come to the Tokyo headquarters by yourself." Still lying in bed, Mrs. Uematsu ate the ice and said that it tasted good.

Two days later, to our surprise, she unexpectedly appeared in the headquarters—that is, the second-floor room over my milk shop. She explained that her husband, who worked at the naval arsenal, was unable to get time off and that she had come alone. We welcomed her and, in a way that combined praise and encouragement, told her that she had a great deal of life-force within her and that the Buddha had summoned it forth.

She returned safely that day; but thereafter, whenever she felt bad, she had one of her neighbors telephone us to come at once. Because we were determined that we must cure her, we always went. But the distance between Tokyo and Yokosuka and the number of times we had to change from train to bus and from train to train made each trip a day-long task. This meant that, on days when we were to go to her house, I had to get up earlier than usual to finish my morning milk deliveries and then to hurry home again to make my evening rounds. Myōkō Sensei and I made these trips almost every other week.

But our efforts were rewarded, for Mrs. Uematsu's health gradually improved. From March of the following year, she was able to come to Kōsei-kai headquarters by herself. Traveling all the way from Yokosuka every day because of her great devotion, she, with Matsuko Gotō, provided guidance to twenty-three households in six months. She had recovered from her illness; and her personal testimony, presented at the time of the completion of our small headquarters building in Wada Honchō, was probably the very first use of this instructional method in Kōsei-kai.

Though there were cases like hers, most of the new members joined as an alternative to seeing a physician and abandoned their faith the moment their illnesses were cured. In a sense, this is not surprising. A well man does not go to see the doctor daily. A person in good health does, however, have a regular physician on whom he calls at the first sign of disorder. Similarly, many people, though not frequenters of temples and churches under ordinary conditions, rely on the assistance of religion in times of frustration, worry, or insecurity. This is important. It is the second phase of faith.

People who wish to take very good care of their health do not wait for disorder to manifest itself but constantly remain in contact with their regular physician and never overlook health-control programs that prevent the occurrence of illness. This obviously is the best way. Faith, too, ought to be regarded in this way. The individual should keep the teachings of the gods and buddhas in mind all the time, should refrain from selfish thoughts and actions, and should live always in accordance with the law of the universe.

I have said that many of our new members left the group as soon as their illnesses were cured or their problems solved. But I am certain that these people, too, had attained the second stage of faith. I even have proof.

When Myōkō Sensei's spiritual revelations—about which I shall write in greater detail later—became a subject of discussion necessitating a police investigation, the detective in charge visited many of our members and ex-members. He told me that, whereas former members of other religious organizations generally abandon faith entirely on withdrawing from the group, our ex-members continued to worship and to read the sutras. He respected us for this; and I found his remark profoundly encouraging, because it showed that our policy of expedience did not stop at the achievement of immediate goals, but led to profounder truths.

In the year before the founding of Risshō Kōsei-kai, the so-called China Incident, the beginning of warfare between China and Japan, occurred. Less than three weeks after the founding of Kōsei-kai, the enactment of the National General Mobilization Law signaled initial preparations for fighting. In 1939, with large-scale military operations between Japan and the Soviet Union at a place called Nomonhan, on the Mongolian-Manchurian border, the abrogation of the commercial treaty between Japan and the United States, and the promulgation of a domestic law for drafting personnel services, the nation approached the brink of World War II.

The conditions of daily life throughout the country grew steadily worse. In those days there was nothing to compare with present health insurance. A protracted illness—like tuberculosis, which was prevalent—meant almost certain financial ruin. We realized that the times were wrong for lengthy, careful doctrinal presentations and that we would have to use more direct methods with new members. Our ideals remained unaltered; but as a new, small group without persuasive powers to influence the masses, we had to offer teachings of expediency to comply with the pressing needs of the people. Our first step in this direction was in the tradition of Reiyū-kai: healing illnesses.

Having Myōkō Sensei at my side was an incalculable blessing. Her powerful spiritual abilities saved countless people from sickness and unhappiness. As a woman who had suffered much, she was able to strike chords of deep sympathy in other suffering women. Ivory-tower scholars and critics may criticize the kind of activity we pursued, but their censure would be less severe if they left their studies to go into the streets themselves to offer help where it is needed.

The innumerable people of the world all have different mental abilities, emotional experiences, and environmental conditions. To save all of them, one must have what, in Buddhist terms, is called the expedience or tactfulness to meet all occasions. Some people interpret this tactfulness as self-seeking, but in doing so they merely reveal the superficiality of their views. The correct way to save the masses and to bring peace to the world is first to relieve suffering and then to guide in the way of the Buddha's Truth to perfection of the personality. Expedience is a correct means to attain ultimate truth.

10.
An Account at the Pawnshop

I WAS poor, but my spirit was full, and my life was glowingly vibrant. After my morning milk deliveries, I immediately went out to give religious guidance and to lead people to a religious life. I never knew what time I would be able to return home. Sometimes it was around nine in the evening; sometimes it was after midnight. On some days, I would have a late supper; but even this was often interrupted. A member would rush in to tell me that a sick person needed me; and bolting my food, I would dash out, probably not to return until very late. In winter, the cold and the biting wind would add to my fatigue. When I finally went to bed, I slept very soundly.

I remember once hearing a knocking on the shutters covering our sliding doors. Turning on the light and looking at the clock, I saw that it was two in the morning. "Who can this be at such an hour?" I asked myself as I opened doors and shutters to find a woman, out of breath from a long run in the dark night roads. "Please come quickly; my baby has a fever. I'm afraid he will die. Please look at him and see what can be done." I changed at once into street clothes.

In those days, there was little medicine in Japan. What there was could not be easily obtained. In many cases, even when medicine was available, money was not. Doctors were few; and for many people, I was the only person they could rely on. I realized this and was eager to fulfill what I considered my mission by helping them. No matter how late at night, when called, I hurried to the side of the person in illness or pain. When the person who needs to be helped is in perfect accord with the person who wants to help, things happen that can be described only as miraculous. People who were so ill that doctors had given them up and others who had long suffered from stubborn chronic sicknesses recovered with my assistance. They and their families always rejoiced with tears in their eyes and thanked me from their hearts.

My own domestic and business affairs were in a desperate state. Because I left the house for guidance and other religious tasks immediately after morning milk deliveries, my bill collecting got behind, and I made no new customers. There were occasions when I failed to pay the milk suppliers on time, with the result that my supply was stopped and I had to find another supplier as fast as I could.

I was too busy to care about my appearance. I wore ready-made trousers bought at an old-clothes store. Since I am very tall, such pants never came much lower than my shins. People often commented on the odd way I was dressed. "These pants, you mean?" I would ask. "Oh, these are just the thing for rainy days. No matter how wet the weather is the bottoms stay dry. I wouldn't be surprised if they became all the rage before too long." "Oh, I see," was the kind of reply I generally got to this explanation.

Of course, I was only joking; but even those sad garments sometimes saved the day for us. Though they brought very little, they could be pawned; and the little they did bring stood between the seven members of my family and starvation on several occasions. Many things from my house were taken to the pawnshop. At formal Japanese-style occasions it is customary for men to wear a kimono with two outer garments: the skirtlike *hakama* and the fingertip-length coat called the *haori,* which is decorated with the family crest. These articles of clothing are expensive, and mine were frequently in the pawnshop. Whenever I had to participate in a formal event, on the preceding evening, I would go to the pawnshop and take my clothes out, only to return them when the event was over.

At the Kawamoto Pawnshop, I became so good a customer that the owner suggested I use an account book instead of the ordinary pawn tickets. I thanked him for the idea; but he said he would benefit by the arrangement, since it would relieve him of the need to write pawn tickets for individual articles. And from that day, for seven years, the Niwano household had an account at the Kawamoto Pawnshop. If one of us took the account book and an article for pawning to the shop, the owner lent money without comment. When one of us took money and the book to the shop, the previously pawned article was returned with equal taciturnity.

This was the way we lived. I was poor, but I was not regretful. I never sent my wife to the pawnshop. Though we were not blessed in the material things of life, I experienced a rich sense of fulfillment because of my work in spreading the Buddha's Law and in saving others from sorrow. As a father, I sometimes felt grieved that my children, who knew little or nothing of what was happening to them, had to suffer. But I suppressed both my compassion for my children and my love for my wife in order to devote all my energy to religious work.

11. Growth in Spite of War

By 1941, the membership of Risshō Kōsei-kai had reached one thousand. It was no longer possible for Myōkō Sensei and me to run our businesses and attend to our religious duties as well. She took the establishment of a government-controlled ice-distribution system as an opportunity to close her shop. Then, one night, in a dream she received divine revelation to the effect that she was to move her residence to a place in Suginami Ward, Wada Honchō, where she would find already standing on the land a house with a statue of the Bodhisattva Regarder of the Cries of the World near its entrance.

She told me about this on the following day, and the two of us set out immediately to find the house. When we got off the bus at the Nakano carbarn, we happened to meet a plasterer with whom Myōkō Sensei was acquainted. He asked where we were going. On learning that we were looking for a house, he said that not far away was a new one he had worked on, and he suggested that we have a look at it. The owner had built it for his son but might be willing to sell.

We found the house at once. Entering the gate, we saw a stone statue of Kannon, the Bodhisattva Regarder of the Cries of the World. Before seeing the inside of the house, Myōkō Sensei knew that she liked it. "There's the statue of Kannon. Why, the house might have been built especially for me!"

The house was small—three modest rooms and a small entryway—but it had a pleasing, bright mood. We visited the owner immediately. Negotiations went smoothly, and in a short while it was agreed that Myōkō Sensei would buy the house for eleven thousand yen. In the largest of the rooms, she installed a shrine to her guardian deity, the Bodhisattva Kokūzō, the Bodhisattva Space Treasury. This room was to be the center of her religious life. (The building, in the old headquarters compound, is now the Myōkō Memorial Hall.)

But even with this small house and the cramped room on the second floor of my milk shop, we lacked space so badly that the construction of a headquarters building became an absolute necessity. As luck would have it, the land next to Myōkō Sensei's house was vacant. Explaining that we wanted it for the construction of a headquarters for Kōsei-kai, we again conducted smooth and speedy negotiations with the owner, purchased the land, and held groundbreaking ceremonies on the eighth of November of that same year.

We did not have a large budget. Myōkō Sensei and I donated our money, and other members contributed to a total sum of sixteen thousand yen. At roughly that time, Myōkō Sensei had another spiritual revelation, in which she was instructed to obtain building materials as quickly as possible. World War II began for Japan about one month after our ground breaking. This immediately caused a severe shortage of materials. But throughout December, anyone who had the money could get what he needed. We decided to spend everything we had on construction materials; and on the twentieth of December, we held ceremonies marking the completion of the major framework. By the middle of January, controls on consumer goods became still more rigid. Building materials were virtually impossible to obtain, no matter how much money one was willing to spend. It was a very close race, but we finished our headquarters, which escaped burning in the war and served as the base for much of our dissemination activities in the postwar period. The timely acquisition of materials and the escape from war damage convince me that the building enjoyed the protection of the gods and buddhas.

Materials were not the only problem. Controls on labor made it difficult to hire even a single carpenter or plasterer. To compensate for the shortage, members did such unskilled labor as clearing the land, hauling lumber, mixing clay for the walls, and so on; but they hesitated to undertake the skill-demanding carpentry. Yet times would not permit such hesitation. Ultimately we had to do much of the carpentry work as well. The efforts of the members were a deeply touching example of the astounding things human beings can accomplish when confronted with the need to surpass the limits of their abilities.

During the construction work, the first American air raids on Tokyo caused great consternation among government officials, who immediately launched air-defense and escape-training courses. It required considerable confidence to go ahead with the construction of a new wooden building under such circumstances. We had confidence. We knew that our building would be safe. Our confidence was different from anything that is possible with limited human wisdom alone.

The building was small; but under prevailing conditions, it took one hundred and fifty days to complete. When I think about it now, I am amazed that we finished it at all. I went to the site and guided work daily. Of course, I worked too. The other members devoted their time and sweat. Using what modest supplies she could obtain, Myōkō Sensei prepared food for us. The building itself, the result of united efforts on all our parts, was later moved to the Kōsei Cemetery grounds.

A shortage of materials brought Kōsei-kai the only member I know of who was won through anger. During the construction work, we had to have two and a half bags of cement. We had received government authorization, but the military took priority in all such matters; and the cement itself was not forthcoming. A man who delivered a load of gravel to the site told us that a certain Mr. Chiba had some cement he was not using. We could persuade him to let us have it and then return the materials when our authorized supply was delivered. We followed this advice, and Mr. Chiba did let us have the cement. Our authorized supply, however, did not arrive. Mr. Chiba complained to the gravel man, who complained to us. There was nothing we could do. Then Mr. Chiba came to us himself, demanding his cement back. All I could do was apologize, and this made Mr. Chiba boilingly angry.

Using the difficult experiences everyone was undergoing then as subject matter, I started discussing the Buddha's Law with him. Looking as if he did not have the haziest idea what I was saying, Mr.

Chiba got angrier. But I remained calm and continued my teaching of the Law. Finally, Mr. Chiba yielded and asked to become a follower of Kōsei-kai.

On the seventh of May, 1942—a bright, warm day—to signify the completion of the headquarters, I hung up over the gate a sign bearing the name of the Dai-Nippon Risshō Kōsei-kai, in letters lovingly written by me. Scarcity of food would have precluded our celebration party if my elder brother had not brought twenty-nine kilograms of glutinous rice from the country. It was the first time he had any contact with Risshō Kōsei-kai. All he had known till then was that his younger brother had started some kind of religious group connected with the Lotus Sutra.

Although I had thought my proper path lay in managing my small business and conducting religious activities, Kōsei-kai's increasing number of members made it impossible for me to pursue this double course. Consequently, feeling that it would be unnatural to run against the ordained current of events, on the occasion of the completion of the headquarters I closed my milk shop and moved into the new building.

12. Training and Trips

NOT VERY long after its completion, the new headquarters building would no longer hold all the people who came for guidance and religious services. It became necessary for members to sit outside on the ground on grass matting. The sessions for groups who gathered in this way came to be known as *hōza,* one of our activities that has remained a basic practice from the inception of Kōsei-kai to the present, though it did not start with a fixed form and has changed from time to time.

The members were so devoted and eager that none of them complained about sitting on the ground or even regarded it as an inconvenience. They made circles of mats around the *hōza* leader. Often two or three concentric circles formed a single group. And when the group became very large, the people in the outermost circles had to stand throughout the discussion.

Members vied with each other for the privilege of being in charge of preparations for the meetings and cleanup afterward. If *hōza* was supposed to start at nine in the morning, these people would arrive as early as five or six, spread the matting, prepare everything, and then stay after three in the afternoon to put things in order again. All this was hard work, but the members pleaded with the leaders to be allowed to do it. They were eager to acquire as much virtue as possible from their efforts, and it was because they were permeated with this desire that they were able to achieve miraculous things.

They were equally devoted to and eager for all the other duties and services of the group, including morning and evening meetings, the observances held on memorial days, and the midwinter austerities.

For the midwinter austerities, they arose at four in the morning every day for thirty days from January to February. The night before, they set out a bucket of water. In the morning, breaking the ice that had formed on its surface, they poured the water over their heads. They then drew other buckets of water until they had emptied twenty or thirty over their bodies. They then read the Threefold Lotus Sutra. Each member practiced this discipline independently in his own home.

As a result of such training, several members developed abilities to receive spiritual inspirations and to invoke the sacred protective mantra. They could quickly cure colds or stomachaches. One of the most memorable of the enthusiastic members of the early period was Ken'ichirō Murata, the head carpenter for the construction of the headquarters building. Murata was very diligent in the midwinter austerities and became especially adept at the invocation of the sacred mantra. He took part in all our pilgrimages to Mount Shichimen (the holy mountain near Mount Minobu, where one of the priest Nichiren's disciples founded a temple in the thirteenth century) and advanced rapidly in *hōza* discussion groups.

Later a training hall was built at the headquarters building, and midwinter austerities were conducted there under a system that called for strict adherence to rules and schedules. People who were late to training were not allowed to enter. Bus service did not exist in those days, and people had to hurry along the cold, windy streets from the nearest train station. If they suspected they were late, they would take off their wooden clogs and run barefoot over the icy ground. If they did arrive late, they found the doors closed and had to content themselves with reading the Threefold Lotus Sutra in front of the door and returning, trembling, home. The leaders did not pamper the members, and the members survived their harsh training and made spiritual progress. The story of one woman should give an idea of the mood in which we lived. I shall let Mrs. Hiroyo Igusa speak for herself in these words taken from an extract of the official records of a meeting of former Tokyo chapter heads held on August 4, 1967.

"When my son, who is now twenty-five, was four years old, I was instructed to join a pilgrimage to Mount Shichimen. On the night before our departure, when I had made all my preparations, I was tested. My small boy suddenly developed a temperature of about forty degrees centigrade. I stayed up all night applying cold compresses to his head, but by morning his temperature still had not dropped. I did not know what to do but decided that I could not neglect my religious faith. Putting on a white pilgrimage kimono, I left the house at about four in the morning.

"Before I had gone far, I heard my eldest daughter calling, 'Mother, come back! Yoshiharu's having a fit!' I returned at once to find my son in convulsions.

"Dreading that the trouble might be very serious, I hurried to the house of Mrs. Ikuyo Morita, the leader of the second chapter—ours—to discuss the matter. She simply turned her back on me and refused to answer my questions. She was waiting to see if I would repent. Then she at last said, 'All right, I suppose you can come one train late.'

"Intending to do that, I returned home. As I was about to take my pilgrim's staff and leave to take the train, my son had another convulsion. It seemed impossible for me to go that day. I called the doctor, who did not know what the cause could be but said that it might be juvenile dysentery and recommended that we wait and watch a while longer. By about nine o'clock, the boy was somewhat better.

"I went to the headquarters, where I met Mrs. Tanaka, of the first chapter. She asked me why I was not on the pilgrimage train, and I explained. She then said that there were many posthumous Buddhist names for the second chapter and that I should attempt to make amends for not going on the trip by copying them. I set about the task eagerly.

"At lunchtime, when I returned home, my son was well and playing happily. I then saw clearly that his sickness had been a test of me. Realizing this, I went to the headquarters to copy out posthumous names for the four days that I knew the pilgrimage would last. But I was not sincere enough. I thought the matter would be settled by my doing this work. I had forgotten my children in the Law, for whom I was responsible. They were on the pilgrimage, and I remained in Tokyo. If I had so much as telephoned them at Mount Minobu. But I did not think of it.

"I was in for a difficult time at the meeting of thirty leaders that took place in the headquarters the day after the group returned. Sitting in the rear of the room and making myself as small as possible, I apologized from the bottom of my heart to both Mr. Niwano and Myōkō Sensei.

"Suddenly Myōkō Sensei called out, 'There's someone very foolish in this room! For the sake of her own child she left her children in the Law alone on Mount Minobu. She says she performed some tasks here to make up for it. Fool!'

"I had no idea such a loud voice could come from such a small body. The whole building seemed to be about to crack from the sound. Trembling, pale, and terrified, I could do nothing but look at the floor.

"When the leaders' meeting was over, we were to spread mats on the ground for a *hōza* counseling session. I was to guide one group, but before doing that I felt that I had to apologize to Myōkō Sensei. I could think of nothing else.

"I happened to meet Mrs. Iwafune, the head of the fifth chapter, and asked her to take me to Myōkō Sensei. Saying that it was all a part of religious training, she agreed to take me to the main room of the building. She opened the door and announced me. Mr. Niwano said, 'Very well, come in.'

"Kneeling with my forehead on the tatami floor and weeping with repentance, I seemed to strike a chord of sympathy. Myōkō Sensei said, 'It's all right; if that's the way you feel, it's all right.' Then she encouraged me to go out and guide my *hōza* group to the very best of my ability. Next she told the head of the fifth chapter to bring me some tea and some dried persimmons.

"But this was not the end of my penance. I next had to suffer the displeasure of the head of my own chapter, Mrs. Morita, who said to me, 'Anyone Myōkō Sensei says is no good is no good. I don't want to have anything to do with you.' For two months she would not speak to me. She would not exchange morning greetings with me and always sat with her back to me in *hōza* discussion meetings. Nothing is more painful than being ignored. A good scolding is much easier to take. Every day I read the Sutra of Meditation on the Bodhisattva Universal Virtue, the so-called sutra of repentance. I lived repentance until finally she began to speak to me again. This trial affected me very deeply. Mrs. Morita must have known that I am rash and tend to take things lightly. That is why she resolved to teach me a thorough lesson. I have not experienced any further tests since then. But that one was both bitter suffering and an extremely good chance to learn from a religious lesson."

This episode reminds me of the experience of a certain Zen priest aspirant who, as part of his training, was given a koan by his master and was expected to reach enlightenment on it in a fixed number of days. He was to sit morning and night concentrating on the koan and, when enlightenment came, to report to the master. According to the rules, if he failed to reach enlightenment, he did not have to go to the master.

But while the trainee was performing zazen, seated meditation, the priest in charge ordered him to report to the master. The trainee objected strenuously; he had not attained enlightenment. But the priest in charge physically dragged him from the training hall. Though a grown man, the trainee wept, clutched at pillars, and did all he could to resist, but to no avail.

Of course, he had no solution to the koan yet and was severely scolded and badly embarrassed when he appeared in the master's presence.

Such an experience convinces the person that he must devote himself entirely and enthusiastically to his training program. Ordinary common sense says that, since the rule requires no appearance before the master without enlightenment, there was no reason to force the trainee to go. But when spiritual renovation and growth are the aims, training cannot be limited by common sense. Sometimes an unreasonable shock must be administered to force the human being to shed his old self and thus reveal his true, inner self, develop his true powers, and manifest his true life-force. It is especially important to give attention to this today, when everything is interpreted in the light of facile rationalism.

Not everyone was permitted to make the important pilgrimage to Mount Shichimen. Those who could go were obliged to purify themselves for twenty-one days beforehand. They could not eat meat, fish, eggs, or milk. They could not use grated, dried bonito, which is used in the bean-paste soup that is important in the traditional Japanese diet. Furthermore, they could not even use pans that had been polluted by contact with any of these foods. For a week before departure they were obliged to conduct the cold-water ritual that was practiced during midwinter austerities. The buckets in which they drew the cold water had to be thoroughly purified by scrubbings with salt. Using an ordinary bath bucket could bring serious retributions on the head of the hopeful pilgrim. The night before departure, with ink I wrote the *Daimoku—Namu Myōhō Renge-kyō*—on the pilgrims' white clothes, which had been brought to me, and set them in front of my family Buddhist altar. On each garment I set a glass filled with fresh water. If the pilgrim had been negligent of spiritual development or if his mind and heart were not in a suitable state, froth would appear in the water. When this happened, he would be advised not to make the pilgrimage. All these strict preparations were necessitated by the harsh penalties inflicted on some of the pilgrims during our first trip.

The first pilgrimage took place in September, 1940. The weather was unseasonably warm. I was leading the party, and Myōkō Sensei was walking briskly at my side. On the way up the mountain, we all became thirsty. Fortunately, beside the main gate of the temple on Mount Minobu was a well. Near the well grew a fig tree, laden with delicious-looking, ripe fruit. In spite of the religious nature of the trip, two of the pilgrims acted like tourists on a hiking excursion and ate some of the figs.

In the inn that night, after supper, these two people came down with severe stomachaches. Myōkō Sensei invoked the gods and was asked the following question: "What is the meaning of stealing on the holy mountain? In such a state of mind, you must not climb Mount Shichimen tomorrow."

We were all shocked. What indeed could "stealing" mean? I noticed that the two ailing people remained kneeling with their faces on the floor. "This must have something to do with them," I thought.

"We ate some figs from the tree by the well," they admitted. So that was what was wrong. Though it was after eleven at night, we all joined in reading the sutra of repentance, the Sutra of Meditation on the Bodhisattva Universal Virtue.

We arose and departed at three o'clock the following morning. The weather was clear as we walked through the inner temples and had lunch at Akazawa before climbing Mount Shichimen. We stayed in a lodging hall of the temple that night and rose and went to the observation platform before dawn. After spiritual-inspirational training, we sat on the gravel, faced east, and read from the Threefold Lotus Sutra. The holy atmosphere of the mountain exerted an indescribably exhilarating physical and psychological influence. As we watched, gradually the edges of the clouds above Mount Fuji became tinged with red, then turned gleaming gold. Suddenly, with an arrow-like shaft of light, the sun appeared, lifting all of us to the pinnacle of excitement and joy.

One of my most vivid memories of pilgrimages to Mount Shichimen is connected with a religious ceremony that I was to conduct. October thirteenth is the death anniversary of the thirteenth-century priest Nichiren, who first uttered the *Daimoku*. On that day in 1945, when the turmoil of the immediate postwar period had begun to settle down, Myōkō Sensei received a divine revelation ordering me to offer an invocation to Shakyamuni Buddha (whose image is the focus of devotion of our organization) on my next birthday, November fifteenth.

In November, Myōkō Sensei was stricken with an attack of erysipelas and was forced to go to bed. I nursed her. Though I am constitutionally strong, I caught a cold, which suddenly developed into acute pneumonia. On the thirteenth and fourteenth of November, I lay ill with a fever of forty degrees centigrade. I was in the inner room of the headquarters building. I could eat nothing. The fifteenth—my birthday—was also the memorial day of the headquarters and the day on which I was to conduct the invocation ceremony. All the officers were happily and industriously making preparations.

My doctor said that I must not think of conducting a service with a temperature, but the most important thing for me was the knowledge that I would be failing my responsibility to the gods and buddhas if I did not.

On the morning of the fifteenth, I awoke at three o'clock. After a cold-water ritual in the bathroom, I wrote a Buddhist plaque, placed it in my domestic altar, and read the Lotus Sutra with all my mind. The fever did not go down. I went back to bed. Then, at nine, I received a divine inspiration: "You are still worried about your wife and children. You have not cut yourself from them. Unless you become as the gods, you will be unable to conduct the invocation ceremony." Then my fever dropped. I was able to lead the service.

Following an unwritten law of those days, I decided to make a pilgrimage to Mount Minobu as a token of my gratitude for having been allowed to carry out my duty safely. Though I still had a slight fever that evening, I performed the cold-water ritual and read the Lotus Sutra. Since I had eaten nothing for four or five days, I had some of the food that had been cooked for the ceremonies. Later that night, I put on my white pilgrim's clothes, took my staff, and joined eighty-seven other pilgrims on a train from Tokyo Station.

To reach Mount Minobu, it is necessary to change from the Tōkaidō Line to the Minobu Line at a station called Fuji. We did so, only to find a landslide blocking the tracks two stops before Minobu. There was nothing to do but walk along the tracks for the remaining eight kilometers.

In spite of the sickness and the strain of traveling and walking, after I visited the main hall and reported on the invocation ceremony, I felt miraculously refreshed. "As long as I'm in such good shape, I might as well climb Mount Shichimen tomorrow," I said to myself. And on the next morning, at the head of the group, I walked up the mountain, chanting the *Daimoku* all the way. It seemed impossible that two days earlier I had been suffering from a high fever and pneumonia. I think I can be justifiably proud that since the foundation of Risshō Kōsei-kai I have never missed an event that I was supposed to attend.

On my return to Tokyo, I found Myōkō Sensei completely recovered from her sickness. She greeted me with the words: "Mr. Niwano, from now on I am going to call you Kaichō Sensei." (The term means "president-teacher.") When I asked her why, she said that, in a divine revelation experienced while I was away, she had been instructed to do so. From that time, she and the other members of Risshō Kōsei-kai referred to me by that title. It was shortly after this that we began calling her Myōkō Sensei instead of Naganuma Sensei.

As I have said, no one was permitted to make pilgrimages to the mountains without reaching the correct stage of spiritual development. But I remember the following interesting story. Though one woman wanted desperately to join a pilgrimage to Mount Shichimen, her chapter head would not permit it. Further, her husband was opposed to her religious faith.

Undaunted, she decided to go anyway. The night of departure, she waited until her husband and children were in bed. Then, leaving a note saying that she would become a better wife for the trip and requesting permission to go, she tossed her white clothes and straw sandals out the window and sneaked from her own house. Dashing to the station, she hopped on the train and hid in the lavatory until it started. Then she appeared before the other pilgrims, pleading to be allowed to accompany them.

Pilgrimages were a strict part of our training. For a number of days beforehand, we performed the cold-water ritual as preparation. During the ascent of the mountain, we constantly chanted the *Daimoku, Namu Myōhō Renge-kyō*. Not only did these trips leave a deep impression on the pilgrims, they also helped cement relations between us and the priesthood of the Nichiren sect of Buddhism and contributed to our development as good members of society. We learned to help each other as much as possible. The strong and young helped the weak and old in climbing and in carrying provisions. (Since food was rationed then, we had to carry our own rice with us.) Usually we chartered one coach on the train. We were always very quiet, reading the Lotus Sutra or conducting calm *hōza* counseling sessions. Before leaving the train, we cleaned up any mess that we had made. In inns we never behaved like guests, but cleared our tables, spread our own bedding, and cleaned our rooms—even the toilets. This was excellent training for the pilgrims. In addition, it created a very good reputation for us among the members of the staffs of the inns and the people with whom they spoke about us. Indeed, many of the people working in the inns and shops we frequented and other citizens of the town of Minobu became members of Kōsei-kai.

In later years, when the membership grew to hundreds of thousands, pilgrimages of this kind became impossible. We changed to a system of group pilgrimages centering on the headquarters. But for those of us who took part in them, the inspiring trips in the early days are precious memories.

13. In Jail

Two or three years after Risshō Kōsei-kai was formed, relations between Director General Murayama and Vice-Director General Ishihara became so strained that Murayama asked to be permitted to resign. I did not want him to leave. In 1940, after much quarreling, Ishihara was the one to quit. (Since I was indebted to him and since he had once been my employer, I have kept up friendly relations with Ishihara to the present. On the occasion of the celebration of my seventieth birthday, I invited him to attend the party held for me at the Imperial Hotel, in Tokyo. As he was unable to come, I visited him on the following day. We sat together for some time reminiscing about the past.)

We continued without further incident for three years and then, in 1943, faced a major trial. On March 13, a mustached policeman suddenly appeared at Kōsei-kai's headquarters and asked Myōkō Sensei and me to accompany him to the police department. Wondering what it could be about, we innocently followed the officer. I was in an ordinary kimono, and Myōkō Sensei had on a short informal jacket over her kimono.

Arriving at the police department, we were immediately imprisoned because, they claimed, Myōkō Sensei's spiritual guidance was confusing people's minds. In those days, what was known as the Peace Preservation Law was in effect. It had been promulgated primarily to control and repress the communist movement, but its effects were strongly felt by the Christians and other religious groups, as well. Realizing that I was the true leader of the Dai-Nippon Risshō Kōsei-kai, the police had arrested me instead of the director general. The detective who interrogated me was familiar with the terminology we use. "You are Mrs. Naganuma's spiritual godparent and as such ought to reconsider the principles you use in instruction," he said.

I replied, "There is nothing wrong with my instruction principles. We have a large number of members, and it may be that some of them have emotional problems and say and do things that are not absolutely correct. But there is nothing wrong with my basic instruction principles."

That was my position, and I stuck by it. The police did not know what to do. They had probably been prepared to let me go at the first indication of compromise on my part. But since I showed no such signs, they kept me in jail for two weeks. During that time, they interrogated me daily; but I never varied from the stand that our principles are correct.

Prisons are never good places. I dare say they have improved; but in the days of World War II they were very unpleasant. My underclothes were full of lice. But I did not let my situation get me down. I regarded it as part of my religious discipline. During my stay in jail, I came to be on good terms with the police. I surprised some of them by making accurate predictions on the basis of their names. Ultimately they jokingly called me the god-man. At interrogation time, they would call: "Come on out, Mr. God-man."

In everything, however, I did not waver from the path dictated by my religious faith and refused even to pretend to compromise. The police were at a loss to know what to do; but since they were unable to find me guilty of anything, after two weeks they let me go. One week later, they released Myōkō Sensei. Explained in outline this way, the incident seems simple, when in fact its internal causes were highly complicated and concerned my domestic situation.

My wife was strongly opposed to my life of religious faith. In the eyes of the world, her disappointment was only natural from the standpoint of a homemaker and the wife of a man who spent all his time helping others. Furthermore, when I gave up the milk shop and dedicated myself entirely to the Law, our way of life became poorer and more difficult. I received very little money from Kōsei-kai. We were forced to make frequent trips to the pawnshop, and we all—my wife and I and our five children—lived in one small room on the first floor of the headquarters building. The room was so cramped that at night when we spread our bedding some of the mattresses curled up against the sliding doors, from which they gradually wore away the paper covering. At about that time, my wife had just had another baby and was forced to remain in bed. Before I went out on guidance missions, I would prepare a large pot of rice gruel and put it on a hibachi charcoal brazier set by her bed so that at least the family would not go hungry.

Throughout this period, I was always either out on guidance or other business with Myōkō Sensei or was discussing the Law with her and other members in the headquarters. My wife must not have liked the idea that I spent so much of my time with other women. It is true that Myōkō Sensei was seventeen years my senior; but after all, she was a woman, as were many of the other Kōsei-kai leaders with whom I was constantly brought in contact. Frankly, there were times when I felt that some of the female members were interested in me. While I was still running the milk shop, I made deliveries to a large restaurant where two waitresses were Kōsei-kai members. These two seem to have made a bet about which of them could catch the milkman first. They tried all kinds of wiles, but I never paid any attention to them. Still, my wife must have known intuitively that something might happen. Nor is it surprising that she earnestly wanted to return to the ordinary way of life of a married couple. Sometimes her longing made her very angry. Once she even ripped up the *hakama* of my formal kimono. The garment was very important to me.

I tried to be as resilient as a willow in the wind, while never compromising my rock-steady inner faith. I felt that I could have understood my wife's feelings completely if she had been married to an ordinary man. But as the wife of a person dedicated entirely to the Buddha's Law, her attitude was unpardonable.

The Kōsei-kai leaders considered my wife an interference in my work, a kind of Devadatta—a cousin of Shakyamuni Buddha who was first his follower and then his enemy but even then was an important element in the Buddha's spiritual development. Some of them insisted that I should be separated from my wife; others sympathized with her. I later learned that Myōkō Sensei had felt that the situation was hopeless until she received divine instructions to clear up my domestic affairs. This happened while I was away in the country at memorial services for my father. I knew nothing about the divine instructions. On my return to Tokyo, a delegation from Kōsei-kai met me at Akabane Station and, instead of allowing me to return home, took me straight to the home of one of the members. There a group of leaders was waiting to tell me that they were going to rent a house in which they wanted me to install my wife and children. The house was in relatively distant Nerima Ward. The announcement came as a great shock. I could not take such a step without consulting my wife. The leaders passed strict judgment on me: I was still too much attached to my wife and children and was not yet sufficiently refined spiritually to fulfill the great mission entrusted to me by the gods. I was instructed to live in Myōkō Sensei's house and was watched so that I did not speak to my wife, who had not moved to Nerima but remained in the headquarters. It was while we were living in this way that Myōkō Sensei and I were imprisoned.

Much later I found that the following circumstances surrounded our summons by the police. My wife wanted me to return to our former way of life. In our neighborhood lived Mrs. Umeno Tsunaki, the head of the Tengu-fudō organization, who was doubtless displeased to see a former student succeeding with another religious organization. With the assistance of the principal of a neighborhood kindergarten and another influential member of the neighborhood, these two women reported to the local police that Myōkō Sensei's spiritual practices were confusing people. Without proof, the police refused to act. The group of conspirators then carried a petition around the neighborhood, collected a number of names, and in this way compelled the police to do something. Of course, at the time of our arrest, I knew nothing of all this.

With the two main leaders of the organization in prison, the membership fell into confusion; and all but two of the chapter heads left the organization. The ones who remained, however, were very considerate and even brought me homemade lunches in prison.

As a further outcome of the incident, the director general of Kōsei-kai, Mr. Murayama, was so frightened that he insisted on being allowed to resign. No pleading would convince him to remain. I had to take his place, becoming president. Myōkō Sensei then became the vice-president.

While the two of us were in jail, some of the members said that Myōkō Sensei should be reduced to the standing of an ordinary member. It was because of her spiritual revelations that the police had investigated and imprisoned us. The members who felt this way further thought that the organization would be better off if it adhered solely to my policies, which were oriented largely toward the Law—the Buddha's teachings. But I put a stop to this by saying that Myōkō Sensei and I had founded the organization together and were deeply related to each other in religious ties. I could not permit such a thing. I continued, "It is because none of you carefully observed or bore in mind Myōkō Sensei's divine revelations that the matter reached the police. The gods are trying to lift us up. If we debase them, we are certain to face retribution." Nonetheless, many of the leaders could not be reconciled. They thought that two leaders would only confuse the membership. People who felt this way left the group. Being caught between the secular needs of the organization and the divine requirements represented by Myōkō Sensei's revelations caused me considerable suffering.

Of course, I neither denied nor undervalued the phenomenon of revelations from the gods, but I felt it was important to protect ourselves from any evil revelations that might be disclosed. Completely accepting divine revelations without question was difficult.

In the course of the midwinter austerities and prayers conducted during the early days of the organization, some members, when visited by the spirits of such animals as foxes, snakes, and badgers, performed grotesque, mad antics that were distressing to see. Even relatively advanced members were unable to do anything about it. But Myōkō Sensei and I could restore such people to their senses by chanting the *Daimoku* and invoking the protective mantra. Although the world of shamanism involves startlingly miraculous things, it is not without danger.

Many of the leaders who left the organization gradually returned to receive my warm welcome and to become top leaders in Kōsei-kai in later years. At some time and somehow, this incident came to be called the first flight of steps in the history of Risshō Kōsei-kai. It greatly reinforced and strengthened the faith of the entire membership.

When I was still a milkman, we made it a policy to accept no alms or charities from members. But sometimes, families felt obliged to express gratitude in some way when illnesses were cured or family troubles settled by means of our help. In such cases, they would place small amounts of money in the Buddhist altar at the headquarters. These gifts usually amounted to no more than ten or fifteen yen a month. I always took the entire amount to the Nakano Police Station as a contribution to the army and navy. I continued this practice regularly each month until 1942. But in May of that year, when I closed the milk shop and dedicated myself to the Law, it became essential to put all money into the Kōsei-kai funds. I am convinced that it was our past record for contributions and awareness of the new circumstances that convinced the Nakano police of our sincerity and prevented their taking action against me and Myōkō Sensei the first time my wife and Mrs. Tsunaki made a report to them.

In passing, it was remarkable that both Myōkō Sensei and I were released from jail on the memorial days of our guardian deities.

14. Widening Fields

Our dissemination work in the regions outside the city of Tokyo began with the Ibaraki Chapter, in Ibaraki Prefecture, founded in 1947, and moved farther afield to Shizuoka, Chiba, Saitama, Kanagawa, Yamanashi, and Nagano prefectures. The program was not planned and organized as it is today but consisted of teaching trips to various areas for the opening of chapters or the completion of training halls. We took advantage of such occasions to call together believers in the local area for sermons on the Law and for leadership training. It is true that, before 1947, I had gone to Myōkō Sensei's home village in Saitama Prefecture to teach; but that did not actually fall into the category of dissemination work for Kōsei-kai. Sometimes I made the trips when Myōkō Sensei received divine revelations that a member in such and such a place was suffering. At other times, it became necessary to go in order to satisfy written requests for guidance on the part of the regional chapters themselves. Because all our work was concentrated in the general region of the Kantō district, around Tokyo, things were fairly easy. Teishirō Okano, one of the directors, and Hiroshi Naganuma, the head of the first chapter, frequently made teaching trips. They would leave for Ibaraki Prefecture at noon, visit three places or so, and return on the last train, which brought them to Tokyo at one or two in the morning.

I distinctly recall the first teaching trip we made to Ibaraki. In those days, there were no taxis. We spread grass matting and one cushion in the bed of a half trailer attached to a bicycle. Myōkō Sensei rode there, and I walked along behind. It was winter. I wore a double cloak—somewhat like an Inverness—over my ordinary kimono and had a white scarf around my neck. At the time, my hair was cropped very short, like that of a Buddhist priest. I did not let it grow out until after Myōkō Sensei's death.

The head of the Ibaraki Chapter—who is now head of the Ibaraki Branch—was Nobuyo Nozaki, one of the pioneers of early regional dissemination work and one of the shining leaders in the history of our organization. A few years ago, she joined me and some other members in a pilgrimage to thirty-three revered temples in the Tokyo area. But she had put on so much weight that she could not make it up the mountains without being pushed and pulled. Convinced that she was disqualified to guide and teach others if she could not follow her own leader up a mountain, she consulted her doctor and lost twenty-five kilograms. When I heard this I was pleased, but not amazed, at her sincerity, for the same devotion has shown itself in all her activities in the chapter. The coal mines in the district where she lives began to suffer financial depression when petroleum became the major source of energy in Japan. One after another, the mines closed, and the population began to fall off. Mrs. Nozaki insisted that hard times like those demand intensified teaching of the Buddha's Law for the sake of the salvation of the people. Thanks to her efforts, as the general population in the region decreased, the membership of the Kōsei-kai chapter increased.

Another of my vivid memories of early regional teaching missions involves a trip to Fujinomiya in March, 1953. We were returning from Mount Minobu in a torrential downpour along a narrow road. On our way, we stopped to give guidance and to teach at a local training hall. Hiroshi Naganuma was carrying Myōkō Sensei on his back. (He and Okano always accompanied us on our teaching trips. Naganuma became famous as the man who carried Myōkō Sensei on his back. If he juggled her or treated her in the least roughly, she complained: "I'm not a piece of luggage, you know.") About one thousand people had gathered. Since not all of them could get in the building, large numbers stood under umbrellas in the rain as they listened to the lectures.

In the earliest days, on our teaching journeys, we always rode the third-class railway coaches with their cramped, wooden-backed seats. Later, arguing that third class was too uncomfortable, the leaders bought second-class tickets for us. For a long time, I was strongly opposed to the purchase of an automobile. "Religious people should go on foot to teach. We're not aristocrats!" I insisted. But as the teaching campaign spread all over the country, the limits of my activity expanded; and schedules became very tight. It was no longer possible for me to cling to this attitude.

In 1949 or 1950, we bought a large German car that seated six or eight people. In this we launched a planned regional teaching program. Dissemination teams including some of the top leaders of the organization took turns traveling afield in the automobile. Sometimes their campaigns carried the teams as far away as Kagoshima, in the southern part of Kyushu, and kept them on the road for as much as a month.

We always put up in the homes of members. Our stay was almost always no more than a short night's sleep. Sometimes there was no time for a bath. It was not unusual for us to dry our underwear as we drove along, since, if we washed it out the night before, it often would not dry before we had to depart to meet the next stop on our schedule. And on our arrival at the next place, we usually had to begin teaching or holding *hōza* sessions without even stopping for a gulp of tea.

We were all deeply sincere, and so were the members we visited. It made no difference that we arrived late at night. There was always a large group waiting for us. With students as earnest as this, the dissemination teams had to stay on their toes.

Usually our meetings were held in the offices of the local branch or chapter. But when these places were too small, we held them in Buddhist temples or Shinto shrines. Sometimes temples or shrines were good enough to request that we meet in their precincts. Holding Kōsei-kai *hōza* sessions in Shinto shrines is an example of the early budding of the spirit of religious cooperation.

People in the regional areas met Myōkō Sensei with overwhelming enthusiasm, many of them nearly in tears. Because of their trust in her spiritual powers, they would call out her name. Indeed, usually two or three people were cured of illnesses by merely crying "Myōkō Sensei!" The simple act of paying reverence to her restored speech to the mute. I realize that people who believe only in Western-style scientific medicine may laugh at what I say, but the facts remain the facts.

The universal determination of all our members was seen in those people who took turns of duty in the Tokyo headquarters. At the time, we operated on a system in which duties were assigned on a rotating basis according to chapter affiliation. For instance, people in the Tochigi and Fukushima prefectural chapters were affiliated with the second headquarters chapter. They came to the headquarters when it was the second chapter's turn to be on duty. Members affiliated with the third chapter came all the way from Kyoto. In spite of the length of time they had to travel, they went straight to work on arriving. We did not even have adequate luggage storage for them. But no one complained. They undertook training and tasks diligently and were happy even to be scolded by the leaders. If it was their good fortune to see Myōkō Sensei from a distance or—even better—to speak to her, these members nearly fainted with excitement. In fact, on one occasion, a person did faint when she saw Myōkō Sensei, a living human being, ascend the platform to deliver a talk. This person had firmly believed Myōkō Sensei to be a buddha. Although this was an extreme case, many members entertained a very similar feeling.

All our members did everything they could to make us comfortable when our travels brought us to their homes. Some went so far as to buy new bedding for us. A fisherman partitioned off a part of the work area of his house and made a bath for us there. His house had formerly lacked one because his family had used the public baths. It was a simple affair, with only a tub. The cold wind whistled through the cracks in the walls. But we were deeply grateful that he had taken the care to make it for us.

The officers of the headquarters education group were not the only people to take part in dissemination activities. Leaders from chapters and ordinary members traveled as far as northeastern Honshu, Hokkaido, Shikoku, and Kyushu to offer guidance to relatives and acquaintances. They joined us in teaching in various towns and villages and were so intent on sharing the saving way of the Law that they refused the most ordinary demonstrations of hospitality. They sacrificed their family lives, cut corners to save money enough for travel expenses, and carried their own food. Their fervor to share the teaching and their great compassion exceed all my powers of description. It is thanks to the efforts of members like these that gradually the light of the Law spread throughout the Japanese nation as Kōsei-kai developed from liaison offices to training halls.

Here I would like to make some comments about Genshō—originally Gennosuke—Sano, a pioneer in dissemination work in the Kansai district (which includes the cities of Osaka, Kyoto, Kobe, and the surrounding areas).

Until he joined Risshō Kōsei-kai, Mr. Sano had worked for a manufacturer of wooden buckets, which were made in Aomori Prefecture and sold in Tokyo. At the time, World War II was in its most violent stages. Metal was unobtainable for civilian use; but because of the air raids, every family tried to have two or three buckets handy for use in fire fighting. This meant that the wooden buckets sold very well.

His wife was ill, and the couple became members of Kōsei-kai in the hope of curing her. I analyzed his name and told him that the company for which he worked would be in trouble in its second year. Although he half doubted me because of the prosperity the company was enjoying, he gave up his position as business manager. It was a good thing. Two years later, the manufacturer of wooden buckets was sued for faulty merchandise. The buckets were made of plywood, which was sound enough as long as it was wet but which leaked badly when allowed to dry out.

Although he had been a materialist, Mr. Sano soon became a man of tremendous religious faith. Intelligent, good at calculations, and blessed with a cheerful disposition, he soon accepted the position of administrative director of the headquarters. Then he became the head of the first chapter and soon the general director of our organization. Because of his warmth, generosity, and seriousness, he did everything he undertook well.

He was eager to pioneer a Kōsei-kai organization in the Kansai district. In spite of his frequent requests to be allowed to undertake the task, I refused permission because I felt that Kōsei-kai was not yet strong enough for such a step. Nonetheless, he persisted; and in late March, 1950, I consented. His intention to do this work was so pure and strong that before receiving permission he had sold his house, earmarked two hundred thousand yen for the dissemination fund, and had copies of the Lotus Sutra mimeographed at his own expense. On hearing this, I was deeply moved by his strong will and his spirit of service.

He and his second wife (his first wife had died, and he had remarried a lady introduced to him by Myōkō Sensei and me) and their three-year-old daughter left Tokyo for the Kansai area, where they moved into a handsome house in Ashiya, between Kobe and Osaka.

At first the lack of members caused them serious uneasiness. But soon they made contact with Mrs. Noriko Okabe, who had been a member when she lived in Tokyo and had maintained a tenuous connection by paying dues of ten yen a month after her move to Kobe. Mrs. Okabe, a widow, had lost her second and third sons in the war and lived with her eldest son and his wife. Sano's fervent teaching soon helped these people form a deeply dedicated Kōsei-kai family, which became the kernel from which a whole range of faithful groups grew in Osaka, Kobe, Wakayama, Himeji, Okayama, and Hiroshima.

It was owing to the efforts of Genshō Sano and his wife that the circle of the Law was widened to include the Kansai district. Many people who worked with him have left testimonials to Sano's kindness and effectiveness and to the consideration and economy of his wife. After laying the foundations for the Kansai organization, Sano returned to the headquarters, where he served as an advisor. In 1974, he died, at the age of eighty.

15. In the Service of the Smallest

I WOULD like to turn for a moment to the period of World War II, when the oppressive power of the militarists extended to all phases of Japanese life, including religion. All kinds of religious organizations suffered from oppression, but because of the militarists' mistaken belief that the teachings of Nichiren (who propagated the Lotus Sutra) and those of the Lotus Sutra (on which his teachings are based) could be put to the service of ultranationalism, less pressure was applied to organizations—like Risshō Kōsei-kai—that professed faith in that sutra.

In truth, the Lotus Sutra, completely the opposite of all power philosophies, advocates respect for humanity, the perfectability of man, and peace for mankind. We did not attempt to take advantage of the ultranationalism then rampant in Japan. Instead we remained a group huddled in a corner and devoted to mutual protection and the preservation and education of human beings. From the standpoint of the militaristic national state, individual human lives were of little importance. As an organization devoted to the respect of individual human lives, we might have become the victims of government oppression. But the military's mistaken interpretation of the nature of the Lotus Sutra proved to be our good fortune.

If we escaped oppression from the military, we were not spared the censure of the mass communication media. One newspaper called us traitors because groups of women came together under our auspices to spend whole days doing nothing but reading sutras when the factories and other enterprises of the nation were crushed with work and crying out for help. While realizing that there might be something in this objection, we clung to our faith because, on closer examination of the issue, we saw that spiritual calm and repose and the healing of psychological wounds also served the good of the nation.

With the intensification of the war, more and more people came to us. And the increase in our membership stimulated the police to interfere with us in more annoying ways. At night, even when no police or air-raid warnings were in effect, they would come to us with orders to turn out the electric lights by which we had been conducting *hōza* sessions. Ironically, this had a spiritually strengthening effect. To take the place of the electricity, we lighted candles, which we shielded with newspaper to prevent their being visible from the outside. Sitting around these lights gave us all the feeling of truly protecting the flame of the Law of the Lotus Sutra.

The noted Japanese Christian writer Reverend Toyohiko Kagawa, who is intimately familiar with the Lotus Sutra, made some pertinent comments about it and the way the Japanese people interpreted it in the days of World War II. In his book *Religion as Life* he says:

"Reading the Lotus Sutra made me happy that Japan has preserved such a fine work for over a thousand years. There is good reason why prince-regent Shōtoku [574–622] and Nichiren endorsed this sutra. The Lotus Sutra is not a philosophical work, but a perfect religion in itself. In this, it differs from the Agama sutras, which the Buddha expounded in the first period of his teaching.

"But I wonder to what extent the Japanese people today realize the teachings of the Lotus Sutra in their daily lives and the extent to which followers of that sutra think its teachings ought to be so realized. The number of followers of Nichiren Buddhism who use the Lotus Sutra as a tool in the service of the militarists and the privileged classes makes me indignant. But I was relieved and overjoyed to see that the Lotus Sutra itself teaches the very opposite of the way such people use it. I was very happy to learn that the true essence of the Lotus Sutra is to be found in the practice and realization of its teachings.

"When I learned that the truest follower is one who humbly reveres even the smallest beings, I discovered that I too might be called a follower of the Lotus Sutra. Believers in this sutra have no reason to fault Christ and his disciples. Indeed, the believer in the Lotus Sutra should rejoice that its predictions have been fulfilled in Jesus Christ."

"Who humbly reveres even the smallest beings." We were the smallest beings, striving to walk hand in hand on the path of life. But even the smallest beings enjoy mighty protection when they bear the grave responsibility of being an emissary of the Buddha. My personal experiences demonstrate the working of this protection.

On August 8, 1941, I received orders to report for military duty. The war between Japan and China was moving into its last phase, and the danger of conflict with the United States was growing stronger. Thirty-four years old, I was strong and healthy. I was prepared to serve from three to five years, if I was not killed in battle. Though my own resolution was to be brave and do the best I could, Kōsei-kai's members were troubled to be deprived of one of their leaders.

But Myōkō Sensei received a divine revelation to this effect: "Niwano will be home within three to five days. It is unthinkable that a man with a great mission should be sent to the front as a soldier. Niwano has not yet been able to abandon himself entirely. Until he does, he will be unable to serve as a true disciple of the Buddha. He must ponder this and leave now."

Reflecting on this severe revelation, I asked myself if my willingness to serve in the military to the best of my ability indicated that I had not completely abandoned myself for the sake of my mission. Perhaps so. If I had given myself to my mission entirely, I would have regarded being ordered to the front as a misfortune.

Be that as it may, it was impossible that I should return in three to five days. With the nation on the brink of a huge war, my personal fate was inconsiderably small, no more than a sheet of paper in a typhoon. Like a typhoon, war sweeps all before it—the good, the bad, the rich, the destitute, the day laborer, the university professor, and everyone else. The leader of a religious organization with about one thousand members does not count at all. No matter what Myōkō Sensei's revelation said, that could not be altered. There must have been some mistake.

I left Tokyo Station at eight in the evening, on August ninth. About a hundred neighbors and members of Kōsei-kai came to see me off. On the following day, I arrived at the Maizuru training base and, for some reason, was declared physically disqualified.

I was struck dumb. At the same time, I experienced a burning sensation throughout my body. My person, which I had considered no more significant than a scrap of paper in the wind, suddenly took on great importance. The Buddha had assigned to one of the smallest beings the mission of saving his fellow small beings.

16. Revelations

SPIRITUAL contacts and divine revelations were an important aspect of the practices and beliefs of Reiyū-kai. Both Myōkō Sensei and I had been trained by Mr. Arai of that organization; and for about the first year after we founded Risshō Kōsei-kai, such revelations manifested themselves with extreme force and frequency. The pronouncements we received came mainly from Fudō Myō-ō, the Bodhisattva Hachiman, Bishamonten, Shichimen Daimyōjin, and the Bodhisattva Nichiren.

I have already mentioned some of the revelations Myōkō Sensei received in connection with me, but the most severe was the order for me to live apart from my wife and children: "Shakyamuni Buddha left his palace when his son, Rahula, had just been born. Niwano, too, you must leave your family. You have six children. In the future, you must not allow your mind to be distracted by either your wife or your children. Unless you can do this, you are not worthy to be called a disciple of the Buddha."

This happened in 1944. At once, I sent my wife and children to my family's home in the country and started living alone, in complete dedication to my religious training. I refused to try to explain myself to the many people who criticized me, because I realized that they could not understand the motivations of a man who had given his whole life to true faith.

I sometimes became lonely for my family. But when I did, a divine revelation would come to this effect: "You still can't separate yourself from your wife and children. What good do you think your attitude will do? The less you worry about them the stronger will be the protection granted them by the gods."

But since I am fundamentally a man of common sense, I would object: "Isn't it natural for a man to think about his wife and children? The Buddha teaches compassion for all sentient beings. If that's the case, it seems that abandoning wife and child, the closest people in the world, violates the teachings of the Buddha. It is a great sin to bring trouble on one's family. It is both inhuman and antisocial." But whenever I reacted in this way, on the following day, Myōkō Sensei would say to me, "Last night you thought about your wife and children and offended the gods, didn't you?" Her telepathic powers were astounding.

Thinking about the situation now, I realize that I was wrong to object in this way. I did it because I was too modest to understand the leadership mission that had been settled on me. In my own eyes, I was no more than an ordinary lay believer.

Even though I remained a layman, in order to become a leader, I had to undergo the same kind of religious discipline as a priest. In 1954, I was able to call my family back to me again; but during the ten years we were apart I made highly important spiritual progress. I was able to study the Lotus Sutra thoroughly and could give myself to unrestricted guidance and instruction of other believers. Had my wife and children remained by my side, I would not have been able to develop in this way. My own experience gave me a striking understanding of Shakyamuni's need to separate himself from his wife and son.

My experience of a life like that of the priesthood enabled me to make a definite choice between the Buddhism of the laity and that of the clergy. From that time, I thought more and more in terms of Buddhism of the laity.

In spite of the six years of harsh ascetic practice prior to his enlightenment, in his first teachings Shakyamuni rejected asceticism and advocated the Middle Path. In the Nirvana Sutra, the last of his teachings, he said, "My teachings are not entrusted to monks and nuns but to the men and women of the laity." By this he meant that the laymen, not the clergy, would bring his teachings to full life. It is most important to know why Shakyamuni, who attained enlightenment after arduous asceticism and who remained apart from his own family for the rest of his life, taught that lay Buddhism would be the true way to protect and apply his teachings.

I am not attempting to sound like a great man. I do not rank my own experiences with those of Shakyamuni, but I too was enlightened to the importance of lay Buddhism after ten years in which I opposed the gods, argued with them, and diligently sought the Truth. By being separated from my family for ten years of struggle and search, I came to realize that faith is real only when it embraces the whole family.

The next divine revelation with great meaning for me had to do with reading. "You have the duty to spread the teachings of the Lotus Sutra to the world. Abandon all other reading and dedicate yourself to it alone." For a time, I abided by this rule. I did not read magazines or newspapers, because they contain information on the changing situation of the world and the divine revelation instructed me not to be distracted by such things. Gradually, however, I came to think that it might be safe to read the works of Nichiren, which are true and do not change with the times. One evening, after going home, I read some of these writings. The following day, Myōkō Sensei said to me, "Niwano, last night you had delusions and read the works of Nichiren, didn't you?" I was too embarrassed to raise my head.

Though I abided by some of the divine revelations, I paid no attention to any that deviated from the teachings of the Lotus Sutra. I would not countenance those sudden flashes of enlightenment that founders of religious organizations are sometimes said to experience. The Lotus Sutra was always the central element. Spiritual powers were recognized only when they assisted in the understanding of the sutra or served to enhance its importance. The Buddha's Law came first; I would not accept even divine revelations that departed from the Law.

For this reason, I had several disputes with the deities. Sometimes, at meetings of the senior leaders of Kōsei-kai, Myōkō Sensei would experience visitations. If I was convinced that they were in keeping with the sutra, I explained to the others. But, if they were unreasonable and unconvincing, I refused to comment. The deities were often enraged and scolded me: "Niwano, if you do not do as I say, I will bring physical harm to you." Still I would not give in, but replied, "Do as you like. Take my life. I have devoted it to my task already."

Judging from my continued good health to this day, I must have been right. No, it was the Law that was absolutely right.

In late March, 1945, when the war was moving into its final phase, I was once again summoned to military service. In those days, even inexperienced men in middle age or early old age were being called up and sent into the expendable divisions. I was resigned to going finally to the hell of battle. But Myōkō Sensei had another divine revelation: "Niwano will come back on the twenty-eighth."

Not completely believing it, I proceeded to the Maizuru training base, where, as a formality, I underwent a physical examination. Looking steadily into my face, the examiner said, "You have important work to do on the home front. People who save the nation on the battlefield and those who save others at home are of equal importance. Disqualified!" And I took a train to Tokyo, arriving at seven twenty on the morning of March twenty-eighth.

Tokyo had been reduced to a wasteland, but our headquarters still stood. About a thousand loyal members continued to come for training and discussions. They wore baggy bloomers or civilian-guard uniforms, had sooty faces, and carried lunches of potatoes or yams. But their eyes sparkled with power. The mood of the place was still bright.

17.
All Came Home

Since the beginning of the war many of our members had been drafted and sent to battle. We saw them all off and gave them each a stomach warmer bearing the words "*Namu Myōhō Renge-kyō,*" "Eternal as Heaven and Earth," and "Many in Body but One in Spirit." Thin slips of paper bearing the name of each soldier and our prayer that he would serve well and safely were pasted on the woodwork in a room in the headquarters. Soon one wall was almost covered with them. From Risshō Kōsei-kai about four hundred fifty men went to war; all of them returned home safe when the fighting was done.

On the fifteenth of August, 1945, a large group of members gathered in the headquarters to hear the emperor's radio broadcast announcing surrender. When it was over, we conducted a lengthy service.

Motoyuki Naganuma had been sent to northern China in November, 1943. Many months after the end of the war, he still had not returned. Feeling certain that he must have been killed, we gave him a posthumous Buddhist name and held services in his memory. Then, in May, 1946, he suddenly turned up in perfect health. Myōkō Sensei and the rest of us were so overjoyed that we thought we were dreaming.

On his return, Naganuma was pained at what he considered his loss of training in religious matters. Risshō Kōsei-kai had developed greatly in his absence, and he felt that he had much catching up to do. From childhood, he had been a diligent, serious, quiet person. His aunt—Myōkō Sensei—often commented on the way in which he preferred to economize by eating other people's leftovers instead of the portion set aside for him. He worked hard, sometimes taking his meals in the kitchen instead of allowing himself the time to come into the main part of the house to eat in a leisurely fashion.

In the days of his youth, there were no flush toilets in Tokyo homes. Waste accumulated in cisterns, which were emptied every month or so by the collectors of night soil to be used as agricultural fertilizer. As more and more members of Kōsei-kai called on Myōkō Sensei, once a month became insufficient to keep the cistern at her house usable. Motoyuki undertook the task of emptying it more frequently himself. He carried the night soil away and carefully cleaned everything for the sake of both appearance and sanitation. He said he was glad that the cistern filled quickly because it meant an increase in Kōsei-kai membership. In whatever spare time he had from work and chores, he was always to be found in front of the family Buddhist altar, reading the Lotus Sutra.

After his return from the war, in spite of our urging him to assume a position of leadership, he preferred to perform humble tasks until he had made up for the time he had lost. The task he selected was emptying the headquarters toilet cisterns and carrying the night soil to places where it could be used as fertilizer.

After a while, however, we succeeded in convincing him to accept a post as a leader. From that position, he steadily rose to become a director. He was indispensable to both Myōkō Sensei and me. His earnestness and selflessness contributed immensely to the development of our organization.

Some of the places to which Motoyuki Naganuma carried night soil were the gardens that Kōsei-kai members cultivated on land left open and desolate as the result of bomb raids. This movement started when Myōkō Sensei and I began using the vacant ground of a primary school adjacent to our headquarters. Seeing the land rank with weeds, we decided that this was wasteful and began weeding and caring for the plants originally set there by the pupils of the school. The crop we raised the first year was divided equally between the owner of the land and the authorities of the school, to whom we carried the produce on bicycles.

The success of this initial project led us to undertake a program of clearing other ravaged land of debris, stones, and broken tiles; fertilizing the ground with night soil; and planting burdock, carrots, onions, beans, potatoes, corn, wheat, millet, spinach, and Japanese radishes. We did the farm work early in the morning before the members of the organization began arriving for religious training. Many of the faithful eagerly helped with the labor, though most of them had never held a hoe before and many of them were seriously ill. All the produce was carefully divided among the owners of the land and the people who did the farming. A certain part was set aside for people in especially desperate conditions. All this food was extremely welcome in wartime, when everything was scarce.

The good relations we established with Mr. Sakuma, the owner of the land adjacent to the headquarters, ultimately led to our purchasing that land and using it for other Kōsei-kai buildings.

18. Living Apart

THOUGH all Kōsei-kai members who had been drafted returned safely after the war, there was still one of our families that could not be reunited: my own. When, on August 12, 1944, I sent my wife and children to live at my family's home in the country in response to a divine revelation received by Myōkō Sensei, my oldest daughter, Tomoko, was twelve, my second daughter, Kyōko, ten, my third daughter, Yoshiko, eight, my oldest son, Kōichi, six, my second son, Kinjirō, three, and my third son, Hiroshi, one. I explained to my wife and children that I was embarking on a severe course of discipline and study of the Lotus Sutra and the writings of Nichiren and that I was sending them to the country, not out of selfishness, but out of a need to help other people. I asked my wife not to worry and to do her best to raise the children well. She nodded in both resolution and understanding.

She had become accustomed to Tokyo. It was by no means easy for her to take six children to live in the country. Still, she did her very best. In Niigata she helped in the fields every day. Toward the end of the war, there were sixteen or seventeen people living in the family house. Assuming the responsibility of cooking and doing laundry for all of them, my wife rose daily at four in the morning and was always the last to go to bed at night. But since she had been raised in the rural area and was used to hard work, the physical aspects of her position caused her little difficulty. The thing that made life most difficult for her was the attitude of the narrow-minded villagers. No matter what reason was given, they regarded her return to the village as indication that she was in some way unsatisfactory. Being looked on as a fifth wheel caused her great suffering.

During the ten years of our separation, I returned to Suganuma only twice: once for a memorial service on the occasion of the death of my father-in-law and once when I was drafted into the military a second time and faced the possibility of grave danger on the field of battle. But though on those occasions I came into contact with my own family, I did not speak with any of them. I preserved my vows of separation. When my young children came to my side and looked into my face, I wanted to embrace them; but I restrained myself. My apparent lack of feeling could not fail to arouse the suspicions and opposition of relatives and villagers. My wife bore all the sufferings, including my share.

I longed to inquire about their welfare and to urge the children to be good students and to obey their mother. But I could not. If I had spoken words of affection and concern to my wife and children, I would have destroyed the effect of the ascetic disciplines imposed on me until then by the divine revelation. Since I could not let this happen, I bottled my feelings up inside myself. Nonetheless, my attitude and rumors about me in the village had an unfortunate influence on the children's minds, especially on those of Kōichi and my third daughter, Yoshiko, when they reached ages at which they were able to make judgments on their own.

The wife of my older brother recalled something about the problems and humiliations facing my wife at this time.

"Very few people truly understand Mrs. Niwano's suffering in those days in Suganuma. But it was great, as this example shows. When he was drafted for the second time, Mr. Niwano came to the village. With him were Myōkō Sensei and a number of chapter heads, all of them women. This caused the villagers to raise their eyebrows. A large number of relatives were gathered in the Niwano house. The presence of five or six women from Tokyo, all strangers to the family, created a decidedly cool atmosphere. (In those times Kōsei-kai was still young and small; and the people of Suganuma had no idea about its true nature.)

"During the visit of these people, the electric lights suddenly went out. One electric line served about six houses. If the people in one house turned on too many lights at one time, it blew the circuit, plunging all five or six houses into darkness and creating general inconvenience. As ill luck would have it, this happened just at the worst time and made the villagers more convinced than ever that all these strangers from the big city were unwanted burdens.

"After the lights went on again, Mrs. Niwano and my sister came out and knelt on the tatami to apologize to a whole row of gloomy-faced relatives. It must have been mortifyingly embarrassing for her. Her husband, from whom she had long been isolated, had visited but would not speak to her or to their children. He was surrounded by a group of unknown women, whose presence soured and annoyed relatives and village friends alike. And on top of all this, she had to apologize humbly for a light failure that was in no way her fault. My heart bled for her."

Although my wife does not like to talk about those days, she did say the following in a newspaper interview that appeared in the *Kōsei Shimbun* on November 15, 1968.

"With the six children, I went to Mr. Niwano's elder brother's farm, where I worked in the fields, day in, day out. Since the separation was the result of a revelation, Mr. Niwano did not communicate with us in any way.

"On the two occasions when he came to the village, he said nothing to me or to his children. Even though it was part of his training, it must have been very hard.

"Having separated himself from wife and children, my husband was engaged in religious training and could discuss nothing with me. When I tried to talk the matter over with other people, they urged divorce. The Lotus Sutra was the only support I had to lean on. I read it every day.

"As I read the sutra in the utter silence and frozen air of winter, when our whole area was completely engulfed in snow, my own voice seemed to be the voice of the Buddha addressing me from the family altar. The Threefold Lotus Sutra clearly showed me the path I was to follow. I decided then that, since Mr. Niwano was engaged in difficult religious training, it was my responsibility to see to it that he had no worries about domestic matters. This discipline lasted for thirteen years."

From time to time during the period of separation, my oldest son, Kōichi, would come to Tokyo to get money for living expenses and from talks with Myōkō Sensei he learned much about me and the way I was living. On his return to the village he would tell his mother what he had discovered. Apparently the part of my training that upset my wife most was the statement in the Lotus Sutra to the effect that, after ten years, the Devadatta (or enemy of the Buddha's teaching) would vanish. My wife interpreted this to mean that she would herself vanish after ten years and became frightened of sudden accidental death or death from serious illness.

Even after the ten years of separation were ended, we did not return to normal family life. For another three years we were allowed to share the same roof but not as man and wife and father and children. Perhaps this period was more difficult for us than the ten preceding years. The children lived with their mother in a room on the first floor. I lived on the second floor. On returning from work or counseling, I went directly upstairs without talking with them. I ate alone. They took their meals downstairs. We could not bathe together, as Japanese fathers often do with their young children.

At the end of the third year, when the prohibition on family life was finally lifted, my wife said to me, "For a long time, no matter how difficult your mission, I thought of you as my husband. Then, just as I had come to consider you Mr. Niwano, president of Risshō Kōsei-kai and not my husband anymore, the ban was lifted."

In the quote from my wife's newspaper interview, the question of divorce was raised. Since it was a serious issue, I should explain what happened in further detail. From my standpoint, the separation was only for ten years. But my wife's family, seeing no guarantee that we would return to normal family life at the end of the ten-year period, were both disturbed and angry at the course events were taking. On several occasions they sent letters of warning to my older brother and to me. My brother, a carefree man, said that I was an adult and should be allowed to do as I liked. But unable to look at it in this clear-cut way, my wife's family held six family councils to discuss our situation. There were times when I began to feel certain that we would have to part for good, and I seriously entertained the idea of letting my wife take three of the children while I took the other three.

I learned later that each time the subject of permanent separation came up, one of the children would fall ill with a rash or injure himself and have a limp for a while. At such times, miraculous cures were effected by my wife's diligent reading of the Lotus Sutra and chanting of the *Daimoku*. As the result of these experiences, the children naturally grew into people of deep religious faith.

Indeed it was faith that enabled us to escape the danger of divorce. My wife and I are both patient, persevering people; but there are limits to human abilities. And our trying conditions would have led us beyond those limits had we lacked religious faith.

For the first year or so after they left the city, the children were amused by the novelty of living in the country and did not suffer. But after the war, when other people who had evacuated to the country for safety began returning to their city homes, my children began wondering why they did not go too. I never wrote to them, and their mother never sent me complaining notes. My daughter Yoshiko, however, did write me sincere letters in which she asked me why I did not summon them home and complained about her mother's hard lot and about being lonely because of the separation from her father.

It was difficult for them and for me. Though I tried to put up with the situation, there were times when I sent notes to Yoshiko asking her to be patient a little longer.

Other members of Kōsei-kai have sacrificed family happiness for their religion. Myōkō Sensei and her husband parted because of her heavy schedule of religious activities, and other leaders in the organization have suffered in similar ways. Recalling their experiences always brings tears of gratitude to my eyes.

It was because of the protection of the gods and buddhas that, in spite of what might be called an unnatural family situation, my children grew to be upright and honorable people. Today they are all happily married and have children of their own. My wife and I are typical grandparents, with sixteen grandchildren. In 1960, I took my wife for a short trip to the seaside hot-spring resort of Atami, a few hours from Tokyo. This was our honeymoon, taken in the thirtieth year of our marriage. The trip made her very happy, and I realized how much suffering I had brought to her.

Today my wife is as essential to me as the air. Recently, when the children gathered, I made the remark that I could not live a single day without her. They all laughed at what they probably thought was the old man's senility. But I meant every word.

My wife gets up at four o'clock every morning for her private devotionals. In order not to disturb me, she never puts away her own bedding. After I get up and wash my face, I fold up both her bedding and mine and put them in the cupboard. Invariably she rushes from the kitchen and thanks me for having put her bedding away. She then begins cleaning the room. This is the way we live now. Our relation is uncomplicated, refreshing, and mutually considerate.

19.
Incalculable Loss

UNTIL the age of fifty, Myōkō Sensei had been so ill that she expected death virtually every day. When she was given fresh life as an outcome of new religious faith, she resolved to devote all her remaining years to the Lotus Sutra. In spite of her age, she worked ceaselessly and without rest for the sake of dissemination activities and the guidance of members of Kōsei-kai. Regarding all the members as her own children, she scolded them when they made mistakes and cared for them lovingly, even in private matters. But her labors ultimately took a toll in weakened health. She sometimes said, "It's as if everyone were tearing at my breasts; but if it brings salvation to them, it will not matter if I fall by the wayside."

Hiroshi Naganuma tells several stories that reveal how she never took her eyes from her duty to the members of the organization.

"Whenever we traveled to other parts of the country on teaching missions, I felt sorry for her and realized how great her task was. As long as members were by her side, her eyes were alive and shining with strength; but they grew lusterless and weary as soon as she was left alone. She could not even go to the toilet without having people follow her and wait in the hall until she came out so that they could resume their discussions. Mr. Niwano is a carefree, open person. This kind of thing is easy for him, but it was very hard for her.

"Sometimes she would ask me to send away people who followed her everywhere; but it would always be with a small gift of whatever cakes we might have or a little money. She frequently said, 'I never seem to be able to rest until I am in bed at night.'

"Once shortly after the war, we made a trip to Nagano. Times were hard, and commodities scarce. The bedding in the inn where we stayed had not been washed for a long time, and the cotton stuffing of the mattresses and quilts was moldy. Fearing that this would be too uncomfortable for her, some of the local members brought soft, fresh quilts from their own homes. Because we were grateful for their kindness, we prepared to use the quilts; but Myōkō Sensei refused, saying that it would be rude to the maids in the inn. When we insisted that she ought to allow herself to rest comfortably at least while sleeping, she finally agreed but instructed us to give the maids a small amount of money, which she wrapped up for them. She did everything.''

But ceaseless concern for the public and private welfare of the people around her finally wore down a constitution that was innately not very strong. Cataracts developed to such a stage that she was nearly blind. She was operated on for breast cancer and was occasionally bedridden for as long as a month because of undetermined illnesses.

Some of her sicknesses had a mystical quality that defied medical explanation. When time approached for religious services devoted to holy mandalas or to tutelary deities, karma in Myōkō Sensei's life seemed to accumulate to cause her to lose her sight or to become physically disabled in some way. After the religious services were performed, however, she would recover as if there had never been anything wrong. This occurred again and again.

After World War II, when I saw that something was seriously wrong with her eyesight, I forced her to consult a doctor, who told her that blindness from cataracts was only a matter of time. For a long while, her sight had been failing, though she had concealed it, for reasons of her own.

When she took part in readings from the Lotus Sutra, she followed unhaltingly. Everyone thought she was reading from the printed text, but it later appeared that she had been reciting from memory. The copy of the Threefold Lotus Sutra that she left at her death is marked and worn from the tens of thousands of readings that enabled her to make the text part of her very self.

At home she knew where everything was so well that she got along even without seeing clearly. When she went out, she was always accompanied by someone. Still, gradually I began to notice odd actions on her part. For example, she would try to put her geta on the wrong feet. At last, when I asked her outright, she admitted that her eyes were growing very weak.

Shortly after the end of World War II, lumps developed in one of her breasts. A doctor examined the lumps because he was afraid they might be malignant. Though he pronounced the tumors benign, he nonetheless decided to remove them. Hospital conditions were highly primitive in the aftermath of the war. Rice steamers were the only things available for the sterilization of scalpels and other surgical instruments.

Some time after this operation, lumps appeared again. This time, the head of the Maeda Clinic, in the Yotsuya district of Tokyo, diagnosed cancer and counseled a second operation: a radical mastectomy. The operation took place on December 22, 1948. Five days later, she insisted on being released from the hospital. And on December 28, she addressed a Kōsei-kai memorial-day meeting. Her spiritual strength astounded us; but her rashness in leaving the hospital had no ill effects, for she recovered from the operation completely. Thereafter, whenever she felt unwell, we sent her to the Maeda Clinic for an examination to find out whether cancerous growths had reappeared.

In August, 1953, she once again fell ill. No one knew the cause, but I suspected a mental influence of the mystical kind that I mentioned earlier. She later wrote an article for a Kōsei-kai magazine in which she explained what had happened.

She said that she had been brought to the sickbed in order to force her to reflect on weaknesses in her own character. The doctor had told her that there was nothing physically wrong; the cause seemed to be psychological. Still, her head was heavy and her breast was agitated. The slightest sound made her nervous. But as she reflected on various aspects of her personality and repented her faults, the symptoms abated. On the memorial day for the formation of chapters and for chapter heads, she felt well. She then remembered the old saying that one must suffer to understand the suffering of others. Her illness had helped her comprehend the hardships endured by the chapter heads, about whom she had frequently complained and grumbled in the past. She went on to express regret for the sharp words and harsh things that she had said to others and to profess the conviction that she, like all the other members, was no more than another seeker of the Truth.

She told of my watching by her bedside during her illness and of my reading to her from the Lotus Sutra. One of the passages I read was from the twenty-sixth chapter, "Dhāraṇīs."

"Whoever resists our spell
And troubles a preacher,
May his head be split in seven
Like an arjaka sprout."

In harboring resentments against me, her godparent in faith, she felt she had been profoundly guilty of troubling a preacher.

Throughout the period of her confinement, the heaviness and pain in her head had refused to respond to ice packs or any other form of treatment. She interpreted this pain as retribution for her having troubled a preacher of the Lotus Sutra. At one point, she wept and apologized to me; and according to her own account, from that time on, her condition improved dramatically. In a dream, she was told the things she had done wrong in various parts of her house. The next morning, she requested that I put things right, ask for forgiveness from the gods, and conduct a purification ceremony. Suddenly, the terrible pain in her head vanished. Her conviction was that she might have died had not the Buddha and I informed her of the sins she was unknowingly committing. She concluded the article by repenting fully and announcing to all the members that it was only through the forgiveness of the gods and buddhas that she had been granted additional life after having committed grave sins.

In the autumn of 1956, her condition deteriorated again. Nonetheless, in the first sixteen days of 1957, she participated in an exhausting round of meetings, services, and other events. The chief surgeon of Kōsei Hospital urged her to slow down and to care for herself, but she would not listen. In late January, she agreed to go to a hot-spring resort for some rest; however, after only two days, not only did she leave, but she made a side trip to a distant training hall. At the urging of her friends, she agreed to go again to a hot spring for rest on February 16. I alone objected to the trip, because the resort selected lay in an inauspicious direction.

On arriving there, Myōkō Sensei felt bad; and on February 22, she began running a fever. The chief surgeon, accompanied by nurses, immediately rushed to her side. She was confined to bed for about a month, at the end of which time she was well enough to return to Tokyo, where she at once entered a large national hospital.

Only a very few people knew that the cancer had reappeared. She was in such pain that she could sleep at night only if given injections. But gradually her blood vessels hardened, making intravenous injections difficult.

After performing my duties at Kōsei-kai during the day, I spent the nights by her bed, reading passages from the sutra and comforting her as best I could. Then her blood vessels softened sufficiently to make injections possible again.

Privately the doctor told me that she could not live past September. Because she wanted to go home and because her house was in an auspicious direction, she left the hospital on June 16. The doctor warned of the likelihood of recurring pain if she went home, but she experienced none.

I reduced my activities to the minimum and spent as much time with her as possible. While she slept, I copied the Lotus Sutra in the next room.

Her condition fluctuated. From time to time, she was able to sit on the edge of the bed and look at the greenery in the garden. She would say, "I want to get well soon. I've promised to visit so many training halls."

But the hope was futile. On July 17, we summoned all the chapter heads, who spoke with her one by one in the room where she slept, the room where she said private devotionals. This was the last public meeting she ever attended. In all these interviews, she never said a word about her own sufferings but urged everyone to be firm and courageous. To those who cried, she said, in her old, familiar voice, "Don't snivel like that. Be brave."

Though she gradually lost appetite and ate very little, as her illness progressed she seemed to be in a brighter mood. She often joked and made her nurses laugh. When she coughed, those of us who stayed with her tried to ease her pain by pressing her abdomen. Ten days before she died, she smiled and said, "No need to do that any more." We smiled too and said, "All right."

At about the same time, the chapter heads asked if they could not see her again. We arranged for a large number of them to wait in the garden. I picked Myōkō Sensei up and carried her to the window on the staircase landing. All the people in the garden brought their hands prayerfully together before their faces in the *gasshō* greeting. Myōkō Sensei returned the gesture with a look of deep warmth in her eyes. It was the last time these people were to see her alive. When a similar group had visited her in her house in July, she had already lost a great deal of weight. As I carried her for this final meeting, I found she was incredibly light.

A few days before the end, she told me that all the responsibilities were now mine. After asking the nurses to leave us alone for a while, she said, "Nothing can be done for me. Don't waste money on treatments. I'll be happy if you read the sutra for me often."

That night she slept deeply and snored. The following morning, the doctor told me that the snoring had not been normal: it was caused by a blood clot in the brain. Myōkō Sensei never opened her eyes again. She died peacefully at six fifteen on the evening of September tenth.

Shortly before her death she had said to me, "When you first gave me religious guidance long ago, I was ill. I thought I was going to die then, but faith in the teachings you offered extended my life by twenty-two years." As she made this remark, her face was calm. A beautiful light illuminated it. I looked at her serene, unclouded countenance and could not help thinking that she foresaw her own death. Her words fell heavy and hard on my heart. For twenty years she had encouraged me, helped me grow, sharply reprimanded me for faults, and believed in me. Once again, I looked at her face, and my entire body seemed to fill with memories.

> "Flowering wisteria, grow longer and longer;
> It is such grief to see you break."

Many of us hoped that the wisteria would, as Ryōichirō Yokoyama says in his poem, grow longer and longer. The Buddha teaches that everything that lives must die and that all who meet must part. Still, the sorrow at the loss of a beloved person passes all expression. When Myōkō Sensei died, I felt like a bird deprived of one wing.

Funeral services were held on September 14 and 15; 250,000 members from all parts of Japan came to bid farewell to this woman, who, in the second half of her life, had been a true bodhisattva of compassion.

It had rained on the day that Myōkō Sensei died. It was cloudy on the first anniversary of her death. The sky was leaden from morning as we conducted memorial services and dedicated a handsome gray stone for her grave. More than six thousand people, including the surviving members of the Naganuma family, chapter leaders, and other members, attended. The mingled voices of the large group filled the sky over Kōsei Cemetery as we joined together in reading from the Lotus Sutra.

I read a message in which I commented on the grief of the more than two million members of Risshō Kōsei-kai at her death and added that we felt the warmth of her presence with us even though she was gone forever from the earth. I said that her great merits were as lights on the path for those left behind. She had been an example for the practice of the teachings of the Lotus Sutra, and in her we had been able to see the goodness of the buddhas and the gods. I explained that the cremated remains of Myōkō Sensei had been reverently protected and cared for by over one hundred senior leaders of the organization for more than forty days after her death and that, throughout that time, the scriptures had been ceaselessly chanted in the presence of her ashes.

On June 1, 1960, almost three years after Myōkō Sensei's death, the ideograms with which the name of Risshō Kōsei-kai is written were altered. Another ideogram pronounced "kō" was substituted for the one we had originally used. The new ideogram is especially appropriate for two reasons. First, it represents harmonious exchange among human beings. Second, it is the one used to write "kō" in Myōkō Sensei's name.

Though her physical being has passed from this world forever, as long as Kōsei-kai exists, the great personality of Myōkō Sensei, a woman dedicated to religion and compassion, will be loved and respected.

20.
From Without and Within

In 1956, Kōsei-kai was forced to survive a serious trial. On January twenty-fifth of that year, the newspaper *Yomiuri Shimbun* published an article boldly accusing Risshō Kōsei-kai of illegally cornering real estate. On February 28, police investigations were conducted at the general business and other departments of Kōsei-kai with the result that our name was absolutely cleared of any implication of illegal proceedings. When they learned this, the staff of the *Yomiuri Shimbun* began attacking other aspects of our organization. For three months, the newspaper stubbornly persisted in printing critical articles that focused public attention on Kōsei-kai. They criticized our way of living in accordance with our faith, the management of our organization, the personal lives of our members, and even the private affairs of Myōkō Sensei. Throughout this distressing period, our organization resisted passively; but we all felt the need to make the facts known for the sake of the honor of Kōsei-kai and of historical truth.

The Kōsei-kai Young Adults' Group established a special investigating team, which made thorough research investigations of all the problem points and compiled the results of their study in the "Report of Investigations of News Published by the *Yomiuri Shimbun*." This report was distributed to the Standing Committee on Judicial Affairs of the lower house of the national Diet of Japan, to the Japan Newspaper Publishers and Editors Association, to the *Yomiuri Shimbun* Company, and to other concerned parties. Its publication finally removed doubt and misgiving on the part of the general public about the probity of Risshō Kōsei-kai.

Nonetheless, the incident had far-reaching repercussions among the members. In the outlying districts of the nation, the shock was so great that the membership dropped from 360,000 households in 1955 to 290,000 households after the *Yomiuri* incident. In the trying days of 1943, the members who remained faithful in the face of tribulation were enlightened to the great Truth of the Lotus Sutra. Even many of those who dropped by the wayside gradually returned and learned to withstand hardship. The same kind of thing happened after the *Yomiuri* incident.

Pressure and attack from established powers inevitably accompany the establishment of new religious movements. But if the religious movement is good and true, its supporters will not shrink from criticism and attack. When confronted with trials, they will burn all the more brightly with the desire for Truth. Hardship and tribulation will become nourishment strengthening the individuals and the organization as a whole. The histories of religions of the past show that this is true, and our own experiences in times of trouble add further proof.

Today our relations with the *Yomiuri Shimbun* are perfectly amicable. For this reason, it seems a pity to have to rake up old grievances. But it must be done for the sake of the accuracy of the record.

From about 1954, after my wife and children had returned to Tokyo, I noticed something strange in the activities of the upper echelons of Kōsei-kai's leaders. An odd mood had been apparent for some time, but it came more vividly to the surface after we had successfully settled the *Yomiuri* incident. Groups of leaders would gather daily for the devotionals in the meeting room in Myōkō Sensei's house. When I would enter the house by the front door, there were people standing in the way to prevent my going into that room. Soon, I began finding the main door locked; only the side door was left open.

When I went to the training hall in the headquarters in the morning, the people in charge of maintaining the registers of posthumous names would suddenly disappear. If I entered the Second Training Hall, the leaders would leave at once. I had no idea what was happening, but I felt lonely and sometimes angry. One memorial day, when I went to perform my half day of duty at the headquarters, I found the training hall empty except for a solitary old woman tending the premises. My inquiry about people's whereabouts was met with the answer that the ceremony had been conducted before a large group on the preceding day. After my own devotionals, I drank tea and chatted with the old woman before going home alone, very sad.

But I accepted this too as part of my religious training. The general membership was unaware that anything was afoot among the senior leaders. Consequently, I was able to smile and teach the Law to them with a light heart.

None of the chapter heads came to discuss the matter with me; they had been told by their superiors that doing so would leave them open to accusations of slandering our faith. By nature, I do not like doubting or analyzing other people. I did not pursue the problem further at the time but simply admitted to myself that, for some reason, I was being ostracized.

Nonetheless, my being shut out from the group was an important matter. I did not know what to do. Reviewing the membership in my mind, I could think of no one who could teach the Law more clearly than—or as clearly as—I. I knew that I had a mission that only I could fulfill. At times, I went so far as to think about withdrawing from the organization and starting all over again. But two considerations stopped me: the humiliation of such an act and the conviction that, without me, Kōsei-kai would deviate increasingly from the true path of the Buddha. Regarding the matter as something that must be left up to the Buddha, I resolved to remain calm and to wait.

In August, the intangible gloom assumed concrete form when all the senior leaders and chapter heads presented me with a written document with the following complaint. "Speaking frankly, we consider the compassionate chastisements of Myōkō Sensei a contribution to general trust and to our spiritual growth. But we feel that both the words and actions of the president of the organization lack firmness and resolution. Because the things he says and does under the attractive name of broad-mindedness cast shadows on our faith, at present we are unable to trust him."

The words "compassionate chastisement" refer to Myōkō Sensei's habit of speaking frankly and severely. This made her frightening to some people. But to those who were devoted to her, the fearsomeness included reliableness and strength and made her indescribably appealing. My personality is very different. I am easygoing and open. These characteristics apparently irritated some of our members.

Flexibility is a characteristic of Buddhism that originated with the founder of the religion. Though Shakyamuni Buddha eagerly sought to lead other people to the Truth, he did not insist that they abandon all previous faith. Indeed, once when a famous man who was a member of the Jain faith heard and believed the teachings of the Buddha and announced his intention of abandoning his old religion for the new one, the Buddha said, "It is not good for a famous man like you to alter his standpoint." When the man nonetheless persisted in adopting the new faith, the Buddha told him, "You must continue to make offerings to the Jain priests as you have in the past." The Buddha put virtually no controls on teachings and left the following words for his disciples: "All phenomena change. You must strive diligently."

This attitude of flexibility remained with Buddhism, which always tends to include indigenous religions when it spreads into new regions and which alters to suit the needs of the times. Sometimes the inclusiveness of Buddhism has produced an apparent disappearance of Buddhism. But I regard this as indication of tolerance and forbearance. When I say that Buddhism has changed, I do not mean to suggest alteration of basic teachings. Buddhism has altered only its external appearance for the sake of the salvation of the people of a given place and time. The point of this somewhat theoretical digression is to illustrate something about my own personality. My broad view of humanity results from an innate trait that has been reinforced by what I have learned from Buddhism. I do not make sharp judgments of others. People who found trustworthiness in Myōkō Sensei's "compassionate chastisements" were likely to look on my approach as vacillating and unreliable. And this caused them to announce lack of faith in me. I believe that this was the major cause, but two contributory factors played an important part in these developments.

First, after the *Yomiuri* incident, I called together an inquiry committee for the improvement of Risshō Kōsei-kai. The body included people from outside our organization. Indeed, there were even some who considered Kōsei-kai wicked and advocated that it be disbanded.

This caused great shock among many of the senior leaders of the organization. Today I can see that, though I included the outsiders in the spirit of what I called broad-mindedness, the senior leaders of Kōsei-kai found my act unforgivable.

Second, some of the members of the leadership group still considered my wife an obstacle and reacted negatively to her. I have written about this in greater detail earlier. To clear up the issue, the leaders presented me with a contract containing these points:

1. In accordance with the origins and aims of the organization, Myōkō Sensei and Mr. Niwano, the president of Kōsei-kai, must always act in agreement.
2. Because of the likelihood of internal disturbances, the wife of the president is not allowed to interfere with Kōsei-kai affairs.
3. Members of the inquiry committee, both those from Kōsei-kai and those from outside the organization, may participate in Kōsei-kai activities only with the unanimous approval of all the chapter heads.

Myōkō Sensei's signature and personal seal were affixed to the document, which was presented to me for signing and sealing. Turning the first page, I found the signatures and seals of Motoyuki Naganuma and the eleven Kōsei-kai directors, including one of my own brothers. In addition, there were the signatures and seals of all one hundred twenty-five Kōsei-kai chapter heads. I later learned that many of these people had been handed the sheet of paper and instructed to sign it, even though they did not understand what it was about. But at the time, I could think only that it represented the will of all the leaders. Since I had no reason to object to any one of the three stipulations, I signed and affixed my personal seal.

But the situation was not as straightforward as it appeared on the surface. Somewhat later, Jōsei Kamomiya, who was educational-research chairman at the time, came to me with the proposal that we designate Myōkō Sensei as the originator of Kōsei-kai teachings and me as the president. I rejected the proposal on the spot.

Since customarily I only explained to the members the divine revelations she had, Myōkō Sensei might seem to have originated doctrines. Her spiritual abilities were undeniable and great; but in terms of teaching, Shakyamuni Buddha was the originator of our organization's teachings. And I was in charge of guiding our members in the way of those teachings. In fact, Myōkō Sensei was my pupil in the Law. She did not like instructor's work and often said so. When it was essential for her to lead a class, she and I often worked out her lesson plan together two or three days in advance so that she would find the task easier to accomplish. Under no circumstances was she the originator of our teachings, and I could not permit a mistake on this fundamental point.

But this did not end the matter. A few of the important leaders of the organization, including one of my own brothers, attempted to convince me to go along with the idea. I refused, and perhaps for this reason a movement got under way to set up an independent organization centered on Myōkō Sensei. The advocates of this step went so far as to prepare a petition to which they affixed their seals in blood. They bought a villa in Chiba Prefecture for the proposed organization. (I visited it later and found it a fine building with a beautiful view.) Before long, however, Myōkō Sensei became ill and was forced to spend all her time in bed. With this, the movement seems to have lost impetus and gradually to have died entirely. I say "seems" because I lack accurate information. At the time, I was ignorant of these activities. I only recently learned who was the leader of the movement. I made no attempt to uncover all the details. I did not regard the movement as something inspired by ill will or ambition. It was pure trust and faith in Myōkō Sensei that led these people to take such steps. None of the leaders in the movement were removed from their positions or in any other way punished. The important thing was for Kōsei-kai to go on as it had in the past.

Teishirō Okano, a leader in that movement, later joined me on dissemination trips. Once, in Kyushu, he and I shared a room at an inn. In the evening, he told me of a fund of forty million yen that had been set aside for the independent organization and asked what should be done with it. I replied that if the money was the property of Kōsei-kai it should be returned to Kōsei-kai funds. I concluded by saying, "That should bring the whole matter to a close."

For a moment, Okano seemed surprised, then he vowed to devote himself entirely to dissemination work until his death. Indeed he has made astounding achievements in this field and has become a highly important member of the Kōsei-kai organization.

The attempt to form an independent group was important. For the sake of the future, it is necessary to clarify the causes. I have reflected on the aspects of my own personality that contributed to the rift. Equally important is the frame of mind of the people who decided to take such a course. I do not like investigations of this kind and am not good at them. But since it is not impossible that such a situation might arise again, in preparing to write this book, I interviewed people who knew what was happening at the time and reached the following conclusions on the information I gained from them.

As I have said, Myōkō Sensei was possessed of outstanding spiritual abilities and, with her combination of the kindness of Kannon and the severity of Fudō Myō-ō, had a much more attractive personality than a person devoted to doctrines and rules, like me. From what I have heard, I assume that respect for her and misunderstanding of remarks she made about me led some of the senior leaders to assume erroneously that she was not in favor of my actions. Because of the deep feelings they entertained for her, these leaders took it for granted that opposing me was the right thing to do. Of course, Myōkō Sensei herself was in the most embarrassing and difficult position. She could not easily tell them to stop what they were doing, since they were devoted to her and to placing her at the head of a new organization. On the other hand, she could not countenance a new organization that meant turning her back on me, because I had been her friend in the search for religious truth for many years. The dilemma caused her great mental anguish that undermined her health and sent her to bed often.

This incident was another of the flights of steps that we have had to mount. But the price we paid to overcome this obstacle was too high. The illness and death of Myōkō Sensei was the greatest trial of my life. It must have been a discipline imposed on me for negligence and pride of which I was not consciously aware.

On the occasion of the completion of a monument on Myōkō Sensei's grave, I presented to her memory the contract I had signed. Then I burned it, and the burden of the entire incident disappeared from my mind as the smoke rose into the sky. Nothing remains of that burden to trouble me today.

It is said that rain firms up the ground. After this incident, the high-ranking leaders of Risshō Kōsei-kai achieved a unity of purpose that has enabled them to become the foundation stone of the entire organizational edifice.

21.
A New Phase

THE LOTUS SUTRA is divided into two sections. In the first half, defined as the "Law of Appearance," the World-honored One, the historical Buddha, Shakyamuni, discusses the organization of the universe, human life, and human relationships on the basis of his experience and enlightenment. This section of the sutra teaches human beings how they ought to live. In the second half, the "Law of Origin," Shakyamuni Buddha expands his teachings. For the first time, he says that the true Buddha exists without beginning and without end and that he himself has consistently preached the Law and taught people throughout the universe since the infinite past.

The Buddha of the Law of Origin—the Eternal Original Buddha—is the basic life-force of the universe; he is the truth, life, and law of the entire cosmos. The teachings of the Law of Origin inform us that by tuning the wavelength of our own lives to that of the universe we can achieve the spiritual state we should attain and become truly happy. The Law of Appearance contains what is often called the expedient teachings; the Law of Origin contains the true teachings. The former is essential for a transition into the latter, but neither teaching is superior to the other: they are the complementary halves of a single Truth.

The early stage of the development of Risshō Kōsei-kai—from its founding in 1938 until 1957—can be compared to the Law of Appearance of the Lotus Sutra. During those years we were cultivating the form of the organization. In 1958, however, I felt the need to shift emphasis to internal growth and in this way to manifest the truth about ourselves, just as Shakyamuni revealed the truth about the universe in the Law of Origin in the Lotus Sutra.

With the death of Myōkō Sensei, Kōsei-kai was deprived of the medium through which to hear the voices of the gods directly; and I interpreted this to mean that we no longer required such a medium. The gods that had revealed themselves to her were no more than Buddhist guardian deities. They were not suitable focuses of devotion for believers in the Lotus Sutra, according to which it is the duty of human beings to abide by the teachings of Shakyamuni Buddha and to perfect their capabilities and personalities so that they can fulfill their missions on earth.

The completely egalitarian Lotus Sutra teaches that not only human beings but all beings in the universe share the potential to attain buddhahood through full manifestation and complete development of their essences, each according to their true natures. When all things, including humanity, have attained this state, we shall achieve perfect peace in the Land of Eternally Tranquil Light, which ought to be the ultimate goal of all mankind.

This is the ideal concept of the teachings of the Lotus Sutra, but it is not sufficient to save man, who is weak and requires spiritual support to be able to live in peace. All things in the world of phenomena are transient, and nothing is permanent enough to serve as a spiritual support except the Eternal Original Buddha, the great force of life that is the origin of the universe. Human beings and all other beings are but visible manifestations of this great invisible universal life-force.

Since the life-force is eternal and indestructible, in essence human life too is eternal, though the manifested physical body dies. A person enlightened to this truth in the deepest part of his understanding experiences everlasting tranquillity. This very tranquillity itself is at the same time the joy of life that throbs in man's physical and spiritual being.

Profound enlightenment to this truth leads to an awareness of the essential unity binding all things into one great family of life. This awareness in turn inspires a deep sense of equality and love for all beings, a greater love that is called compassion. A person who is compassionate in this sense is truly valuable, and a society of such people is a paradise. This is fundamental in the teachings of the Lotus Sutra. Living daily in correct spiritual and physical attunement with these teachings inspires the joy of living with the Eternal Original

Buddha, generates love and compassion, and eliminates the need for the kind of spiritual support provided by revelations from protective deities.

At the New Year observances in 1958, I made a declaration of my intention to move actively into a new phase in which we would make known the truth about our faith. The first step was the affirmation that the main focus of devotion for Risshō Kōsei-kai members is the Great Beneficent Teacher and Lord, Shakyamuni, the Eternal Buddha.

It took two decades for Risshō Kōsei-kai to reach the stage at which this truth could be made manifest. But that requirement for time in reaching the level of maturity is in keeping with much that is said in the Threefold Lotus Sutra. For instance, in the opening sutra, the Sutra of Innumerable Meanings, it is said, "In forty years and more, the truth has not been revealed yet." This means that the Buddha did not reveal the whole truth for more than forty years after he had attained enlightenment. In "Faith Discernment," chapter four of the Lotus Sutra, there appears a story that is in some respects comparable to the parable of the prodigal son in the Christian New Testament. A wealthy man has a son who leaves home to lead a profligate life. The son falls on evil days and finds refuge at the home of a man of wealth. The son does not know that this man is his father. Though the father forgives his son at once, he requires him to work at menial tasks for twenty years before revealing the truth of their relationship and allowing his son to come into his patrimony.

When the time came for Kōsei-kai to manifest its true nature, I decided to take a number of important steps. First, because study and education are vital, I realized that the way for us to make the Truth clear to others was for each member to study the contents of the Lotus Sutra thoroughly and to put its teachings into practical application in all phases of daily life and in society at large. To bring about a nationwide pooling of energy for the practical application of these teachings, I revised the structure of the branches of our organization. The basic concept on which the former education and leadership system rested was the godparent-godchild relation: the person advanced in study was the godparent, and the person led by him was the godchild. I intended to revise this system. Further, I wanted to improve the nationwide organizational structure by establishing what might be likened to a diocesan system. Although some people insisted that these changes would cause agitation among the members, I was not afraid. I had already seen the strength of which our organization is capable in time of trouble, and I had faith in it.

22.
My Eldest Son

ON MY fifty-fourth birthday, in 1960, it was publicly announced that my son Kōichi would succeed me as president of Risshō Kōsei-kai. At the time, he was a student in the Department of Buddhist Studies at Risshō University (which is unrelated to Kōsei-kai). The decision to follow Japanese tradition and make the presidency a hereditary position was made by a council of chapter heads from the entire nation, in accordance with the regulations of Kōsei-kai. To Kōichi, the decision came as a shock. He said, "My father has undergone a continuous course of ascetic disciplines. He founded the organization. He blazed the path and brought the teachings of our faith to many people. I lack the kind of experience in discipline that he has. I have achieved nothing and am unsuited to be the next president of Risshō Kōsei-kai." I found his modesty and his strict attitude toward himself moving. At least, he did not merely accept the presidency without resisting. He was willing to examine himself and his fears directly.

Kōichi is a sincere, studious, and straightforward person. He was young when this decision was made, and he was completely unwilling to compromise with himself. I did not find it unusual that a man of religion like Kōichi should be disturbed by the offer of the presidency. It would have been odd if he had experienced no suffering and uncertainty. I told him, "I have traveled my own path and have founded the organization. As the second president, you must travel your own path." But still Kōichi continued to think about the matter.

I once met Yasuharu Ōyama, a master of the game of *shōgi* (sometimes called Japanese chess), and he told me that he had not the slightest intention of allowing any of his children to take up *shōgi*. When I asked why, he explained: "If I had reached only some of the higher degrees of the game, I would have allowed my children to pursue it because it would have been possible for them to go farther than I and to fulfill the wish for a perfection that I had not attained. But since I am a master, I have gone as far as is possible. If my children undertook to learn *shōgi,* no matter how hard they tried, they could never do more than attain the level I have reached; they could not surpass me. I think it is wrong to force children to carry this kind of burden all their lives."

What Ōyama said about his children and *shōgi* revealed the strictness and the limitations of the fields of activities in which things depend on winning and losing. It revealed something even more important, since it made me see clearly that there are no limits to Buddhism. For all people and in all places, its truth is inexhaustible. Ōyama's remarks indicated the resolute will of a father who does not want his children to copy what he has done because he wants them to grow and develop constantly. Steady progress is the most important thing in life. The Buddha teaches that it is not the person who walks in the Buddha's shadow that is closest to him, but the person who fervently seeks the way. For a believer and a practicer of the Lotus Sutra, even though the course may be slow, it is vital that daily progress in self-refinement be made. The person must be farther along the way tomorrow than he is today and still farther along the way the day after tomorrow than he will be tomorrow. My wish for my son was not that he follow the path I have followed, but that he continue to grow and develop as he follows the path ordained for Kōichi Niwano.

Risshō Kōsei-kai was founded March 5, 1938. Kōichi was born on the twentieth of the same month in the same year. He grew up with Kōsei-kai and experienced many tests and trials with the organization throughout his infancy, childhood, and adolescence. During the summer vacation of his first year in primary school, he went with his mother and brothers and sisters to the country.

Before our separation, there had been countless happy family moments with Kōichi and the other children. I remember a field day at the school of his older sisters. I was persuaded to go and took the whole family. I participated in a parents' obstacle race consisting of running a little way from the starting line, picking up and putting on a mask, and then raising a sandbag to the shoulders before running on to the finish line. I have strong legs; and at that time my work made me accustomed to lifting and carrying. When I won the race, Kōichi was so delighted that he called out, "My father came in first! My father came in first!" It made me happy to see how proud he was.

When he completed his master's degree at Risshō University, in 1968, Kōichi first went to work at the Lotus Sutra Cultural Research Center, headed by Nichijin Sakamoto. Later, after leaving that center, he came to work at the Kōsei-kai headquarters. At that time, I brought my son together with the chief director, Motoyuki Naganuma. I do not have the slightest idea what they talked about during their first meeting; but afterward, Kōichi's outlook brightened.

Because he had experienced the suffering and complications of hesitation in the face of his own task, Motoyuki Naganuma understood the predicament Kōichi found himself in when it was decided to make the presidency hereditary. Kōichi understood Naganuma too and had confidence in him as a leader. This relation enabled Kōichi to assume a positive attitude toward the heavy responsibility of becoming the next president. He was given added emotional stability by his marriage to Ayako Kakeba.

My heart was warmed as I watched my son and his bride at the impressive wedding celebration, attended by members of Kōsei-kai from all over Japan. The service took place in Kōsei-kai's Great Sacred Hall, on January 22, 1967. During the celebration, "Prediction of the Destiny of Arhats, Training and Trained," chapter nine of the Lotus Sutra, was read. In this chapter, the Buddha predicts the future buddhahood of his own son, Rahula.

Rahula was said to be a person who, though enlightened, concealed his blessed state and lived with ordinary people in an ordinary fashion so that he might lead them to enlightenment naturally. This personality is virtually that of my son. On the day of his wedding, in gratitude to the Buddha for the happiness of the newly married couple, I addressed these words of Shakyamuni to them: "The two of you must not walk the same path."

On the surface, this might seem an inappropriate way to congratulate and encourage young people about to begin married life.

But I wanted Kōichi and his bride to understand the deeper meaning of the Buddha's words. The pioneer is always alone; when he travels in a party, he himself is the only person on whom he can constantly rely. For the person who sets out to carry the truth of the Law to others, the decision and determination to act alone are of the greatest importance. Resolution to carry out one's mission without assistance is the only way for true development. The person must be prepared to face the isolation of loneliness. Shakyamuni Buddha requires that people who propagate his teachings have the strength to face isolation. In married life, the strength and the willpower to walk one's own path are the source of true cooperation and mutual assistance.

I have profound trust in my son Kōichi. I believe that he has undergone severe trials in order to reach an understanding of the gravity of his own fate and his own karma. Neither I nor anyone else can know what this understanding has cost him, but I am firmly convinced that the discipline to which he has submitted himself will someday bear fruit.

In 1970 my son Kōichi changed his name to Nichikō, when he became head of the dissemination department of Risshō Kōsei-kai. He is fervently active throughout Japan. At the age of thirty-seven, Nichikō adopted as his motto: "Heaven helps those who help themselves."

23.
Recovery and Invigoration

On January 3, 1958, I traveled to the Kōsei-kai training hall in Yokohama. The morning was cold, and the dry wind characteristic of the Kantō district was blowing over the patches of thin ice that appeared here and there along the road. In spite of the chill, the members gathered at the training hall filled the room with the warmth of enthusiasm. The eyes of everyone present glowed with determination to carry out the vow to manifest the truth. My call to walk forward hand in hand for the sake of spreading the Law and of employing the Law to build a bright and peaceful society on earth met with overwhelming approbation. The strength of the response filled me with renewed courage and will. Nor were the vigor and eagerness to go forward limited to the Yokohama membership. In the next few weeks, I traveled to several places in the Kantō area and as far afield as Kobe. Everywhere I found such vitality and such rapid growth that even the extended traveling of my tour did not tire me.

On my first night in Kobe, I stayed in a hotel; but on the next day, I changed my plans and decided to sleep at the local training hall. When I arrived in the company of Teishirō Okano, head of the instruction department, the people in charge of the training hall were very surprised to see us. Okano and I immediately changed our Western-style clothing for the padded kimonos brought for us. My kimono was too short—I am a tall man; Okano's was unequal to his girth—he is stout. Nonetheless we were comfortable enough. The next thing we wanted to do was go to a public bath. Slipping on wooden geta at the rear entrance of the hall, we went out into the twilight. The streets were busy with evening activity; children were playing a game that is not unlike king of the mountain.

Soon I noticed a barbershop and suggested a haircut and shave before our bath. The small shop was empty. There was no need to wait. Noticing the shortness of my kimono, the young barber expressed concern that I might be cold. He at once covered my legs with a blanket. The unsolicited considerateness of a young man I had never met was very much appreciated. The conversation with the barber and the haircut and shave refreshed me greatly.

Leaving the barbershop, we headed for the bathhouse, which we found very crowded. There is a mood prevailing in the old-fashioned Japanese public bath that relaxes a person and makes it easy to hold conversations with perfect strangers. I suppose it is that abandoning clothing human beings also abandon false pride and enable themselves to speak freely with one another on a basis of humility and equality. Okano and I enjoyed that mood in the Kobe bathhouse before we returned to the training hall for the night.

When we arrived in Nagano, it had begun to snow. By the next morning—the day of the scheduled conference—the world around us was silver. The wind that sent the snowflakes dancing was very cold. Although it was chilly outside the training hall, the mutual trust and friendliness of the members, who had traveled far to come to the meeting, filled the room with a mood as warm as springtime. In Nagano, as in Kobe, I stayed at the training hall. At night, after taking a bath, I was walking to my room when the glass sliding door to the corridor suddenly opened, revealing the somewhat stern face of a young man who said that he had a favor to ask: would I come in for a few minutes?

I looked into the room where he was and found twelve or thirteen other young people preparing for the conference scheduled for the next day. Signboards and placards for the discussions were already in place.

"Is this the Young Adults' Group room?" I asked.

I received an affirmative answer. At once some of the people in the room brought a large hibachi brazier. I sat on the tatami floor next to it, and the young people gathered around me in a circle. As soon as I said that I was willing to answer any questions they might put to me, one young man spoke up boldly, "It seems to me that there is a great deal of difference between attempting to progress when one knows the way and trying to go forward without knowledge of it."

"You pose fairly hard questions, don't you?" I said. "What is your name?" He told me without hesitation, and I offered to analyze his future on the basis of his name. As it turned out, the young man's fiancée was present; I offered to do the same thing for her. But since it seemed unfair to perform this service for only two people, I agreed to make name analyses for everyone. This brought glowing looks of happiness to the faces of the young people. As I proceeded with my task, I did everything I could to encourage spiritual growth in my audience. Their pure, keen receptiveness seemed to generate stimulating waves that flowed back to refresh me. So enjoyable was the experience that I did not notice the passing of time. But before long Okano came to warn me that it was getting late. Making all the analyses I had promised required another hour, and it was eleven thirty when I finally returned to my own sleeping quarters.

My experience with that group of young people, seated in happy communion around the hibachi, reinforced my conviction that the brains and strength of youth are major forces in the progress of Kōsei-kai. Young people are the flag bearers in our drive to manifest the true nature of our beliefs.

During the conference on the following day, I had this say to the members of the Young Adults' Group: "Sometimes young people who have accepted a religious faith encounter contradictions and confusion in the realm of practical affairs. But it is the merit of youth to be able to overcome such difficulties and constantly to advance through study that leads to the fundamental elimination of suffering and perplexity. Many of the most famous scientists in the world have made independent discoveries and have invented things of importance between the ages of fifteen and twenty. The ability to do this reveals that, because it is pure and good, the spirit of youth can approach truth directly.

"You young people are filled with energy and with the power to absorb things. This is why I want all of you to read at least part of the Threefold Lotus Sutra daily. Even a few lines are enough if you are very busy. But try to read the entire sutra once a month. If you do this, in three or four years you will make new spiritual discoveries within yourself. These discoveries will be an inspiration to you and will bring great light and good tidings into your life. Remember that we make our own happiness. And with this in mind, go forward with determination."

This statement was part of my attempt to bring to each member in all branches of our organization the vital importance of study of the Lotus Sutra to the development of an elevated outlook. Although contact with the Law through direct experience is important, study too is a major goal of our program of revealing the truth. I hoped to begin with the Young Adults' Group and strove to bring an awareness of this goal to each member of our organization. As part of this campaign, I traveled to more than forty Risshō Kōsei-kai chapters throughout Japan. In cities, towns, and villages, the reaction to my call was astounding. Many new members joined the organization; and in new and old members alike enthusiasm grew for the study and education program. Gradually, the new organizational structure took shape and gained firm acceptance. In this and other ways, Kōsei-kai slowly recovered from grief at the loss of Myōkō Sensei and made bold strides forward.

For six months, I was on the road all the time. But I felt that my efforts were only what was to be expected of me. Moreover, I derived great satisfaction from the opportunity of coming into close contact with Kōsei-kai members all over the nation. Their enthusiasm for the Buddha's Law not only made me extremely happy, but also gave me an increasing assurance that my judgments and actions were not mistaken. At about this time, I began working on *Buddhism for Today*.

24. In Other Lands

In June, 1958, when the revised education program of Kōsei-kai was reaching its first stage of completion, I went to Brazil, where the local government and that of Japan were jointly sponsoring a festival that summer to celebrate the fiftieth anniversary of the arrival of the first Japanese immigrants. Prince and Princess Mikasa and Japanese representatives in the fields of politics, economics, religion, art, and sports were to attend. Kōsei-kai had already been requested to make use of the merits and strength of religion to assist the immigrants to Brazil to be diligent and persevering; and when Motoyuki Naganuma and I were chosen to represent our organization at the celebration, which was to be held in both São Paulo and Rio de Janeiro, we decided that it would be an excellent opportunity to gain firsthand information on conditions in Brazil.

For a long time, I had wanted to learn about the religious activities in other lands in order to use my new knowledge in the work of Risshō Kōsei-kai. One of my most cherished dreams was allowing religion to serve as a way to establish peace and mutual good will among all the peoples of the world. In addition to visiting Brazil, I wanted to go to other countries in North and South America to examine cultural and religious life. I was convinced that the intangible harvest from such a journey would help Kōsei-kai to move forward and would contribute to the forming of ties of peace among the nations of the world.

Our party departed Japan for Brazil on June 8, 1958. After passing through Hawaii and San Francisco, we arrived in São Paulo on the evening of June 11. From the very outset, we were busy. On the day of our arrival, we immediately attended a welcoming party held by the *São Paulo Shimbun,* a Japanese-language newspaper. On the eighteenth, there was a memorial mass at the Catholic church as part of the celebrations. On the twentieth, we visited a kindergarten, primary school, junior high school, and high school operated by the Catholic church; on the twenty-first, we attended a meeting of a local union; and on the twenty-second, we went to a meeting of Brazilian members of Kōsei-kai. It was my first trip abroad, and everything I saw and heard was a new experience. Everywhere we turned we found warm welcome and considerate hospitality that gave me a deep admiration for the world that Japanese people had managed to build in another land. But we saw plenty of evidence of the sufferings and hardships the Japanese immigrants have had to endure.

On June 18, 1908, the Kasado-maru, the first immigrant ship between the two nations, arrived in Brazil with 781 Japanese on board. But in the first year, the coffee harvest—the major source of work and income—was bad. Japanese immigrants found it necessary to borrow money, and many of the debtors fled with the consequence that the reputation of the Japanese was bad. Further immigration from Japan was halted. By and large, the failure of the first immigrants was the outcome of ignorance about the Brazilian climate and way of life. But few of the early immigrants intended to remain in Brazil permanently. Many of them wanted to make quick, easy fortunes and return to live the high life in Japan. Lacking the spirit needed for pioneering, when they were forced to face debt and hardship, they faltered and later absconded.

After the passage of some time, however, immigration was once again permitted. This time, the Japanese who came to Brazil were burning to work and to make their adopted country their permanent home. They broke their ways into the dense forests. Living in crude huts, they felled the mighty trees; and sweaty and dirty, they suffered and worked to build farms with their own hands. Because of the labor they put into the land, the Japanese immigrants became deeply attached to their farms. And as they observed the newcomers' energy, industry, and ability to persevere, the native citizens of Brazil began to recognize the merits of the Japanese immigrants, who gradually came to enjoy a more stable way of life and greater trust from their neighboring Brazilians. Today people of Japanese descent occupy posts of importance in the agricultural, industrial, technological, and commercial fields. They are active in organizing and managing business and industrial unions, and they are numerous on state and city councils. Throughout the country, they have, and strive hard to deserve, the reputation of being highly industrious and completely trustworthy.

The experiences of the Japanese immigrants to Brazil have much to teach. For the sake of pioneering virgin land, the human being must take hoe in hand and break the ground little by little; but if his agricultural efforts are to bear fruit, he must have love for his task. Because he must battle against primitive conditions in a land that is not his original home, the pioneer is often beset with loneliness. His plight is in some respects similar to that of the active Buddhist. One must be patient and diligent in order to lead people into the ways of self-development and constant vigilance against laziness and error. Doing this through the Buddha's Law is the way of the bodhisattva. Just as the selfish and weak pioneer fails in his task, so it is impossible to make the Law of Buddhism blossom and bear fruit in the wilderness by means of self-interest and weakness. The early immigrants who went to Brazil in search of nothing but quick riches were frustrated and forced to flee, whereas those who went with steadfastness and firm faith braved the hardships of the forests and received their rewards in the form of flourishing farms.

It took the Japanese immigrants fifty years to establish a reputation for industry and good faith. It remains to be seen how long it will take Kōsei-kai to be properly understood by society and the world. But my knowledge of the experiences of the immigrants made me deeply aware of the need for us to believe that the day will come when we are understood and that we must neither hurry nor be slow, but must walk together boldly and in a spirit of unity.

Brazil is a Catholic nation, which means that the social lives of the people are inseparably tied to religion and that everything the people do is influenced by religion. In the physical and the spiritual senses, towns and villages generally center on the church. Many of these buildings are architecturally and aesthetically valuable. The care lavished on the churches and the length of time—sometimes forty or fifty years—devoted to their construction indicate depth of religious feeling. As I looked at Brazilian churches and listened to their histories, I found my mind traveling to Tokyo, where, at that time, Kōsei-kai's Great Sacred Hall was under construction. The plans had required numerous corrections and even complete redrawings.

Those of us connected with the building of the Great Sacred Hall examined the architects' drawings with the utmost attention, but I felt that there were still things to be learned from such venerable religious structures as the ones I examined in Brazil. Each time I visited a church, as I looked up at the steeple, I thought, "To make the Great Sacred Hall even closer to perfection, we ought to incorporate the good points of buildings like this one." Motoyuki Naganuma would observe my pausing at such times and would ask if there was anything wrong. I would then smilingly explain that each time I stood in front of a church my mind flew back to Tokyo. Indeed, virtually everything I saw and did on the trip to Brazil recalled Japan and Kōsei-kai to me.

In the evening, Catholic priests in Brazil drive in automobiles through towns and villages in outlying districts to preach and carry their teachings to the people. No matter how remote the area, these priests engage in their work gladly and without complaining. Even small children are educated in religious sentiments, and the seeds sown in these young minds grow and produce increasing interest in religion throughout Brazilian society. I attended mass in Brazil five or six times, on Sundays and on weekdays; and I was impressed with the presence in the congregations of people of all ages and social classes.

I was especially interested in the choirs of small, white-clad children who took part in services. Participation by the very young is highly important because the ideas and the memories implanted in the mind of a human being at an early stage in development remain throughout life. The child of a poor family that joyfully works for the good of others in an atmosphere of light will grow into an adult of generosity, with a great capacity for understanding. On the other hand, the child from a strife-torn, unharmonious home is unlikely to grow into a cooperative, altruistic person. Clearly the influence of the environment on the child helps determine the direction in which the personality grows. And this explains the difference between the adult raised in a religious setting and the adult from a home in which religious matters are thought to be of no consequence.

I saw shortcomings as well as good points in the state of religious affairs in Brazil. For instance, there is no other religion in the nation that can rank on a par with Catholicism. The people therefore must often yield to Catholic authority, and many of the ceremonies of the church have become excessively formalized. Nonetheless, the Brazilian custom of training young children to take part in religious observances has something to teach us.

Rio de Janeiro is a beautiful city, especially when seen from an airplane that is just about to land. The deep blue of the sea and the modern buildings ranged in front of gentle, green mountains surrounding a white crescent of beach create a picture of great loveliness. The statue of Christ standing with outstretched arms atop Sugar Loaf Mountain off the shore is one of the things justifying the description of Rio de Janeiro as one of the three most beautiful ports in the world.

Motoyuki Naganuma and I frequently commented on the immensity of Brazil. Unlike Japan, where many kinds of scenery are to be seen at once because of the smallness of the islands, Brazil has vast stretches of unbroken plains and virtual seas of rolling mountains. Nor is this surprising, since Brazil occupies nearly half of South America and is about twenty-three times the size of Japan. It ranges in climate from the tropical rain forests of the Amazon Basin, near the equator, to the temperate zones, around 32° south latitude, where frosts occur in winter. Perhaps nothing gives a Japanese a more overwhelming feeling of being in an unknown world than standing on the banks of the Amazon, which waters an immense tract of land along the roughly 6,400 kilometers from its headwaters to the point at which it empties into the Atlantic Ocean. On the sixth of July, my party and I crossed the Amazon at its mouth, where it is impossible to see from one side to the other.

As we stood watching the great flow of green water, my mind went back to the rivers in the part of Japan where I was born. My birthplace is a small village in the mountains. The sloping land is covered with terraced agricultural fields. In winter, rivers, mountains, fields, and farmhouses are covered with a thick blanket of snow. The local inhabitants have no choice but to sit indoors most of the time, waiting for the return of spring. In Brazil, for thousands of years, the sun has beat down hard on the unpenetrated rain forests. Not a single snowflake has fallen there. Yet, though the climates and ways of life are different, the inhabitants of both lands share a common humanity. The peoples of Brazil are various: there are peoples of black, white, brown, and yellow skins. There are people of Italian, German, Arabian, Persian, and Japanese ancestry, as well as the native Indians and people of Portuguese descent. But no matter what our skin color or national background, all of us are insecure and confused when we must combat loneliness, sorrow, and conflict, all of which are part of the human predicament. Only religion—only the True Law—can save human beings from this condition. In this sense, the people living in the mountain villages of Japan are exactly like their fellow human beings in the hinterlands and rain forests of Brazil and exactly like all other human beings everywhere. The only thing that crosses all boundaries of nation and race to bind the hearts of human beings together is religion. This thought glowed in my mind as I traveled about under the skies of foreign lands. I have always believed that this is true, and while I was in Brazil I was even more strongly convinced that I am right.

On leaving Brazil, we traveled to Paraguay, Argentina, and Chile. On August fourth, we went to the United States, where we visited Washington, D.C.; San Francisco; other parts of California; and Niagara Falls. Then on August twenty-second, about two and a half months after our departure, we arrived safely in Japan. Many members of Risshō Kōsei-kai came to welcome me home at Tokyo International Airport. Their greetings and the feeling of being home again made me warmly happy that I was born Japanese and that I enjoy the support and companionship of many fellow believers in Buddhism.

That night, my wife prepared a home-cooked meal of typically Japanese vegetables, spinach in sesame sauce, broiled fish, and sakè. "How does Japanese food taste after such a long time away?" she asked me. I told her that it tasted delicious and that I was happy to be home in our fine country. Luxurious food in handsome restaurants is good, but the tastes and smells of home-cooked vegetables touch the heart. And nothing seems to quench the thirst of a Japanese as well as sakè. I enjoyed all of those good things that night as I sat quietly telling my family of the experiences I had had in other lands.

25. New Structure

THE YEAR 1960 marked a great turning point in the history of postwar Japan, for it witnessed the rapid development of industrial productivity, the modernization of agriculture, and the liberalization of trade that were to pave the way for the high-level economic growth of the following decade. Material wealth increased. Consumption of goods came to be regarded—arrogantly, perhaps—as a virtue. And with the increasing use of machinery, many phases of life became more convenient.

At the same time, an attitude that economic growth and the pursuit of material wealth are of paramount importance swept over the Japanese islands. Because of their greedy race for affluence, the Japanese people were ridiculed by the peoples of other nations as economic animals. Instead of seeking true happiness, many people looked no farther than the gratification of immediate desires. And for the sake of their desires they used whatever means came to hand. In Japan and elsewhere the results of such behavior have been destruction of the natural environment in the name of development, pollution of many parts of our world, and, ultimately, threats to the continued existence of mankind itself. In that year of violent economic growth, I wrote an article for the magazine *Kōsei* in which I made an appeal to the membership of our organization in connection with the establishment of a new Kōsei-kai organizational structure.

Since the birth of Risshō Kōsei-kai, organizationally it had been divided into chapters, district groups, and neighborhood groups. This structure and the lineage of spiritual guidance involving the relation of godparent and godchild in faith were characteristic of Kōsei-kai. This basic organization had been the main artery through which we had been able to build a solid body of more than two million members. It had produced great results and had been the firm basis on which we had participated in religious disciplines and practices in a spirit of unity.

But because the vertical organization from chapter to district group had been too much emphasized, too little exchange had taken place among chapters and district groups, with the result that the organizational structure itself had almost lost its progressive nature. In consequence, even though they were members of the same Kōsei-kai, some people from one chapter or district group occasionally tended to react negatively to the educational and guidance practices of other chapters and district groups.

This had an effect on the natures of the chapters themselves. Little horizontal exchange took place among different district groups and neighborhood groups. And that in turn had a negative effect on the spreading of our teachings. In the regional chapters and information centers, many staff members came originally from the Tokyo chapters. In other words, the personnel composition of the regional chapters in some cases was heterogeneous. Naturally, much of the fault in the situation was the result of lack of thoroughness on the part of the senior leaders and failure to allow the true teachings of the Law to permeate the most distant parts of the organization. Another difficulty arose from excessive responsibilities for the chapters. Although we had established a responsibility limitation of two thousand households for each chapter, in fact, many chapters had to be responsible for the guidance and training of three, four, or even five thousand households. Furthermore, the number of leaders was extremely small. Many of the people filling leadership positions were relatively inexperienced in the teachings of the Law. In addition, we needed to attempt to do something about the insufficient guidance that had sometimes been provided for individual members.

The leaders of Risshō Kōsei-kai—an organization that takes as its motto "many body but one in spirit"—devoted deep thought and consideration to the problem with the result that we proposed a reorganization on the basis of a national system of regions. The aim of this system was to build a strong, densely related, yet resilient educational network by putting the right people in the right places throughout the country in an organization that is balanced horizontally and vertically.

The idea for this reorganization of the educational system had been in my mind for a number of years. The older system called for sending teachings into the provinces and outlying districts from the central headquarters in Tokyo. Chapters to carry out the work were established all over the country. But this system had shown signs of allowing the strength of the guidance and instruction to stagnate. This and alterations in Kōsei-kai made necessary by changes in the times convinced me that fundamental organizational revisions were needed.

After the announcement that the time had come for us to manifest the true nature of our organization, I traveled throughout the country visiting the training halls and information centers in order to learn how guidance was being conducted. I saw that, in spite of the self-sacrificing efforts of the leaders and chapter heads, results commensurate with their efforts were not forthcoming. This made me even more deeply convinced of the need for revisions.

Risshō Kōsei-kai values a relationship between a person offering guidance and the person being guided that is comparable to the relation between parent and child. From the emotional standpoint, this is beautiful. But from the standpoint of the need to fulfill the Mahayana teaching of salvation for all beings and from that of the desire to make contributions to rural Japanese society, a wider view is required. Furthermore, the day is certain to come when Risshō Kōsei-kai of Japan will become Risshō Kōsei-kai of the whole world. For the sake of that day, we must have a leadership system that is based on a balanced relationship among intellect, emotion, and will.

The system that we devised to meet these needs is as follows. Japan is divided into thirty-three areas. The branches—of which there are now over two hundred in the nation—are supervised by the area directors and are divided into various units, from chapter down to *hōza,* or counseling groups. Each *hōza* group has its own leader, as well as district, neighborhood, and block leaders who are responsible for maintaining liaison.

Obviously when old patterns must be broken and an organization must be revised, there are people who find it difficult to break with the ways they have grown accustomed to. While understanding the theoretical need for a new organizational structure, people often feel insecure when alterations must be made in the practical affairs of daily religious training. In the case of our organizational revisions, I was often asked if the changes in the area structure would not weaken the old ties between godparents and godchildren in faith. I replied that, even though the organization changes, the relation between parent and child in faith is permanent. The bond between these two parties who are together in the Law of the Buddha is eternal. In the future, this relation must be further strengthened as the parent and the child work together to perform the roles of bodhisattvas by helping all sentient beings to find salvation. After a talk of this kind, members usually understood the importance of the steps we were taking. But many members lived in remote districts to which my explanations could be carried only indirectly. These people wrote many letters expressing heartfelt distress at the new organizational structure. Other signs of upset and displeasure were manifested in other parts of Kōsei-kai. But I regarded all this as no more than the birth pangs of a new structure. Without the pain, the sorely needed renovations and progress would be impossible. I was convinced that the members of Kōsei-kai had the strength and intellect to withstand suffering for the sake of the future of our organization.

26. An Act of Dedication

WHEN Risshō Kōsei-kai proclaimed the intention of manifesting its true nature, we made another decision. We elected to adopt a representation of the Great Beneficent Teacher and Lord, Shakyamuni, the Eternal Buddha, as the focus of devotion of our organization. We requested the artist Ryūsen Miyahara to paint a picture of Shakyamuni on silk. It took more than a year to complete this great work. But we were soon forced to take certain steps in relation to it. A painting on silk has a guaranteed life of only about fifty years, whereas a wooden statue can be preserved for more than a thousand years. For this reason, it was decided to commission a wooden statue of Shakyamuni, which would be installed on the main altar of the fourth-floor worship hall of the Great Sacred Hall when it was completed.

We commissioned the master sculptor Shinkan Nishikido to produce the statue; and in 1959, I vowed to make a handwritten copy of the entire Threefold Lotus Sutra for inclusion in a compartment within the statue. I made this vow because of something in the writings of Nichiren about dedication ceremonies for paintings and statues of the Buddha. It is said that if copies of the sutras are set in front of painted or carved representations of the Buddha, the thirty-two signs characterizing the Buddha body are complete. I felt that it was essential to make our representation of the body of Shakyamuni absolutely complete by including in it the heart of his teachings, the Lotus Sutra. Although placing printed copies of the ten scrolls of the Lotus Sutra inside the statue would have satisfied the requirements set forth in the teaching of Nichiren, since I am a person who reveres the Law and worships the Buddha, such an act would not have satisfied my own desire. I therefore resolved to devote myself wholeheartedly to the undertaking of copying the sutra.

But I had been extremely busy since 1958. First, we had launched the new religious practices and training program, which demanded that I travel extensively all over the country. Then I had made the trip to Brazil, other South American countries, and the United States. And when I returned to Japan, I found it necessary to continue traveling about the country to encourage the membership. In 1959, I continued making trips to outlying districts to stimulate support for the progress of the "Teaching and Practical Religion in Unity" program. Toward the end of that year, we launched the program of extensive organizational reforms that I mentioned earlier. Though the project of copying the sutra was on my mind all the time, I was unable to find the leisure to sit down quietly to do it. But in July, 1960, the carving of the main image of Shakyamuni was seventy percent finished. I no longer had any time to lose. Although there was still much to do in connection with organizational and educational reforms and although summer was already at its hottest, I made up my mind to get to work on the copying at once.

First I needed a model from which to work. I studied the copy that is known as the *Chōmyō-ji-bon,* another called the *Heiraku-ji-bon,* and a version I own that was copied by the twelfth-century nobleman Fujiwara no Motohira. But none of these seemed to be what I was looking for. Then, recalling the copy made by Sukenobu Arai, I took out the book and almost gasped with amazement at its excellence.

Arai copied the sutra in eight scrolls three times. The first copy he made was unfortunately destroyed in World War II. It is the third copy that still survives. Because he was an outstanding calligrapher (who used the art name Genshū) as well as an erudite scholar of Chinese ideograms, Arai produced a book that has dignity and elegance. Technique can be mastered with training, but elegance cannot be learned. The personality of the individual and his mental and spiritual character manifest themselves in the kind of dignity found in Sukenobu Arai's copy of the Lotus Sutra.

Sukenobu Arai had instructed me in the profound and eternal teachings of the Lotus Sutra. It was therefore with a sense of the

With Myōkō Sensei during the New Year holidays of 1946, when I first put on the Buddhist monk's robes I would often wear as part of my religious training during the next ten years.

September 6, 1948, the ridgepole-raising ceremony for the Former Main Worship Hall. Myōkō Sensei and I are on the roof at the left.

With Myōkō Sensei in January, 1949, shortly before celebrating completion of the Former Main Worship Hall.

Hōza *groups meeting in 1951 in the Second Training Hall, built when the Former Main Worship Hall became too small.*

By 1953 the Second Training Hall had become so overcrowded that hōza *groups were meeting on its roof.*

Our dissemination trips, which began in 1947, brought us to this farmhouse in Nagano Prefecture, where over five hundred people had gathered.

On these trips Myōkō Sensei and I eventually traveled by second-class coach, much more comfortable than third class.

On February 24, 1956, Myōkō Sensei and I participated in the ground-breaking ceremonies for the Great Sacred Hall.

Myōkō Sensei died September 10, 1957. The path fr her house to her gate was lined with wreaths on t fifteenth, when her plain coffin was carried in a pala-quin to the Former Main Worship Hall for funer-services.

Among the mourners in the ritual procession precedi-the palanquin was Myōkō Sensei's nephew Motoyu-Naganuma, carrying the memorial tablet bearing h posthumous name.

Following the funeral, the hearse carried Myōkō Sensei's plain coffin, past throngs of mourners lining the streets, to the crematorium.

October 27, 1957, Motoyuki Naganuma carried Myōkō Sensei's ashes from her home to Kōsei Cemetery.

At the graveside services for interment of Myōkō Sensei's ashes, I performed the duties of chief mourner.

By January 15, 1958, four months after Myōkō Sensei's funeral, work on the Great Sacred Hall had progressed strikingly.

About a year after Myōkō Sensei's death the framework of the roof was completed.

But the Great Sacred Hall, which Myōkō Sensei had longed to see, was not finally completed until March, 1964.

From mid-July through early Octo 1960, I copied Sukenobu Arai's ha written version of the ten scrolls of Threefold Lotus Sutra.

妙法蓮華經如來壽量品第十六
爾時佛告諸菩薩及一切大衆諸善男子汝
等當信解如來誠諦之語復告大衆汝等當
信解如來誠諦之語又復告諸大衆汝等當

This gold on dark blue painting, illustrating the contents of the sixteenth chapter of the Lotus Sutra, is one of the works Ryūsen Miyahara executed to be mounted with my calligraphy.

The ten scrolls of the Threefold Lotus Sutra ready to be placed in the statue of Shakyamuni, the Eternal Buddha.

Writing the dedicatory text in the cavity of the statue on November 26, 1960.

Placing the sutra scrolls in the statue on December 8, 1960.

Dedicating the sutra scrolls.

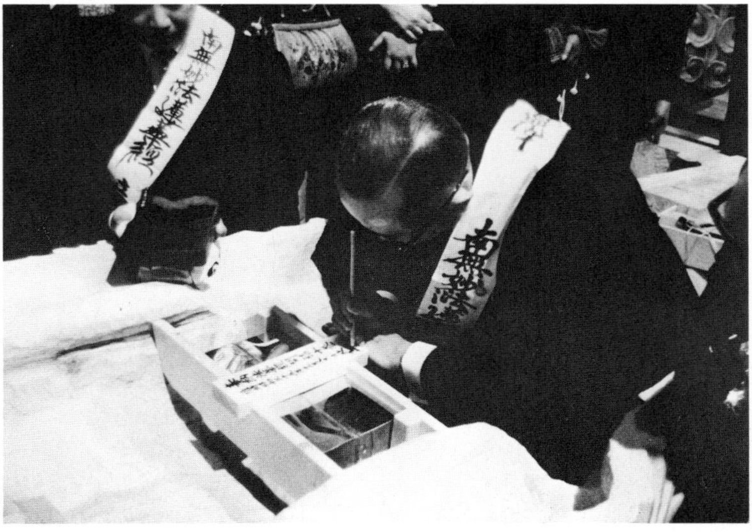

The completed statue was enshrined in the Great Sacred Hall on March 4, 1964.

tatue of the Eternal Buddha accompanied by the Four Great Bodhisattvas, ready to be gilded and lacquered.

At Varanasi I was fascinated by the Ganges holy to Hindu believers.

Paying our respects at the Maha Bodhi Societ India, in November, 1964, on my fifty-ei birthday.

I was moved by this view of the great stupa of the Mahabodhi Vihara, which marks the site where Shakyamuni Buddha attained enlightenment.

ding in the nearby Nairanjana River, where Shakyamuni bathed, was inspiring.

It was very rewarding to be able to address the first World Conference on Religion and Peace, in Kyoto, on its opening day, October 16, 1970.

During the first World Conference on Religion and Peace, fruitful workshops, like this one, brought people of many religions together for the first time.

In Hue, in December, 1970, representatives of the Unified Buddhist Congregation of Vietnam accompanied the fact-finding delegation from the Japan Religions League.

About five thousand people greeted us at a village temple in Quang Tri.

During my visit to China, in April, 1974, I was able to meet with Buddhist, Catholic, Protestant, and Moslem leaders at the temple Guang Ji Si in Peking

and to tour the eight-hundred-year-old temple and view its treasures.

Men and women of religion from throughout the world gathered in Louvain in August, 1974, for the second World Conference on Religion and Peace (top).

They worked together in sessions like this one (bottom).

On September 5, 1974, on the way home from the conference, I was able to meet with Pope Paul VI and give him a report on its proceedings.

Receiving the honorary Doctor of Laws degree from the Meadville/Lombard Theological School in March, 1975.

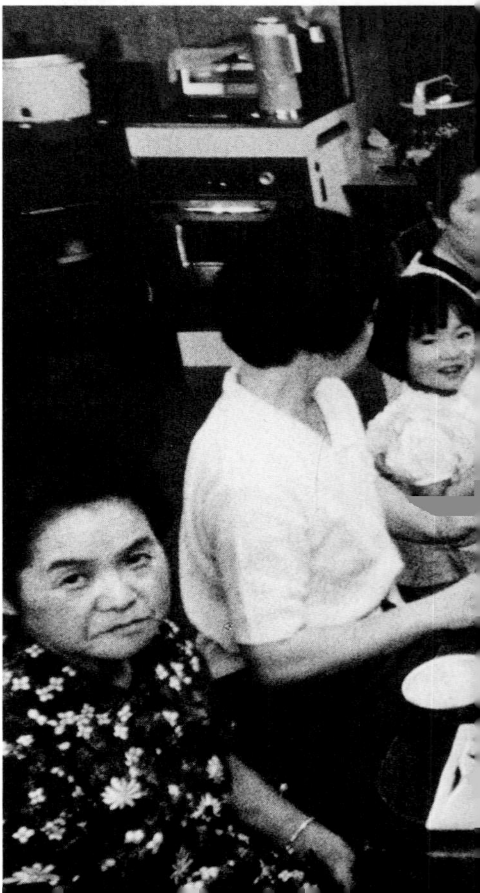

Gen Ōtsuka

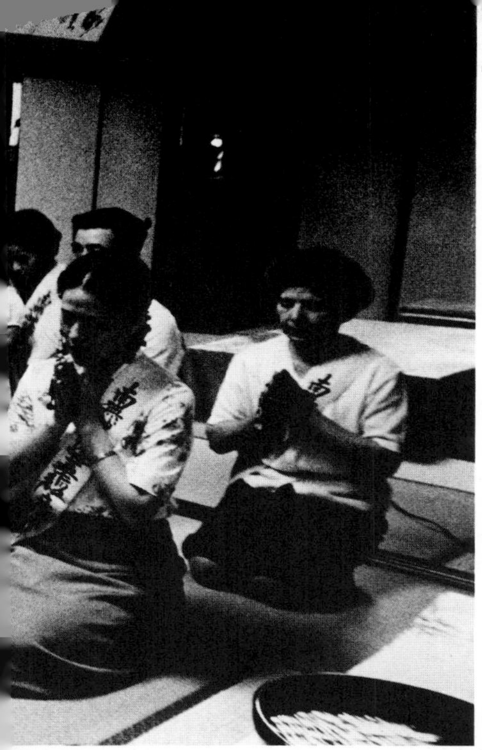

Gen Ōtsuka

Our family shares devotionals together in the evening before supper

which we eat in the kitchen.

wonderful law of causality in the world that I composed myself to use his version of the sutra in producing my own copy.

I employed a kind of handmade paper called *torinoko,* which resembles vellum. Since the sutra was to be arranged in scroll form, I selected a format of fifty vertical lines of fifteen ideograms each for a single sheet. I calmed my mind as I began work and decided to put my entire spirit in each written ideogram.

Practically no rain fell that July. The soil of the garden was baked to a powdery white in the blazing heat that lasted day in and day out. The very leaves on the trees seemed to wither and droop. Because the current it created stirred the papers I was working on, I dispensed with whatever comfort could be obtained from an electric fan. When the occasional breeze came in the window, it was like a blast from the desert; it did nothing but intensify the heat. As I sat writing, sweat rolled from my forehead and down my arms. My back was soaking wet. The brow of Mrs. Kayo Iwafune, who helped by grinding ink on the ink stone, was sprinkled with beads of perspiration. Her work was arduous. Although vigorous rubbing of the ink stick on the stone produces a thick, dark fluid, the quality of the liquid ink is poor, since the particles suspended in the water are too coarse. Gentle rubbing, which gives the required fine, smooth suspension, is demanded. But in the heat of summer, the liquid on the ink stone evaporates quickly, producing an unusable sticky syrup. Mrs. Iwafune's attention was constantly demanded to prevent this happening.

Mrs. Iwafune, my secretary, whom I affectionately call *Obaa-chan* (granny), has shared the hardships and good times of Risshō Kōsei-kai since its founding days. When I was working on the copy of the sutra, I would sometimes put down my brush gently and pause in the hope of giving her a rest from her labors at the ink stone. But usually my hope was not fulfilled, for a guest would almost always appear each time we decided to stop for a moment. Nor were such arrivals surprises, since there was a mountain of important matters for me to deal with every day. As I have said, the reorganization of Kōsei-kai had been in effect for only six months. Consequently, problems in connection with it arose frequently. There were many things to decide in relation to the construction of the Great Sacred Hall. In addition, there were decisions to make about acquisition of land for the branches and for the building of training centers. The duties of new leaders and personnel problems in schools and hospitals, as well as countless other matters, constantly demanded my attention. Obviously these duties left me little time for copying the sutra; but my work on the project had to be finished no later than the middle of September, since the carving of the statue was proceeding according to schedule. To make affairs still more pressing, the person who was going to mount the sutra pages in scroll form requested that I give him the work as quickly as possible, since the mountings would have to be thoroughly dry if they were to be enclosed in an airtight compartment in the statue.

I increased the speed of my writing, but my work became much more difficult because the ink dried so fast that it caused the paper to warp. Sitting in the formal Japanese position—which, when held for a long time, makes the back and legs tired and sore—I wrote at a low desk. The heat that persisted for days made me sweat, and the sweat ran into my eyes, which smarted so painfully that I had to wash them every hour. Motoyuki Naganuma, Nenozō Hayashi, and Granny Iwafune all counseled me not to overtax my strength in the heat and make myself sick. Each in a different way, they all suggested that I go somewhere cool to continue my copying. At first, I refused because I hesitated to leave the headquarters when everyone was working hard on the new organizational changes. "You will ruin your health," they all insisted; but such an argument failed to convince me. Although I have been healthy and strong since childhood, the strain of the circumstances under which I was working at that time was beginning to tell on me. Nonetheless, consideration of my own health alone would not have been sufficient to force me to change my mind and leave the headquarters had the senior leaders failed to remind me that, at the pace I was making then, the copying of the sutra would not be finished in time for the dedication ceremonies. Realizing the disappointment this would cause the more than two million members of Kōsei-kai, I decided to heed my counselors' admonition and go to a cooler, calmer place where I could devote myself entirely to the project. On the afternoon of July 26, Mrs. Iwafune and I left for a villa known as the Sammai-sō, located on the lower slopes of the mountains at Sengokuhara, in Hakone, southwest of Tokyo. In this fairly remote place, the air was cleaner and the temperature much lower than in Tokyo. I felt certain that I would be able to finish my task on time working in such an environment. "Now to work," I whispered to myself as I looked at the cool green of the trees and breathed the refreshing air.

My habit was to arise at five in the morning, wash my face, write my diary entry for the previous day, and then listen to a radio program called "Human-life Reader." After folding up my bedding and putting it away, I would open the shutters and windows and admit the fresh cool morning air. I do not eat breakfast. After light exercises and a bath, I was physically and mentally prepared for my morning religious observances. When they were concluded, I would sit at my desk, ready to begin.

I was impatient to work for even one more hour and to add even one more ideogram to the amount already written. But each ideogram demanded concentration if the work was to have the proper spiritual tone. The conflicting demands for speed and care created a nervous tension that lingered long. At times, I found sleep impossible and got up in the middle of the night to continue work. My shoulders and back grew tired and painful. Accumulated fatigue weakened my eyesight. The desire for speed showed in the quality of my calligraphy. Unlike painting and sculpture, which use form and color to achieve their ends, calligraphy can call only on the resources of line and black and white. With these limited means, the calligrapher must express himself. This means that his spirit must be in each letter. After reflecting on this and on my condition at the time, I decided that the only way to achieve my goal for quality in the time allotted to me would be to entrust myself and my writing to the Buddha.

I decided that for the sake of relief from tension, I should rest in the morning and afternoon. In the second rest period of each day, I took easy walks. This new working arrangement proved to be for the better. The tension and weariness left me. The pain in my back and legs ceased; and my eyes, which had seemed on the verge of collapse, regained their normal powers. Many of the difficulties I had experienced in Tokyo no longer plagued me. For instance, the paper stopped warping and wrinkling. During the writing of the fourth and fifth scrolls of the sutra, my bodily condition was good. I felt the establishment of a rhythm in my mind, and it became a pleasure to move the ink brush across the paper. As I continued my work, I said thanks, for I knew that the good conditions I was enjoying were merit obtained through the grace of the Lotus Sutra.

One day, I had an experience that moved me with a realization of the power of the teachings of the Lotus Sutra to inspire warm contacts in people who have never met before. After finishing lunch, I changed into a cotton kimono, took a walking stick, put on geta, and departed for a walk. The summer sun glittered on the yellow flowers in the roadside grass, where bugs were chirping. Dazzling white clouds were piled up beyond the mountains, and a cool breeze was blowing down the slope. As I walked along, I met an elderly woman with a cloth tied lightly around her head. As she bowed politely to me in greeting, I saw that she had a refined face. I said hello and expressed both my pleasure at seeing her well and my hope that she would continue in good health for many years to come. "Thank you, Mr. Niwano," she surprised me by saying. "How does she know me," I thought. And as if sensing my puzzlement, she explained that she had been a member of Kōsei-kai for twelve years and that she was extremely happy to have an opportunity to meet the president of the organization in person. As she brought her hands together in the *gasshō* greeting, I responded with the same gesture and with a sense of gratitude for the Lotus Sutra, which had brought us together.

Although in the daytime we could sometimes hear the noise of traffic on the highway below us, at night there was not a sound. Sleeping deeply in the silence of the mountains and waking fresh in the clear morning helped me to work well and smoothly. Mrs. Iwafune made my work possible by cleaning and cooking for me. Kōsei-kai members in the vicinity saw to our provisions, and a young member of the organization delivered the newspaper to me each morning. It was always wrapped in paper and secured with a rubber band as protection against soiling and against the morning dew. This kind of unassuming and quiet work by many people encouraged me in the copying of the Lotus Sutra, as did the moral support of the entire Kōsei-kai membership.

On the eighth of September, as autumnal winds began blowing in the mountains, I finished copying the tenth and final scroll. It had taken me 55 days to copy the 69,384 ideograms of the text. At the conclusion of the tenth scroll I appended the following dedicatory inscription.

1. Expressing joy at the connection with the Lotus Sutra;
2. The goal of the foundation of Risshō Kōsei-kai;
3. Growth into a prominent group in our home country;
4. Initial work on the building of the Great Sacred Hall and on the creation of the statue of Shakyamuni, the Eternal Buddha;
5. Manifestation of the Truth in Risshō Kōsei-kai (focus of devotion, teachings, religious practices);
6. Honoring achievement in the five practices of a teacher of the Law;
7. The significance of including the sutra in the image of the Eternal Buddha;
8. The representation of the Eternal Buddha accompanied by the Four Great Bodhisattvas [Eminent Conduct, Boundless Conduct, Pure Conduct, and Steadfast Conduct];
9. The enshrinement of the image of the Eternal Buddha for the sake of all mankind and our spiritual elevation;
10. Declaring our vows throughout the three worlds;
11. Our vows for the salvation of the whole universe.

On this day of good omen in October, 1960

On the occasion of the completion of a copy of the full ten scrolls of the Threefold Lotus Sutra

Nikkyō Niwano
Disciple of the Buddha
First President, Risshō Kōsei-kai

Presentation of handwritten copies of sutras to religious institutions is not novel in the history of Japan. In the twelfth century, for the sake of their happiness in this world and the next, the powerful Heike family copied the Lotus Sutra and other sutras, had them richly mounted in gold and silk, and presented them to Itsukushima Shrine, near Hiroshima. Conditions under which this set and others were copied differed from those prevailing in my case. First, in the instance of the Heike scrolls, each person participating in the project copied only one scroll. Furthermore, most Japanese sutra-copying projects of this kind were undertaken in the name of the worldly well-being of the family or individuals doing the writing.

It is true that some of the dedicatory texts accompanying other copies of Buddhist sutras are longer than the one I wrote, but none is more filled with the devotion and spirit of the author. When the copying work was finished, I was happier than I have ever been in my life.

In addition to the dedicatory text for the sutra itself, I composed the following for the wall of the cavity in which the scrolls were to be stored.

> Hail to the Great Beneficent Teacher and Lord, Shakyamuni, the Eternal Buddha.
>
> This is humbly to pray for the perfection of the personalities of all of the faithful and for the peace of each home, of society, of the nation, and of the whole world.
>
> November 26, 1960
> Nikkyō Niwano
> First President, Risshō Kōsei-kai

The copies of the ten scrolls of the sutra were mounted and bound in dark blue ornamented with gold representations of the Buddha preaching. The pictures, which were done by Ryūsen Miyahara, illustrated the contents of each scroll. When all this had been done, the ten scrolls were exhibited on the third floor of the Second Training Hall (currently the Young Adults' Group headquarters).

Ceremonies for the dedication of the sutra were held in the studio of the sculptor Shinkan Nishikido on December 8, 1960. Representatives of twenty-four chapters of Risshō Kōsei-kai looked on as the sutra and a copy of the Japanese edition of my book *Buddhism for Today* were enclosed in a compartment in the chest of the statue. Fifteen years earlier, on October 13, 1945, on the six-hundred-sixty-third anniversary of the death of Nichiren, we had made the great vow that Shakyamuni would be the focus of devotion for Kōsei-kai and that the teachings of the Lotus Sutra should spread from Kōsei-kai to the entire world. At last, the image of Shakyamuni for the new Great Sacred Hall was complete. My body trembled with profound emotion as I brought my hands together in prayer before the image, the very soul of which was the Lotus Sutra itself.

27.
Delegation for Peace

At a meeting of religious leaders devoted to banning nuclear armaments, Emillian Elinov, patriarch of the Eastern Orthodox Church in the Soviet Union, said, "The enthusiastic efforts and the great sacrifice all of you are making in your sincere call for world peace are priceless. Without doubt, one day, historians will devote a special page to your acts." These remarks were made in 1963 to a delegation of eighteen religious leaders from Japan who traveled for forty days to ten nations, including the United States, England, and the Soviet Union. I was among the group, which was headed by Masatoshi Matsushita, a representative of the Christian faith and at that time president of Saint Paul's University in Tokyo, and by an honorary chairman, Reverend Rōsen Takashina, a representative of the Buddhist faith. During our travels we visited leading politicians and religious leaders and presented to them our request for total abolition of nuclear arms. Although people differed in the way they expressed themselves, everyone we spoke with felt that Japan, the nation that had suffered atomic attacks in World War II, should take the initiative in the movement to ban such weapons.

This attitude reflects a stand I have long taken. We must never forget the 300,000 people whose lives were wiped out at Hiroshima and Nagasaki in brief moments that have become the most horrendous tragedy in the history of mankind. Each year, memorial services are held to pray for the repose of the souls of the victims of these holocausts. But the days must be more than memorials: they must become days of prayer for the peace of the entire world. We Japanese have the right and the obligation to appeal to the world for the banning of nuclear weapons.

Since the end of World War II, some of the nations of the world, including the United States, England, and the Soviet Union, have continued experimenting with nuclear energy and have developed stockpiles of nuclear arms. These nations are the very ones that ought to realize the fearsomeness of weapons capable of converting the entire planet into a graveyard. They are the nations that ought to be painfully aware of the need to prevent the outbreak of a nuclear war that is almost certain to have the most horribly destructive effects.

In the days of which I am speaking now, a strong feeling had begun to spread in many nations to the effect that experiments with nuclear energy and the production of nuclear arms must cease. In April, 1963, the sinking of the American nuclear submarine Thresher in the Atlantic Ocean aroused fear throughout the world. People in the United States raised their voices against nuclear weapons, and in England a one-hundred-kilometer march was organized in protest against them. On August 5, 1963, the United States, Great Britain, and the Soviet Union signed a mutual pact for the partial banning of the testing of nuclear arms.

In Japan, however, owing to differences in ideology and political position among its participants, the movement against nuclear weapons lagged. Because we realized that this must not happen, the delegation of religious leaders I mentioned earlier felt it to be our duty to assume the front ranks in this movement. From my standpoint, one of the most moving and satisfying aspects of this delegation was the opportunity it offered for religious leaders from the East and the West to join hands in a common appeal for peace.

One of the most basic aims of Risshō Kōsei-kai is total dedication to the fulfillment of the long-cherished wish of all men and of the Buddha for the peace of the family, society, the nation, and the world. When time came for the trip, I was especially busy because of the imminent completion of the Great Sacred Hall. Nonetheless, realizing that the undertaking was the first step toward a significant drive for peace, I decided to take part. Our first stop was Rome, where we had an audience with Pope Paul VI. We presented to him a copy of our plea for peace, which included the following three proposals.

1. To ban totally and unconditionally the testing of nuclear weapons.

2. To ban totally the production, preservation, and use of nuclear weapons.

3. Through the peaceful utilization of atomic power based on international cooperation, to overcome the unequal distribution of wealth and to promote the welfare of all the peoples of the world.

In words that I, as a religious man, felt were filled with warmth and meaning, the pope expressed his agreement with our proposal and said that, though he was incapable of exerting political or economic power, he could direct pleas to the hearts of men.

In the more than thirty-four hundred years that have passed since mankind first made a clear record of his civilization, it is said that there have been only two hundred sixty years in which there has been nothing recorded concerning a war. While hating its killing and bloodshed, peoples of the past have fallen victim to war. Still, believing that even such sacrifices hold hope for an ideal future, human beings have continued on the journey toward peace.

Religious leaders of the past too have called for peace but have failed to make clear distinctions between the needs of their own national groups and the welfare of all peoples. Forced to sense their own powerlessness in the face of opposing forces, they have been unable to abolish war. Consequently, many people have lost faith in religious leaders and have abandoned religion itself.

The man of religion is neither a politician nor an economic authority. He must be a support for the people he teaches. Religion must plant courage and the hope to live in peace in the hearts of its followers. I have always insisted that the man of religious faith must base his thoughts and actions on the essential nature of religion and must then persist in striving to bring about peace. On visiting the Vatican, I found that the position of the pope agrees entirely with my own on this issue.

Rome, the Eternal City, is central in the long history of the Christian religion. It boasts precious ruins of the very distant past; but in addition to relics of great historical value, the city is filled with works of art and architecture that bear witness to the important place of religion. I was surprised to learn that the marble, brick, and concrete ruins of the ancient city date from as long ago as the third and second centuries B.C. The aqueducts, great public baths, Colosseum, and other remains from the past deeply impressed on me the technical skills of the ancient culture of the West and the energy of the people of Rome.

But the greatest impression made on me during the trip was the one I gained from my visit to the Soviet Union. Even aside from my work as a member of the delegation, simply traveling to the Soviet Union meant a great deal to me personally. The Communist Party imposes on itself thorough devotion to a spirit of service, to a love of the party, and in all things to put the party first for the sake of satisfying the needs of many people. Although their standpoint differs from mine, these people give themselves to their work with a fervor that I must admire.

We had hoped to meet Nikita Khrushchev, but unfortunately this was impossible, since he was away on a tour of agricultural inspection. After we had given a copy of our peace proposal to Patriarch Elinov, we attended church services, where an old woman approached me and motioned that she would like to take my hand. I gave it to her. Blinking her eyes, she looked as if she wanted to say something to me. I understand no Russian; therefore, verbal communication was impossible. Still, her eyes spoke to me; and I think this is what they said: "Welcome to our country. Religion can bring together the hearts of all peoples. As long as human beings remain alive, religion will be important."

In the United States, we met U Thant, then secretary-general of the United Nations. This moderate man, who had a calm light in his eyes, expressed assent to our proposal. Later we met a spokesman for the U.S. Department of Defense, who briskly explained to us why he considered it necessary that the United States maintain a stockpile of nuclear arms. After listening to him, I said, "It may seem slightly prejudiced for a representative of a nation that has no nuclear arms to speak this way. In calling to you for the banning of nuclear weapons and the establishment of world peace, we are speaking as representatives of the voices of God and of the Buddha. Leaders like you must listen to those voices." Then, with a look on his face suggesting that what I had said touched him, he replied promptly, "Your declaration is right. I understand that. And I realize that we must listen to the voice of God."

Even people who are restricted politically because of connections with governments wish to live in spiritual security and peace. Since man's history has been one of repeated bloody conflicts, it might seem that war is part of human fate. But we human beings create our own history. I am deeply convinced that the common prosperity and improvement of humanity can be achieved only if our efforts in that direction are rooted in religion.

The delegation for the banning of nuclear weapons traveled for forty days through ten nations. Though treaties of partial disarmament were signed, in those times mutual distrust between the East and the West had by no means been eliminated; and conditions in all the nations we visited were severe. Furthermore, the work of our delegation did not go as well as we had hoped in some instances because religious leaders in Europe poorly understood religious conditions in Japan. Nonetheless, this initial encounter between our religious world and that of the West, with which there had been little previous contact, was an achievement of great significance. The pope and religious leaders in other countries vowed to support our plea, but even more important was the feeling we had that people were beginning to be willing to join hands and work together for the sake of world peace.

Too often people of religion remain locked in their own group; and instead of trying to understand the viewpoints of peoples of other religious persuasions, they engage in futile conflicts among themselves. In the case of our delegation for the banning of nuclear weapons, however, representatives of Shinto, Buddhism, and Christianity joined hands for a common purpose. That was one of the most meaningful elements of the undertaking. Junkō Sase, head priest of the temple Shōgen-ji, in Shimane Prefecture, and a member of our delegation, said, "I have traveled abroad on several occasions in Buddhist groups; but usually individuality has been given precedence over religion to the extent that I doubted the dignity of the mission. This trip, on the other hand, has left me with a much better feeling than I have experienced from similar trips in the past."

In Japan, we rarely have opportunities to discuss religion with representatives of other faiths. During the forty days of our journey, the members of the delegation discussed things; and as an outcome of our talks, we came to understand each other better. When Carlyle said that religion is like the stars in the heavens, he did not mean that there are as many religious sects as there are stars. He was speaking of the way in which the value of religion becomes increasingly greater as the human condition becomes graver, just as the light of the stars grows stronger when night is darkest. These words were in my mind as, after returning home from the trip, I made a report at our family altar. Although this trip was not directly connected with the later World Conference on Religion and Peace, repeated experiences of the kind provided by our delegation undoubtedly contributed to the development culminating in that conference.

28.
A Starting Point

On that morning, according to custom, I awakened at five. Listening carefully, I heard the branches of the trees rustling. "It rained last night. I wonder how the weather is today," I thought. Rising and opening the window, I felt the refreshing breeze of a May morning flow into the room. The rain that had fallen in the night had stopped, leaving a blue sky and floating white clouds. I felt the wind and said to myself, "This breeze has come from fresh spring greenery." That was the memorable morning on which ceremonies were to be held to commemorate the completion of the Great Sacred Hall of Risshō Kōsei-kai.

After my private morning services, I changed into formal clothes. This always seems to brace me mentally and physically. My wife and eldest son, Kōichi, too put on formal clothes; and when we met, they seemed to be somewhat tense. Soon the automobile that had been sent for us arrived, and we got in and rode away. My wife said, "I'm glad the rain has stopped, though the wind is a little strong." "But," I replied, "it is a fine wind."

There was a great throng of people in the vicinity of the Great Sacred Hall, and many happy and emotion-filled faces crowded around our car as we drove up to the entrance.

My first duty was to turn on the votive lamps in the Precious Stupa surmounting the Great Sacred Hall. The switch for these lights is located in the control room on the first floor. Prior to switching on the lights, I cut the red and white ribbons stretched across the control-room door and at the switch itself. There was not a sound as I moved to the control box. For the sake of making certain of the moment, I glanced at my wristwatch. Then I turned on the switch.

At exactly eight forty-five on the morning of May 15, 1964, the eternal lights on the top of the Great Sacred Hall were illuminated.

Then, accompanied by a group of senior leaders of the organization, I went to the rooftop to see the lights and, more important, to see the roof itself. On the center pole, the purple flag of Kōsei-kai fluttered in the wind. Looking down to the Haramitsu Bridge and the thoroughfare beyond, I saw masses of people moving toward the building. From as far as Hokkaido in the north and Okinawa in the south members came to celebrate the completion of the Great Sacred Hall. Looking at them, I felt my heart grow full; and without my being prepared for them, tears filled my eyes. In my mind, I called out to Myōkō Sensei to observe the fervor of the members and the splendid hall that their sincerity and enthusiasm had built. I wished that she had lived long enough to see the day.

On February 24, 1956, ground-breaking ceremonies for the hall had taken place. During the following eight years and three months, the members devoted good wishes, fervor, services, and money to a project, the completion of which marked a very important step in the history of Risshō Kōsei-kai. As I thought of these things and of Myōkō Sensei, a sense of great warmth welled up in my breast.

The changes in the buildings used as the headquarters and main hall of worship of Kōsei-kai tell much about the growth of the organization. When Kōsei-kai was founded, in 1938, its headquarters was a room on the second floor of my house; but we quickly outgrew that space and, in 1942, moved into a small building, with eighty-three square meters of floor space, that we had constructed. Throughout the period of World War II, this building served our needs well. (It has since been moved to Kōsei Cemetery.) After the war, however, membership increased at such a rate that the old building soon became too cramped. A movement got under way to build a new structure, but because of the conditions prevailing just after the war, a building permit was not immediately forthcoming. We did get permission, however, to move an already existing building to a different site.

We bought a training hall that the military had used in the Tokyo suburb of Hōya, transferred it to another site, and converted it into what is now called the Former Main Worship Hall. Alterations were completed in 1949. Although we thought that, with an area of 528 square meters, this building would be large enough, as soon as it was finished, we saw that we had miscalculated. Before long, three times as many people as could be accommodated in the large hall were attending services, and every day groups were forced to spread mats on the ground outside and sit on them for meetings.

To do something about this situation, we planned to build another worship hall that would be two stories high and that would house facilities for wedding ceremonies, a discussion room, and a library. But we quickly saw that the continuing increase in the membership made it impossible to accommodate a library. We therefore altered our plans and decided to build a three-story, reinforced concrete building and to devote the entire space to rooms for discussion meetings. This we did three years after the completion of the Former Main Worship Hall. But even with the new building, before long the path between the two halls was packed with people each time a meeting or worship service was held.

The choice of a site for the new headquarters of Kōsei-kai was made in a very simple way. I took Myōkō Sensei to the plot I had in mind. It was located in a place now called Wada Honchō. Though today it has been considerably built up, in 1964, it was still largely rural fields and groves of trees. The land that was to become the site of the Great Sacred Hall was a small hill, in the middle of the southern slope of which was a pine tree about forty years old. At the bottom of the hill flowed a small stream.

"What do you think?" I asked Myōkō Sensei. "Perfect for our purposes, isn't it?"

"You seem to like it," she replied.

Dandelions were blooming on the land on that late spring day. Picking some of the golden flowers and narrowing her eyes as she looked toward the hill, Myōkō Sensei said, "If you like it, I have nothing to say against it." And that was the way the site was selected.

The ground-breaking and land-purification rites, accompanied by readings from the Lotus Sutra, were conducted on February 24, 1956. Although the winter sun shone, the bitingly cold, dry wind made my ears sting. Myōkō Sensei, who stood next to me throughout the ceremonies, did not complain. At one point, she turned to me and said, "Let's finish the building as fast as possible, in about a year if we can.'' I was curious to know why she was in such a hurry, but all she would say was, ''We must hurry. Let's make the biggest and most modern hall of worship we can.''

From first to last, I remained firmly insistent that the Great Sacred Hall must be an architectural manifestation of the teachings of Risshō Kōsei-kai. I adopted this approach because I knew that the building would be an object of intense interest and concern to nonmembers, as well as to members. For this reason, as long as it stands, it must be the main place of worship of the Lotus Sutra and a sanctuary of the Law. I felt that the building should manifest the principles of truth, goodness, and beauty. I decided that the hall must be round because the teachings of the Lotus Sutra, by which we live and work, are as perfectly complete as a circle.

Construction work got under way on the day following the ground breaking. Funds for the project were provided by donations from members all over the nation at a time that was not necessarily favorable for the giving away of money. In 1956, much was said about the final conclusion of the immediate postwar period of social and economic chaos. The Japanese economy was gaining strength; life was becoming stable again; and electrical appliances were being used by more and more people. The following year saw a slump; but by the end of the year, things took a turn for the better. Nonetheless, life was not easy for the ordinary people; and greed and selfish interest were becoming increasingly apparent in business and daily life. It was against such a background that funds were contributed for the building of the Great Sacred Hall.

Incidents occurred in connection with this project that made me realize how fortunate we are to have members of deep faith. A young girl in middle school sent two hundred seventy-five yen to the Kōsei-kai liaison office and accompanied her contribution with this letter. ''I made a promise not to use all my spending money on our school trip and to give three hundred yen to the building fund for the Great Sacred Hall. But when I got home and counted what I had left, I found that there was only two hundred seventy-five yen. I had spent twenty-five yen of the money that I had promised to donate. I apologize, and I feel very ashamed to admit this in front of our family altar, to my ancestors, and to Myōkō Sensei and President Niwano. My contribution is small, but I hope you will accept it.''

There is more to the story. When this schoolgirl's classmates began preparing to take their trip at the end of the school year, she found that she would be unable to go because of the financial straits of her family. Her elder sister, who was working in Tokyo, heard of this and, realizing the disappointment her sister would feel if deprived of this trip, which is something that all Japanese schoolchildren look forward to eagerly, saved her own spending money and sent it home for the younger girl's travel expenses. It was from this money that the young sister resolved to save three hundred yen for the building fund. She promised that she would do this in order to put to best use the money that love and affection had inspired her sister to give her.

Probably all her classmates vied with each other to see who could purchase the biggest and best souvenirs and gifts for family and friends. But this one girl, checking her meager funds, saw that she must spend carefully if she was to save the promised three hundred yen. Even so, she overspent by twenty-five yen and felt compelled to apologize to Kōsei-kai for breaking her word. The purity of heart that inspired her to write a letter of apology reflects the humility of people who live by the Buddha's Law.

In 1957, the good efforts of another needy member of Kōsei-kai led us to coin the motto "A Homemade Savings Bank Is a Prayer for the Sacred Hall." The widow of an army major who was killed in World War II was forced to raise her three children by doing day labor. She wanted to make a contribution, even a small one, to the building fund; but since she received only three hundred fifty yen a day in wages, she was in no position to offer much. The leader of her neighborhood group suggested that she save the one or two yen she got in change from purchases or the five or ten yen she could save by walking instead of taking the bus and allow these coins to accumulate. She agreed to do this and made a savings bank from an old medicine can, into which she vowed to put ten yen each day. This much she felt she could manage to spare. She even wondered why this idea had not occurred to her before.

Each morning after her private devotional services, which she held at six o'clock, she dropped ten yen into the savings bank and experienced great happiness as, slowly but surely, the container grew heavier. Hands that were roughened by hauling gravel and by road construction gradually collected a widow's mite that was more precious than the larger gifts made easily by the rich.

Another deeply moving incident concerning the donation of funds has to do with a one-thousand-yen bill mailed to headquarters by a blind woman, sixty-three years old. Shortly after marrying, she had lost her sight; and this had made her short-tempered and cross. Frequently she misunderstood her husband's good intentions and upbraided him. Fights between them were frequent until she began to learn about the Buddha's Law. Then she came to understand her husband's kindness for what it was and to be grateful to him for it. Convinced that it was the Law that had made the change for the better in her life, she wanted to do something to repay a small bit of the debt she owed. Being blind, however, she could not go from house to house on leadership or guidance work. When she heard of the building fund for the Great Sacred Hall, she saw a chance to be useful. As a young girl, she had learned to weave the straw sandals that are called *waraji*. Turning her hand to this work again, she soon discovered that her blindness was not an insuperable barrier. Weaving these sandals involves several processes. First, the straw must be pounded to make it soft. It must then be woven into a kind of rope, from which the flat sandal is made. Finally, cloth is used to make the thongs that hold the sandal to the foot. This elderly woman did all these tasks herself. The only assistance she had was from her husband, who matched the colors of the cloth for the straps, a task that she was unable to perform.

On very good days, she could make two pairs of sandals; but ordinarily one pair—or only one sandal—was the limit of her output. She made the astoundingly large number of seven hundred pairs, sold them all for one thousand yen, and donated this money to the building fund.

I have never met this woman, but in my mind's eye I can see her seated on a grass mat in the front entrance to her home, pounding straw, weaving the rope, and making sandals day in day out. I can see the sweat running down her back in the sultry summer. I can feel the chill rising in her legs in the windy cold of winter. And the reward for all those many days of hard work was freely given to the Great Sacred Hall.

Unselfish contributions from all kinds of people helped bring the project to a successful completion. An elderly farmer cut medicinal herbs, sold them, and gave the money monthly to the building fund. An old woman, sixty-five years of age, weeded rice fields and sent all her earnings to Kōsei-kai. A twelve-year-old girl saved the five- and ten-yen coins that were her spending money and, on seventeen occasions, contributed them to the fund. I know of many young boys who delivered milk or newspapers and contributed their earnings. All the instances that I have mentioned are only a few of the countless examples of people who collected trash, saved a yen a day, started coin banks, and did all kinds of things in order to contribute so much as one pane of glass or one bag of cement to the building. Tens of thousands, hundreds of thousands, of people in all parts of Japan moved me very deeply by displaying the purity, enthusiasm, and beauty of heart and intention of those who respect and treasure the Buddha's Law. The Great Sacred Hall was completed because of the pure fervor and the accumulated offerings of Kōsei-kai members all over the nation.

The ceremonies to commemorate the completion of the Great Sacred Hall were held in the main auditorium, located on the fourth floor of the building. Flagbearers carrying the banners of all the chapters of Kōsei-kai departed from the Former Main Worship Hall and marched to the auditorium of the new building. They filed solemnly into the room to the strains of classical Japanese music and placed their banners around the room. From the balcony, the choir sang ceremonial music. The women in the choir were dressed in pure white and the men in formal black suits.

Against the upper part of the curtain in the front of the hall is a huge green lacquer bodhi tree sprinkled with jewels. As the Kōsei brass band played solemn music, the curtain, adorned with a pair of phoenixes with wings spread as if about to fly to heaven, rose. Thunderous applause greeted the appearance of the huge statue (nearly seven meters tall) of the Great Beneficent Teacher and Lord, Shakyamuni, the Eternal Buddha. The statue is gilded and lacquered in five colors. Behind the statue is a wall of jasper from Kyushu. This stone, which is more beautiful than marble, retains a high polish for a long time. Gifts of flowers and incense were presented, and fifty girls in long-sleeved kimonos carried flowers to the stage.

After readings from the Lotus Sutra, I rose and went to the

platform. Being the first person to speak in the new auditorium filled me with emotions and tension that are difficult to describe.

"Today, the Great Sacred Hall, long awaited by the millions of members of Risshō Kōsei-kai, is complete; and in it has been enshrined a statue of Shakyamuni, the Eternal Buddha. As we enjoy the happiness and excitement of the moment, we must all remember something very important. From this memorable day, Risshō Kōsei-kai takes a step forward in the movement to bring the Law to other people. We must make the Great Sacred Hall a sanctuary for the salvation of mankind. In order to do this, we must refine our hearts in accordance with the scriptures, act in keeping with them, and prove ourselves to be the bodhisattvas that are prophesied in the Lotus Sutra to spring up out of the earth."

I had already made remarks of this kind on several occasions in connection with the new building—for instance, at the ceremony to commemorate the completion of the framework and at the services held to dedicate the new image of Shakyamuni—because I wanted to impress on the members and especially on the leaders the need for all of us to strive to grow and improve in order to make ourselves worthy of the Great Sacred Hall, a building with significance for the whole world.

Following my remarks, Kyōjun Shimizutani, head priest of the temple Sensō-ji, in the Asakusa district of Tokyo, made a brief speech.

"I am extremely happy at the completion of this hall of worship, the finest of its kind in the world. The Lotus Sutra is the pinnacle of all Buddhist teachings. For a religious group that strives to live correctly in accordance with the spirit of that teaching to build a hall of worship like this one reveals the will of the Buddha. Today people all over the world are in pressing need of the spiritual teachings of Buddhism. It is said that faith arises from solemnity. The solemnity filling this hall today suggests that all the faithful here are being guided in the correct way and that they will not fail to guide others in the same way.

"I am especially impressed to see young men and young women taking part in these solemn ceremonies. Their presence gives me a sense of freshness that I have not experienced before. I am convinced that their ardor and their burgeoning strength and talents will be absolutely necessary to society. I ask that all of you work boldly for the realization of our ideal.''

I agree with what Kyōjun Shimizutani said about solemnity and feel that religious architecture must be solemn, significant, and elegant. Furthermore, it must symbolize the basic sources of religious faith of the group for whom it is built. Inside and outside, religious architecture ought to stand for the basic principles of the religion it serves. For the sake of producing a hall that meets these requirements perfectly, repeated revisions of the plans and design for the Great Sacred Hall were necessary. At the time of the completion of the foundation, I traveled to Brazil and other countries in South and North America, where I had chances to observe the architecture of the Catholic Church and of other religious organizations. I studied architectural history as well, and my reading and on-the-site observations provided me with much valuable reference material. On my return to Japan after the trip, I halted the construction temporarily at the point at which the window frames were being installed on the eighth floor because I wanted alterations made. I adopted this policy because I felt building the kind of structure we needed was more important than hurrying.

The basilica of Saint Peter's in Rome, one of the largest and most important churches in the Christian world, was by no means built in a hurry. Construction on it began in 1506. The building was called finished in 1626, though further construction continued until 1667. Most of the churches of the West are made of stone, and almost all of them are richly decorated with sculpture illustrating persons and incidents related to the Bible and to Christian faith. The cruciform plan of such Gothic churches as Notre Dame de Paris and of Renaissance buildings like Saint Peter's is a symbolic representation of the cross on which Christ died. In short, religious architecture often expresses—and ought to express—the teachings of its religion. Religious architecture that ignores such expression is no more than a physical body without a soul. The need to represent the nature of our faith in the Great Sacred Hall led to the circular plan, which symbolizes the perfection of the Lotus Sutra.

I have named the bridge leading from east to west on the third-floor level of the Great Sacred Hall the Haramitsu Bridge. The Buddhist term *haramitsu* (*paramita* in Sanskrit) signifies the crossing over from the realm of transience and the cycle of births and deaths to the realm of nirvana. I feel that it vividly expresses both the basic nature of Buddhism and the characteristic nature of our organization. People who cross the Haramitsu Bridge to the Great Sacred Hall do so because of their wish to build the peaceful world of nirvana and because they want to understand the Law that enables them to fulfill this wish. I hope people who walk on this bridge will bear this thought in mind.

The Haramitsu Bridge terminates at the stairway leading up to the lobby of the main auditorium. At the head of the stairs are three large lacquer paintings. The picture to the viewer's right is of the Bodhisattva Manjushri riding on the back of a lion. This picture serves to remind the viewer of the need to abandon ordinary wisdom and to clad ourselves in the wisdom of Manjushri, which is based on the elemental meaning of Buddhism. The picture to the viewer's left shows the Bodhisattva Maitreya riding a white ox. This picture is included to remind the viewer that, like this bodhisattva of compassion, we must abandon selfishness and strife and cultivate a merciful heart. The picture in the middle is of the Bodhisattva Universal Virtue, who is riding a white elephant with six tusks. The tusks represent the six sense organs—eyes, ears, nose, tongue, body, and mind. The white elephant symbolizes immense strength applied to the purification of the six senses. The picture is an illustration of my belief that, for the sake of perfection of the character, one must undergo religious disciplines, even at the cost of one's life.

Briefly, the message of the three pictures is this: first, understand the essence of the Buddha's Law by means of superior wisdom; second, effect a spiritual revolution on the basis of Buddhist articles of faith; third, carry out religious disciplines at all costs for the sake of the perfection of the character. Reflecting on this message prepares us to enter the central auditorium of the Great Sacred Hall and to come into the presence of the statue of the Buddha enshrined there. Moreover, it is the kind of religious attitude that I desire for the members of Kōsei-kai.

In religious buildings in the West and in Japan, when ceremony is the major function, a single-story design is usually employed to ensure that everyone has a view of the altar or other important space. But the Great Sacred Hall is not a place of ceremony; it is a hall for discipline and training oriented toward acquiring an understanding of the innermost meaning of Buddhism. For that reason, architecturally it breaks with tradition by being eight stories tall. The only parts of the building directly related to ceremony are the main auditorium on the fourth floor and the seats for distinguished guests, which occupy part of the fifth floor. Almost the entire remainder of the building serves *hōza* counseling meetings.

Ceremonies are not the driving force that will lead to salvation. Daily discipline and assiduous application in *hōza* meetings are the fount of salvation taught in the Lotus Sutra. These activities must constitute the basis of any religion that is meaningful for our times and that will remain meaningful in the future. Furthermore, these activities are a characteristic feature of Risshō Kōsei-kai. They set us apart from all other religious groups in the world.

The earnest efforts of Kōsei-kai members in all parts of the nation enabled us to complete the Great Sacred Hall. But the completion of the building must remind us of the danger of becoming complacent and of allowing our efforts to slow down. It is said that an organization begins to disintegrate from the moment it reaches completion. Religious groups are thought to begin a process of atrophy almost on the day on which they complete the construction of a great edifice. Why is this true?

I believe that it is because once the long-cherished idea of erecting a building for religious purposes has become a reality the members of the faith set their minds at rest and become satisfied with their past achievements, while allowing themselves to become totally preoccupied with caring for the building their efforts have created. It is not so much that members of a faith allow themselves to become part of a rigid establishment as that they become mentally and physically absorbed in the building itself. This is the cause of atrophy and of withering in a religious organization. On the day of the completion of the Great Sacred Hall, I made comments intended to prevent our members' falling into such bad ways.

"Recently it seems to me that a part of the membership is leaving the entire responsibility for the spreading of our faith to the leaders, chapter heads, and a few other people in authority. This is an extreme example of the way to cause faith to rigidify. Even Buddhist groups with long histories of tradition sometimes become so accustomed to relying on the head priests and their sermons as the sole ways of spreading the faith that they bog down in a set of lethargic habits from which they find it impossible to break away.

"I have further noticed a tendency to allow the same person always to take the lead in discussions. Of course it is our system to have leaders in *hōza* meetings, but to allow the leader to assume all the responsibility while the others contribute little or nothing is still another step on the road to atrophy. I understand that some Christian organizations too are concerned about excessive reliance on preaching and teaching by pastors and priests.

"I do not want us to follow the road to atrophy that other religious organizations have followed. I do not want us to dig our own graves."

At the conclusion of these words, a great burst of applause shook the Great Sacred Hall. I interpreted the reaction to be a fervent vow to make that memorable day a starting point for continued, united progress in the Law. It was a powerful vow to go forward; and as I listened to it, I felt a new sense of resolution welling up in my heart.

29. Holy Places

As THE silver body of our aircraft descended to Calcutta airport, the sun was setting. It must have been about seven o'clock in the evening. As we left the plane and approached the simple airport buildings, the smell of parched earth met our nostrils. It was November, 1964. The monsoon had ended, and India was in what is said to be her most pleasant time of the year. Still, it was as hot in Calcutta as it is in midsummer in Japan. In the waiting room—which reminded me of the kind of place one finds in the Japanese countryside—old-fashioned fans revolved slowly near the ceiling, forcing down a current of air so warm that it only made us sweat more profusely.

Eager to greet us were priests of the Maha Bodhi Society of India, including the vice-president of the society, Madhoram Soft, the venerable Nayaka Maha Thera Jinaratana, and Masayuki Takahashi of the temple Nihonzan Myōhō-ji, in India. The Indian priests, who wore the traditional saffron-colored robes of Theravada Buddhism, presented a lei of jasmine flowers and another of marigolds to each member of the group as signs of sincere welcome to India. Looking at the robes and smelling the heady fragrances of the flowers, I realized that these Indian priests and I shared the same religious faith. Suddenly I felt that I had truly arrived in the land where Shakyamuni was born.

After shaking hands with Nayaka Maha Thera Jinaratana, I encountered some people I was surprised and pleased to see. Shortly after our arrival three Japanese had burst into the room. When initial greetings with the representatives of the Maha Bodhi Society were over, these three people bowed slightly to me and expressed their welcome and their happiness at seeing me in good health. They were members of the Toshima and Ōta ward chapters of Kōsei-kai in Tokyo and had been sent to India in connection with work. Two of the three, a married couple, had been living in Calcutta for six years; but the third, a married woman who had come to India with her husband more recently, had ridden for five hours on a train in order to come to the airport to greet me.

Although for twenty years I had cherished the desire to make a trip to India, the homeland of Shakyamuni and of Buddhism, that wish had been difficult to fulfill. Indeed, as little as a month before the trip, I had no plans to go. But suddenly, in connection with the one-hundredth anniversary of the birth of its founder, Anagarika Dharmapala, the Maha Bodhi Society of India invited me to visit their country.

We organized a pilgrimage group consisting of nine members of Risshō Kōsei-kai and including my wife and my oldest son, Kōichi; it was the first time that the three of us had ever traveled abroad together. On the day after our arrival in India, I celebrated my fifty-eighth birthday. On the morning of that day, we made a tour of the Indian Museum, where we saw Buddhist sculpture dating from the second century B.C. to the thirteenth century of the Christian Era. All the works impressed the viewer with the age and splendor of Buddhist culture. The statue of a triple lion at the entrance to the museum reminded me of similar statues at the four corners of the Precious Stupa on the roof of the Great Sacred Hall in Tokyo. In the afternoon, we visited the headquarters of the Maha Bodhi Society.

Dharmapala was born in Colombo, Ceylon. His mother, Malika, who was a devout Buddhist, often prayed for the prosperity of Buddhism in Ceylon. She promised that if she had a child he would be devoted to the practice of the Buddhist religion. After she made this promise, Dharmapala was born. Although the family was well-to-do and the father, a businessman, saw to it that his son attended the Christian schools thought to be suitable for children of wealthy Ceylonese of the time, Dharmapala's mother educated him in the reverence for the Three Treasures and the Five Precepts and gave him ample opportunity to study the Four Noble Truths of Buddhism. Once, when Dharmapala traveled to Bodhgaya in the company of a Japanese priest named Kōzen Shaku, he was appalled at the desolation of the grounds and at the ruin of the great stupa. Realizing then that if such a distressing condition was allowed to persist priceless Buddhist antiquities would be lost forever, he made up his mind to preserve and rebuild important Buddhist monuments throughout India. After founding the Bodhgaya Maha Bodhi Society of India, Dharmapala devoted the remainder of his sixty-nine years of life to this great project.

Today, the Maha Bodhi Society, which carries on Dharmapala's work, is a group of people who are trying to restore Buddhism to prosperity in the land of its origin. Madhoram Soft, the vice-president of the society, told me that he and his fellow members look to Japan as an advanced nation from which they can learn. He expressed his hope that Buddhists in both countries would join hands to work for world peace. I said that the teachings of the Buddha are able to transcend barriers of race and nation to bring peace to mankind. As he listened to me, Madhoram Soft had a glow in his eyes that reconfirmed my conviction that he is a man of true religious faith.

On returning to our hotel, we found that the management had prepared a birthday cake for me. At the celebration that ensued, the band played Japanese songs; and I expressed my surprise and delight at being able to have a birthday in India. I said that the wish of the Buddha had probably made such a thing possible and added that the birthday party would be a memory that I would long treasure.

The sky was the deep, cloudless blue of southern lands on the day that we traveled by bus to Bodhgaya. We rode on the tree-lined highway that had been paved as part of the commemoration of the two-thousand-five-hundredth anniversary of the birth of the Buddha. We saw small hills on our left and seemingly endless agricultural fields on our right. As we approached the outskirts of the city, the great stupa of the Mahabodhi Vihara came into view on our left. Exclamations of excitement filled the bus, and I experienced slight tension as we came closer to this stupa that marks the site where Shakyamuni Buddha attained enlightenment.

Bodhgaya is a quiet forest of vast trees whose branches interlace overhead to provide welcome shade. From among the trees the great stupa rises to a height of about fifty-two meters. The massive and elegant building is made of blue tiles coated with lime; the blue shows faintly through the lime. It was first built in the third century B.C., during the reign of King Ashoka. It was rebuilt in the fourth century of the Christian Era by King Samudragupta and was repaired in 1880. As I slowly raised my eyes to the stupa, I thought of the millions of people who have enjoyed the same view during the thousands of years that the tower has been in existence. And it seemed to me that I could sense, rising upward from the very ground on which the tower stands, the silent voices of the people who had revered the teachings of the Buddha and had died firm in the same spirit of reverence.

After removing our footwear—as is the custom at holy Buddhist places in India—we entered the great stupa. I lighted incense and offered it before the seated statue of Shakyamuni in the inner room of the tower. Then readings from the Lotus Sutra began. We all took part in the readings, and our voices filled the building. At the conclusion of reading, we went out to tour the grounds. On the north side of the stupa are eighteen stone lotus platforms that were made to represent the eighteen lotus flowers said to have burst into bloom after the Buddha walked about at the conclusion of the meditation that led to his ultimate enlightenment. To the west of the stupa is a bodhi tree that appears quite ancient. Under the tree is the Diamond Seat, the place where Shakyamuni meditated and attained enlightenment.

More than two thousand years ago, at the place I visited on that memorable day at Bodhgaya, Shakyamuni became the Buddha after six years of ascetic discipline. At dawn on December eighth, according to tradition, this event—the greatest and most important in the history of mankind—took place under a tree on the very spot where I stood. As I put my hand on the trunk of the tree planted there now and gently closed my eyes, an image of the Buddha experiencing enlightenment under the pale light of the morning star traversed the millennia to reveal itself to me. Opening my eyes again, I saw my son Kōichi standing with gaze fixed on the golden statue of Shakyamuni in a niche in the wall behind the Diamond Seat. Then I saw my wife standing with hands raised together in prayerful attitude in front of the Diamond Seat, and my heart filled with joy at being able to visit these holy places in the company of my own family. My next thought was of the membership of Risshō Kōsei-kai, whose support made our trip to India possible. I found myself wishing that every member could make the same pilgrimage.

A few hundred meters from the great stupa at Bodhgaya flows the Nairanjana River, which passes through open plains dotted with dense groves of trees. One of these groves is called the Forest of Asceticism because it is the place where Shakyamuni and five monks engaged in religious ascetic practices before he attained enlightenment. In the distance rises the mountain called Pragbodhi. The young prince Siddartha, who was later to become the Buddha, left his home, his beautiful wife, Yashodhara, and his son, Rahula, to enter an ascetic way of life in the hope of finding enlightenment. For six years, he engaged in severe austerities only to discover that asceticism does not bring enlightenment. On discovering this truth, he rose, bathed in the Nairanjana River, and sat down under a tree. A village maiden named Sujata came to him and gave him milk and gruel to eat. Refreshed by this food, he resolved to continue his search for enlightenment. To this end he climbed Mount Pragbodhi. Finding the pinnacle of the mountain unsuitable, however, he descended, went to Bodhgaya (near present-day Gaya), and sat under the bodhi tree where he finally attained enlightenment.

When I stood on the banks of the Nairanjana River, it was low because the rainy season was over. Still, its crystal clear water reflected the bright light of the sun. I took off my shoes and waded into the water, which came to just below my knees. The coolness of the river was stimulating and seemed to carry me back to the distant past.

India is a land where poverty reigns supreme. On first acquaintance, Calcutta impressed me with the kind of desolation that I recall in the Tokyo of the days immediately after World War II. In the business parts of town, small dirty shops are crowded together. In the shops, where miscellaneous articles of trade are heaped under dim electric lights, two or three men can be seen gazing idly out into the streets. The city is packed with people, many of whom are as thin as rails and clothed in no more than simple rags. The instant an automobile pauses at a stoplight, beggars flock around and begin rapping on the windows. Day and night, in front of the train stations and in the various plazas, tens and hundreds of people of the lowest caste loiter. Some of them lie on the bare ground staring in front of them with dry, empty eyes. They have no homes, no work, not so much as a small square of land to cultivate. Most of them suffer from chronic malnutrition. They exist in a living death of semistarvation.

My wife often asked me how all these people survive if they do no work. It is amazing that they manage to face each new morning. Nor are they numbered in the thousands or even the hundreds of thousands: in India today there are more than seventy million people who fall into the lowest social caste. Yet Buddhism teaches that all men are equal, that all men can become buddhas. Jawaharlal Nehru once said that Buddhism died a natural death in India. After Buddhism perished there, the majority of the Indian people became believers in the Hindu faith; and it is the Hindu faith that today supports the rigid, irrational system of castes.

I had an opportunity to visit a temple at the Hindu holy place of Varanasi. In front of the imposing white building was a red curtain, and in front of the curtain were six men who intoned a magical liturgy as they swayed to and fro and struck the gongs they held. Finally the red curtain opened, revealing a statue of a strange goddess painted all white except for crimson lips. What I was witnessing appeared less mystical than fantastic. But the scene of people bathing in the Ganges was more surprising still.

The abundant waters of the Ganges flash reflections of the light of the hot southern sun. At the riverbanks, the water is muddy brown. In places along the shore concrete steps have been built to lead down into the water. Large numbers of men and women descend the steps into the river daily and wash their faces, rinse their mouths, or submerge themselves entirely. Upstream is a place on the river where women do their laundry. Not far from the bathing steps is a crematory, from which the ashes of the dead are cast upon the river. To our minds, these scenes on the river were only odd; but from the viewpoint of the Hindu believers, the Ganges is holy. To have one's ashes mixed with its waters is an ultimate happiness. Consequently, the followers of the Hindu religion wash their faces, drink the muddy river water with a sense of gravity, and happily bathe in it. These people are sincere in their belief, although to me it seems only an unenlightened custom.

Customs alter with the nation. There are a large number of Ceylonese and Tibetan Buddhist priests at the holy Buddhist places in India. At one of these places, a Tibetan priest approached me and thrust his long tongue out at me. "What can he mean by sticking out his tongue at a person he has never seen before?" I asked myself in consternation. I later learned that for Tibetans thrusting out the tongue symbolizes a sign of respect and a vow to speak only the truth.

Pasted on walls and fences in many places in Indian towns, I spied brown objects about fifteen centimeters in diameter and about the shape of a large cookie. In the center of each was a handprint. I wondered what these things might be; they did not look edible. Inquiry revealed that they are cow dung, the sole source of fuel for many people in India. Whenever they find a piece of cow dung in the streets, women pick it up, mix it with grass, and press it against a wall or fence, where it soon dries. When it has dried, the women collect it, add it to the other dung cakes in their baskets, and peddle the fuel from place to place. India is vast and has an immense population. I could not help thinking that, if the people would use everything as economically as they do cow dung and if they could know the joy of diligent labor, the nation might well experience rebirth.

I spent the night before my trip to Mount Gridhrakuta in a rest-house in an old royal fort at Rajgir, in the state of Bihar. The fort is surrounded by five mountains, of which Gridhrakuta is by far the highest and the most beautiful. The name of the mountain, which means Vulture Peak, derives from an imagined resemblance between its shape and that of the bird. The Buddha is believed to have expounded many sutras—including the Lotus Sutra—on Mount Gridhrakuta. The other members of the party and I arose and participated in sutra readings at six thirty on the morning of our trip. We did not board our bus, however, until nine o'clock. Rajgir was the capital of the ancient kingdom of Magadha. To the north of the old fort is the new fort built by King Bimbisara, a notable ruler of Magadha. Bimbisara is said to have erected a building in a bamboo grove where he heard the Buddha and came to believe his teachings. During the lifetime of the Buddha, however, Bimbisara was imprisoned and subsequently murdered by his own son Ajatashatru.

On the way from the old fort to the new one are a number of

ruins, some of which we visited on our way to Mount Gridhrakuta. At ten in the morning, we arrived at the stone-paved road called the Way of Bimbisara because the king had it paved so that he could be carried over it to the mountain to hear the Buddha. Moving up the fairly steep road, we chanted the *Daimoku, Namu Myōhō Renge-kyō*. As we went higher, the royal fort came into view.

At the top of the mountain is a plaza, on the edge of which is a brick ruin said to be the platform from which the Buddha delivered the Lotus Sutra and other teachings. I was deeply moved by the sight of this platform because it brought to my mind's eye a vivid impression of the time when the Buddha was alive on this earth. I made an incense offering on the platform, brought my hands together in prayer, and meditated profoundly for a few moments before beginning to read from the Lotus Sutra. As I stood there in silence, I felt strength welling up from deep in the earth. Reading the sutra as I stood on top of Vulture Peak and looked at the greenery of the neighboring mountains gleaming in the blazing sunlight was an experience that will always remain precious.

After a brief rest, we examined some caves in which Ananda, Maudgalyayana, and Shariputra, major disciples of the Buddha, have left traces of their religious pursuits. Then we descended to the base of the mountain. Even after we had left it, Mount Gridhrakuta remained a joy in our hearts.

Sarnath is famous as the place at which the Buddha first rolled the Wheel of the Law, that is, where he preached his first sermon. The Maha Bodhi Society built a middle school and a high school in Sarnath some years ago and planned to construct a college there as part of the celebration of the centennial of the birth of Dharmapala. We visited the grounds of the schools during our trip to Sarnath; and as we entered the gates, all seven hundred of the students gathered in the courtyard rose as if at a signal and welcomed us with voices filled with youth and strength.

After we had toured the school facilities, I was asked to decide the position of the foundation stones for the college. Agreeing to do as requested, I followed my guide to a trench dug to a depth of about two meters. In the bottom of the trench I laid five bricks, on top of which construction workers would later pour concrete for the foundations. At the conclusion of this brief ceremony, I was thanked and asked to make a few remarks. I felt that I must comply. As I spoke to the young people from the high speaker's platform, I could not help believing in a Buddhist relation that led to my making a speech for the first time in India at the place where the Buddha first rolled the Wheel of the Law.

Some time after this experience, I learned that to be invited to attend the ground breaking of a school is among the highest honors an Indian can afford his guest. I was happy that the Maha Bodhi Society had been courteous enough to invite a delegation of Buddhist believers from Japan to take part in such a prestigious occasion. I was further pleased by the profound significance I attached to concluding our pilgrimage in India on the site of a school devoted to stimulating the prosperity of Buddhism in its homeland.

The name of India is said to come from a Persian word meaning "the land of the Indus River." This river has undoubtedly played an important part in the development of India. It was on its shores that the Indus Valley civilization—possibly the oldest in human history—emerged and reached a level of urban sophistication that entitles it to be ranked with the ancient civilizations of China, Egypt, and Mesopotamia. In more recent times, the Indus valley has produced such great leaders as the Hindu poet Rabindranath Tagore, the advocate of the theory of passive resistance Mohandas Karamchand Gandhi, and the great politician Jawaharlal Nehru.

Today, however, religious evil has sent roots deep into the very daily lives of the Indian people to create conditions of appalling poverty and famine. Why did Buddhism, which originated and once prospered in India, fail there? Perhaps the upper classes did not react well to the Buddha's teachings of universal equality. Perhaps the lower classes failed to understand the greatness of the Buddha's teachings, even when they were permitted to come into contact with them. The conjunction of these two factors may explain the failure of Buddhism and the gradual rise of Hinduism in India. Reflecting on the condition of India made me intensely aware of this truth: no matter where the Buddha first taught, unless the people understand its meaning and put it to practical application, the Law, which is otherwise a priceless treasure, has no value. A great Buddhist teacher in the fourth century A.D. prophesied that the Buddha's Law would come to be closely related to the Orient. Just as he foresaw, today, we in Japan have the good fortune to be bathed in the light of the Law. When I saw the way in which Buddhism can be said to exert hardly any influence at all in India today, I became even more deeply impressed with the gravity of the mission of Risshō Kōsei-kai. For the sake of the protection of the Law—one aspect of our mission—and as a way of demonstrating gratitude to Shakyamuni, I proposed establishing an arrangement whereby serious Indian students may come to Japan to study Buddhism so that they may carry the teachings to their homeland again.

30. The Handshake of Pope Paul VI

ON A SUNNY March day in 1965, I received an invitation to attend a session of the Second Vatican Council, to be held in Rome in September of the same year. I knew that Vatican I—the previous meeting of the Roman Catholic Ecumenical Council—had been convened nearly a century earlier and that attendance at these meetings is limited to prelates of at least the rank of bishop. I was invited by the Vatican internuncio in Tokyo to attend as a special guest and as a representative of Japanese religion and of the Buddhist faith. It was the first time in the history of the Catholic Church that a member of another faith had been invited to participate in an assembly of its leaders. Of course, I was honored; but at first I was unable to understand why the pope had singled me out.

The history of the Roman Catholic Church is a long one, filled with glory and with trouble. The Protestant sects that arose at the time of the Reformation and developed rapidly thereafter have been branded as godless heretics and demons by the Catholics. The disputes and strife between Rome and the Protestant Christian groups led to warfare and great suffering. But how significant are the fundamental differences among these factions? The African native who has been exposed to the missionary activities of Catholics and Protestants probably thinks, "We have heard the teachings of all kinds of pastors and priests; but in the final analysis, they all seem the same to us." This simple attitude penetrates to the very heart of religion and sharply reveals the ugliness and foolishness of exclusivism. In recent times, members of the clergy, confused by this kind of view of the Protestant-Catholic question, have given serious thought to the issue and have examined their own opinions on it. The outcome of their soul-searching has been what is called the ecumenical movement.

This movement got under way to inspire Protestants, Catholics, and all branches of the faith to reunite and move forward together toward a peaceful world. In his now famous encyclical *Peace on Earth,* proclaimed in 1963, the late Pope John XXIII took initial steps toward this goal by calling for a reunion of the "separated brethren" (the new name used for the same Protestants that had once been called "people possessed by the devil"). Pope Paul VI, continuing in the direction established by John XXIII, took the additional step of conferring with Patriarch Athenagoras of the Greek Orthodox Church. The outcome of those talks was a joint communiqué expressing regret for the 911 years during which the two churches had excommunicated, criticized, and otherwise injured each other. The same communiqué made a call for new advances in a spirit of union. After this historic resolution of long-standing differences, the pope exchanged messages on the subject of peace and unity with Visser't Hooft, secretary-general of the Protestant World Council of Churches. Because the ecumenical movement was to be an important topic at the Vatican Council, the meeting was the object of considerable worldwide interest.

Shakyamuni asked why certain groups of people should consider themselves the possessors of the truth while regarding all others as blinded by falsehood. Why is it impossible for people of faith to meet and discuss issues openly without prejudices and fighting? Basically religion ought not to lead to the exclusion of others. On the contrary, it ought to promote love for self, love for the other, and the view that the self and the other are in a real sense one. Division and strife among the adherents of different religions are unnatural. All men of religious faith should study together and discuss issues in unity in the hope of contributing to the achievement of peace. Because I feel this way, I have repeatedly asserted the necessity of religious cooperation.

As one step in this direction, I urged the unification of at least the subgroups within Nichiren Buddhism. With this in mind, in 1951, I helped form the Union of the New Religious Organizations in Japan; but the times were unpropitious for such a move in the late forties and the fifties. I was called nonsensical for attempting religious cooperation. There were even people who said that I had launched such a project because I lacked confidence in my own religion. But as time passed, growth, diversification, and intensification in modern technological and mechanical civilization had the psychological effect of turning people away from exclusive, self-righteous religious attitudes. It came to be believed that religion must abandon complacency and parochialism and transcend boundaries of nation and race to work for the happiness of all men. In this ideological climate, in the midfifties, even Japanese religious organizations began to show signs of moving in the direction of general cooperation. Although the movement was late starting, it proved to be a dawning that led to the development of the Peace Delegation of Religious Leaders for Banning Nuclear Weapons.

The spirit of religious cooperation has now begun to spread throughout the world, just as a realization of the importance of union had spread earlier throughout the branches of the Christian faith. I learned that the exceptional invitation of a Buddhist to attend a meeting of Vatican II had been extended to me in recognition of the work my colleagues and I had done in the past in the name of religious cooperation. This meant that the world was beginning to take note of the activities of Risshō Kōsei-kai. Realizing that the invitation was not only a fortunate thing, but also a chance for deepening mutual understanding among all believers in Buddhism and all members of the Christian faith, when a formal invitation was extended to me in August, I immediately replied to express my eagerness to attend.

The day of my departure for Rome was heavy with the lingering heat of September. The sky was cloudy and the air was hot and humid owing to the influence of a typhoon that had approached the shores of Honshu the day before. The lobby of the airport was steamy and uncomfortable, but before long something happened to bring at least psychological refreshment to me and the many people who had braved the weather to come to see me off. Murmurs of pleasure arose from the group around me as my third daughter, Yoshiko, came in, leading her young son by the hand. My grandchild held a bouquet of carnations in his small hands. He offered them to me, saying, "For granddaddy." I thanked him and thought to myself as I gazed at his shy face, "The movement I am taking part in must persevere for the sake of this boy, of other children like him everywhere, and of peace for all men. I must do whatever I can to ensure that these young people are proud in the teachings of the Lotus Sutra when they reach adulthood."

Although it seems to be part of the city of Rome, Vatican City, located on the Vatican hill above the Tiber River, is in fact an independent state. Its front entrance is the piazza of Saint Peter's Church. No one who visits Rome can fail to be overpowered by the splendor of this building and by the grandeur of the colonnade, central obelisk, and two huge fountains of Saint Peter's Square. Though it is the smallest state in the world (with a population of about one thousand) its authority—even to influence international politics—is comparable to that of the Soviet Union or the United States because it is the home of Saint Peter's and the pope (who is the bishop of Rome), the greatest church and the most important religious leader for over five hundred fifty million Catholics throughout the world.

Within the Catholic Church the pope exercises absolute religious authority. Jesus said to the first bishop of Rome, "Thou art Peter, and upon this rock I will build my church," and charged the chief among his disciples to "feed my sheep." Since Peter's time, his successors as bishop of Rome and vicar of Christ have been the head—the pope—of the Catholic Church. At the Vatican Council of 1869–70, the doctrine of papal infallibility was proclaimed. According to this doctrine, when speaking as head of his church on matters of faith and morals the pope is infallible.

The session of Vatican II that I attended was opened on September 14, 1965. The following is a description of the event as written for our monthly magazine *Kōsei* by Kinzō Takemura, who was then head of the publishing department of the Kōsei Publishing Company.

"Some twenty-five hundred bishops clad in scarlet robes and scarlet hats had gathered from all parts of the globe to attend the meeting in Saint Peter's. Together with them, in splendid array, were the cardinals of the Church, heads of the monastic orders, and authorities from theological seminaries. President Niwano sat in the front of the gathering. His dark formal suit and the white Buddhist prayer beads he held in his hand captured the attention of many people who were eager to see this representative of a non-Christian religion.

"To the sounds of liturgical music and in a rainbow of light cast by the stained-glass windows, Pope Paul, clad in pure white, entered; and mass was celebrated in the central part of the cathedral. With his prayer beads gleaming in his hands, President Niwano closely observed the proceedings of the Vatican Council, a highly important assembly within a church that has traditionally refused to confer with other religious bodies. I was deeply moved by this event, which took place on the morning of September 14, 1965, and which signaled the gradual opening of a door that had remained closed throughout the history of the Christian church."

Following mass, the pope made an address in which he modestly commented on his own failings and said that he felt it was his responsibility as God's representative on earth to bring the love of God equally to all men and all religious faiths. During the sermon, which lasted roughly one hour, the pope spoke convincingly about peace and the movement for religious unity. But the most impressive of his remarks was: "The popes in history have been guilty of causing schism in the Christian faith. Today is no time for splits in Christianity or disagreements among the religions of the world. This is our chance to join hands and walk together in the direction of peace." He was describing the mission of all religious people, who must understand each other and cooperate in order to contribute to world peace. The pope of the Catholic Church was expressing a wish that I have cherished ever since the founding of Risshō Kōsei-kai, though my dream has found little understanding in Japan. For a long time, thrilled by a warmth resulting from the knowledge that my dream was understood by him, I gazed at the stern, but gentle, profile of the pope.

When I visited the famous Vatican Library, I saw on display a letter sent three hundred years ago to Pope Paul V by the Japanese warrior and feudal lord Masamune Datè (1567–1636), who dispatched an envoy to Rome in 1613. As I looked at the document, I conjured up a picture of Datè's envoy and retainer Tsunenaga Hasekura (1561–1622), clothed in the *haori* coat and the skirtlike *hakama* and with his hair bound in the old-fashioned way, as he gave the letter into the hands of Paul V. I was struck with the wonderful connection between that man and me. He had brought a document from Japan to Pope Paul V; three centuries later, I brought another document from Japan to Pope Paul VI.

Originally I was scheduled for an interview with Pedro Arrupe, the general of the Society of Jesus, on the fifteenth of September, but this proved impossible, for I was suddenly informed that I was to have an audience with the pope at five o'clock in the afternoon on that day and that I was to make necessary preparations. Since the council session had only started, I had no idea that the pope would have time to see me so soon.

We met in a marble-walled room. The pope, who was again clothed in white, rose upon seeing me enter and welcomed me by name. I replied by saying that I was honored to be with him. I raised my hands and the prayer beads I was holding in a Buddhist greeting. Then the pope extended his hand, shook mine, and finally took it between his, where it remained throughout the audience.

"I know what you are doing for interreligious cooperation. It is very wonderful. Please continue to promote this wonderful movement," the pope said to me. As he spoke he looked in my eyes. His voice was low, calm, and grave.

Continuing, he said, "In the Vatican, too, the attitude toward non-Christian religions is changing. It is important for people of religion not to cling to factions or denominations but to recognize each other and pray for each other." My heart was warm as I realized that the true meaning of religious cooperation can be seen in mutual prayers among all people of faith. The Buddhist must pray for the Christian, and the Christian for the Buddhist.

"I shall exert my best efforts for the sake of world peace," I said to the pope. He replied, "God will surely bless you in the noble work you have undertaken." And I was refreshed and encouraged by the sincerity and truth of what he said. Our audience ended on my wish that the pope would someday visit Japan.

As I left the room, I could still feel the warmth of the pope's handclasp. That had been no ordinary handshake. It was a flesh-and-blood representation of mutual understanding between the religions of the East and the West, between a Buddhist and the head of a church that has long been known for exclusivism. I believe that our handshake proved to be the starting point of the creation of a new kind of religious relationship.

All the way from the Vatican to my hotel, I reflected on my joy at finding that the pope and I agree on religious cooperation. These thoughts led me to consider some of the basic similarities between Christianity and Buddhism. The love of God of which the pope had spoken in his opening message to that session of the Second Vatican Council is the same thing as the compassion advocated by Buddhism. The pope insists that the love for the neighbor taught by the New Testament must be interpreted to mean love for peoples everywhere, no matter what their nationality or race. Shakyamuni taught the same thing about compassion.

As Shakyamuni insisted, the true teaching is only one. From the time of my visit to Rome, I began to see that the idea of one true teaching embracing all teachings might be the bridge that could connect Christianity and Buddhism and perhaps all religions. The resulting contacts might make possible a world conference of religious leaders for the sake of peace. I started to have budding faith in the realization of my dream from that time forward. The ideal of the pope and the meaning of his words are in accord with my belief that religion must save not only the individual, but all humanity.

Ordinarily, I fall asleep very quickly, no matter where I am; but on the night of my audience with the pope, I lay thinking with open eyes for a long time after going to bed. In our time, the role of religion is more important than at any other time. The world is torn between two opposing ideological camps. The fires of war still rage. A civilization devoted to scientific progress, materialism, and excessive concentration on the economic aspects of life and a desiccation of spiritual culture have created social problems that urgently demand the most careful attention. Dark clouds of danger engulf the world.

These reflections caused me to think about the way Kōsei-kai must travel. This in turn recalled the words Myōkō Sensei had spoken to me some twenty years earlier: "You are a believer in the Lotus Sutra. You have learned the truth of the universe. You must therefore apply the basic morality of that truth in developing your buddha-nature and in fulfilling your mission to save mankind." When I first heard those words, I did not seriously think that the world would come to recognize the Lotus Sutra. But at the Second Vatican Council, I had a chance to meet and talk with many religious leaders, including the pope, the general of the Society of Jesus, prelates of the Catholic Church, and Tatsuo Cardinal Doi, of Japan. In our talks, I was surprised to find that there are more points of agreement than of disagreement in our ways of thinking. Turning all these things over in my mind, I kept asking myself, "Are things all right as they are going now? How can we change Risshō Kōsei-kai of Japan into Risshō Kōsei-kai of the whole world?" I lay awake a long time that night.

I returned to Japan on the evening of September 24. Following a meeting with the reception committee and with journalists at Tokyo International Airport, I went directly to the Great Sacred Hall of Kōsei-kai. On both sides of the Haramitsu Bridge, which leads to the building, crowds of members waved their hands in warm welcome to me. The auditorium too was filled with people as I walked to the altar to make a report of my trip to the Eternal Buddha and to make an announcement.

"The pope of the Roman Catholic Church has recognized our organization and has said that the work we are doing will surely receive God's protection. The burden Kōsei-kai must bear in the drive for worldwide religious cooperation is heavy. We cannot fulfill our mission if we remain concerned with the salvation of the individual alone or with no more than the welfare of our own organization. I feel that the spirit of Myōkō Sensei, who has found eternal sanctuary, congratulates us on our work and encourages us to go on."

Tremendous applause broke the silence that had reigned in the hall. As the wave of sound rolled over me, I stood motionless for a few moments in front of the altar.

31.
Unity the Goal

BECAUSE I am often questioned on the subject, I should like to make a few comments about the origins of the Union of the New Religious Organizations in Japan and on the relation between it and the Japan Religions League.

The Union of the New Religious Organizations in Japan was founded in 1951. In the period immediately following the close of World War II, religious freedom was granted to the people of Japan; and new religious organizations sprang up with great frequency and vitality. But the prevailing social trend was to ridicule and abuse these groups, even without attempting to understand what they were about. Banding together in the Japan Religions League, the older, more established religions were able to work together for their common benefit by conducting negotiations with the general headquarters of the Occupation authorities and with various Japanese governmental organs. The new religious organizations, however, were isolated from one another and were therefore open to attack from the press and from other branches of society. But as time passed, the new organizations became so important that the older world of Japanese religion could no longer ignore them. As the new groups grew in size and significance, the need for a body to unite them became pressing. The Occupation authorities found it difficult to remain in contact with these groups as long as they existed in isolation. At one point, the head of the Occupation's department of religious affairs approached Tokuchika Miki, president of the Perfect Liberty organization, with a proposal for the establishment of a liaison office for the new religious groups. By this time the new religious groups themselves had become aware of the need for a body that would work for their common advantage and their protection.

In August, 1951, the Perfect Liberty group, Risshō Kōsei-kai, Sekai Kyūsei-kyō, the Seichō-no-Ie Foundation, and Ishin-kai formed the Union of the New Religious Organizations in Japan. At about the same time, leaders of Ananai-kyō, Shūyōdan Hōsei-kai, Tenshin-dō, Ishin-kai, and the Seichō-no-Ie Foundation met to make preparations to establish a joint body called the Japan League of New Religions. Later discussions between these two groups resulted in their amalgamation in the Union of the New Religious Organizations in Japan.

Prior to the formation of this union, Kōsei-kai had participated in a council of organizations of the Nichiren Buddhist sect. This council, which included Nihonzan Myōhō-ji Daisanga, Hokke-shū, Myōchi-kai, Bussho Gonen-kai, and Myōdō-kai, came into being for the sake of unity among various Nichiren groups because some religious bodies professing faith in the Lotus Sutra had been condemning other organizations professing faith in the same sutra as heretical and wicked.

I argued that the temple on Mount Minobu, as the head of Nichiren Buddhism, is responsible for indicating the teachings that can help followers understand the true spirit of Nichiren, the founder of the sect that bears his name. Mount Minobu must teach the way in which we are to interpret the Lotus Sutra and how we must behave in regard to the focus of devotion. But the council reacted coolly to my proposal and requested that I refrain from discussing unity in religious teachings and that I permit each religious organization to follow its own inclinations in such affairs.

I realize that the issue of teachings is of paramount importance and that unity in this issue is extremely difficult to achieve in a council. Nonetheless, I insist that a council lacking firmly established principles in matters of teachings sacrifices its major significance and strength. For me, it is an ideal and an unwavering article of faith that, though the ways in which it is expressed may vary, religious truth is and must be the same. Consequently, I believe that we ought to rally around the one truth and abandon petty differences; but I found no one at the Minobu council to agree with me.

If the other members of the council were going to hold out for the validity of the teachings of their individual groups, I gradually came to see that I had no choice but to do the same. Our members continued to make pilgrimages to Mount Minobu, and eighty households in the town of Minobu became members of Risshō Kōsei-kai. This greatly enraged the authorities at Mount Minobu; and in 1950, we were reprimanded and accused of having led people in Minobu to forsake their affiliation with the Nichiren sect at Mount Minobu.

In the following year, we were visited by Shūten Ōishi, of the Ministry of Education, in connection with the Union of the New Religious Organizations in Japan. Ōishi called first on Tokuchika Miki, of the Perfect Liberty organization. But we all three met later and agreed on the desirability of forming an organization of new religious groups. I said at the time that if the organization made public the teachings of each member group and sponsored joint study programs it could come to have great significance. Miki objected that if teachings became a premise of our action we would be unlikely to achieve the unity we required. I could see his point. After all, even the members of the Nichiren sect had found it impossible to achieve unity in teachings among themselves. Obviously it would be much more difficult for an aggregation of diverse religious organizations to attain unity in such matters. Still, I felt that we all had much to teach each other and much to learn from each other. "All who see, hear, recognize, and know the sutra shall approach enlightenment."

The first step toward mutual discussion and learning is certainly the act of joining hands in unity. Because I was convinced that this is true, I decided that Risshō Kōsei-kai should participate in the Union of the New Religious Organizations in Japan. Myōkō Sensei objected that it would be a bad idea to join such an organization so soon after having been accused of undermining the Nichiren sect. The senior leaders of Kōsei-kai agreed with her. Against this background of opposition, I nonetheless insisted on joining, though my hopes for success were not high at the time.

But events took a decided turn for the better. The union, which had started with only twenty-four member organizations, grew to sixty in a year. All but two or three of the major new religious organizations joined. Our hope was to make the union an organization that contributes to the creation of an ideal nation and a world of peace. This hope has grown stronger with the passing years.

The generally accepted view is that the public will pay no attention to a new religious federation for five or ten years after its foundation. The prejudice that new religions are cheats taking unfair advantage of people when they are weak is deep-rooted. But in the spring of 1952, less than a year after its founding, the Union of the New Religious Organizations in Japan was admitted to the Japan Religions League.

The Japan Religions League is an organization of Buddhist, Shinto, and Christian groups. During the war, it came under severe governmental control and later disbanded. In June of 1946, however, it got a fresh start with the goal of promoting close cooperation among Buddhist, Shinto, and Christian organizations for the sake of using development in religious movements in the building of Japanese culture and worldwide peace.

In January of 1965, the Religions Center was opened by the Japan Religions League. Some people have criticized this center for being politically inspired, but I am in favor of it. Today human beings are in danger of losing an important part of their humanity because of overemphasis of material well-being and underemphasis of spiritual values. The Religions Center can, I believe, accent the vital importance of a true spirit of religion and can contribute to the development of a national popular faith and to the further strengthening of religious cooperation. It is said in the Nirvana Sutra that the people who do not believe in the Buddha's Law and therefore fall into evil ways are comparable to the full expanse of the whole earth, whereas those who believe in the Buddha's Law and attain buddhahood are comparable to a patch of land no larger than a fingernail. The Religions Center is striving to improve this situation by bringing about the unification of all religions. It has already evoked responses from educators, parents' associations, the field of learning, and the financial world.

In April of 1969, I was elected chairman of the board of directors of the Japan Religions League, which, in 1970, sponsored the first World Conference on Religion and Peace. In spite of a tendency to regard it as something of a salon-conference, that meeting became a steppingstone for further growth. I am deeply grateful to the Japan Religions League for sponsoring it. As time passes, the Japan Religions League and the Union of the New Religious Organizations in Japan are increasing their usefulness as they continue to work in closer harmony.

32.
Three Full Days

In November, 1965, after my return from the meeting of the Vatican Council, I made a trip to my home village of Suganuma. It was the first time I had been there in a year and a half. The season of autumnal foliage had already passed, and the mountain trees were bare as they awaited the arrival of winter. The red earth of the six kilometers of unpaved, winding road from Tōkamachi to Suganuma lay bathed in the pale sun of late fall. Perhaps for strangers from the city this road is rough and sad; but for a person raised in the area, its color, the nature of the sunlight, and the smell of the dried grass are familiar and dear. I like to return to the land where I was born and raised as often as I can because being there and breathing the pure air of unspoiled nature help me recover the spirit I had when I was a child. As I recall times gone by in my native village, I am able to observe myself calmly and quietly. But I rarely have a chance to relax there long, for I am able to make these trips only in the limited amount of time I can spare from my religious duties.

The occasion of that particular visit was to hold memorial services for the fiftieth anniversary of the death of my grandfather Jūtarō Niwano and for the thirty-third anniversary of the death of my uncle Shōtarō Niwano. Memorial services for both men were conducted by the priest Tetsuei Maruyama from the temple Shinjō-in in Tōkamachi.

On the night of my first day home, we sat around the brushwood fire in the central hearth of our house and listened to the sound of the icy, sleety rain falling in the darkness outside. My elder brother turned to me and said in a soft voice, "There are only twenty-three families in Suganuma now."

In the past there had been forty-two families in the village; but it seems that increasing numbers of young people were running away from home in the hope of bettering themselves and escaping from the severe conditions of rural life. Wrapping their belongings in cloths, they would sneak from their houses when their parents were unaware of what they were doing. Not all of the runaways stayed away, however. There were even cases in which young men left and came back as many as five times.

As long as some of these people returned, the village did not suffer much. But after World War II increasing numbers left for the more convenient life of the city; and with the passing years, Suganuma has become a sadly wasted place. Though I realized that this phenomenon is nationwide and that rural villages all over Japan are losing their population, it made me sorrowful to hear that Suganuma had dwindled to half its former size.

On the following day, we made a trip to the cemetery. On our return, I found two of my classmates from primary school days waiting for me. Smiling and commenting on how none of us had changed, we immediately started reminiscing about the snow houses we used to build and the wrestling matches we used to hold. No matter how old one grows, carefree conversations of this kind always start up at once when old schoolmates get together.

As we sat laughing over old times, we heard a voice from the entranceway. I went to see who it was and found Mohei Ikeda at the door. Though he had grown old, had a wrinkled face, and walked with a cane, the smile on his face was still warm and bright. "I heard you were back and came to have a look at you," he said as I put my arm around his shoulder and led him to the hearth. Both of my classmates greeted him courteously. Being considerate of the elderly is an old tradition in Suganuma. Mohei called me by my boyhood name, Shikazō, when he said, "The village has become a lonely place. No more young people around to do the *kagura* dances. Things were at their best when you boys were young. I'd like to watch Shikazō do the *tengu* dance one more time." While speaking, he seemed to be looking at clouds on the top of a faraway mountain peak.

The two most common family names in the village of Suganuma

are Niwano and Ikeda. Mohei's family is the head of all the Ikedas in the area; and he was in charge of the ceremonial dancing that took place during the festivals held at Suwa Shrine, where the guardian deity of our village is enshrined. Mohei Ikeda had been my dancing teacher when, in my young years, I learned the lion and *tengu* roles for the festivals and took lessons in beating the drums that are an indispensable part of Japanese ceremonies of this kind.

After two or three cups of sakè had begun to show in his face, Mohei began to talk more expansively about the past. Turning to me, he said, "Your dancing was good. You were skillful and more eager to do well than most other people. If I showed you something a couple of times, you remembered it. You were too tall for the role of the woman, but you were a first-rate *tengu*. I really liked watching you work—but now I don't have anybody to teach."

While I listened to him, I remembered practicing dance movements as I walked to the mountains to cut weeds or when I rested from work in the fields. Mohei continued: "Your sword dance was good too, and you could sing. Not the kind of voice you use in reading sutras now. You had a cool, strong voice. And when you put on makeup, tied a towel around your brow, and danced, all the village girls blushed, looked shy, and sighed." Then Mohei's voice grew faint and trailed away.

When the young people liked to dance and sing at the festivals, the village was lively. The old traditions flowered afresh then. I remember those times clearly. Mohei's talk made me sentimental about the old days, but it also seemed to tell me something profound about the village and about the nature of the Japanese approach to religion. From ancient times, the people of Japan have gathered together to pray to nature and to the gods for good harvests and again later to offer thanks when the harvest is in. We sat talking for a long time without being aware of the late hour. As I listened to Mohei's recollections, I sensed a kind of comfort that he and other poor country people derive from religious observances of the kind represented by shrine festivals. This feeling reminded me of something I had once written: "The ancient religion of the Japanese people took the form of worship and celebration of the infinite divinities of the natural world. Such nature faith and reverence for ancestors created the sentiments that fostered Buddhism in Japan. It was reaching this substratum of the Japanese mind and spirit that enabled Buddhism to take firm root here."

The next day, I visited Ōike Primary School, which I had attended. In those days the school was very small and had only about twenty pupils. Denkichi Daikai was principal and teacher as well. In my day, I wore straw sandals, carried my lunch in a wooden box, and wrapped my schoolbooks in a piece of cloth. Today the school is large. It contains both primary and middle schools. Food is served in the cafeteria, and none of the pupils wear straw sandals or know what a wooden lunch box looks like. But the natural setting still includes all the things I remember.

The natural environment exerts the greatest influence on children in their formative years. Understanding our contact with nature and reverence for one's ancestors lead to the development of the buddha-mind, without the person's being consciously aware of the process.

On the day of my visit to the school, about one hundred fifty young people gathered to hear me make a talk that lasted about thirty minutes. During the speech, I made the following remarks: "When you do something bad, something that your conscience says you ought not do, it lodges in a corner of your mind and makes you spend a gloomy, dark two or three days. But when you do something good, you feel bright and cheerful. I want you to remember this and to behave always in a way that makes you bright and cheerful."

The eyes of my young audience looked unwaveringly at me, and in them I saw all kinds of possibilities for the world of the future. I spent only three days in my home village, but the contacts I had there with the natural setting and with old friends made the three days very full and meaningful.

33. Steps in the Right Direction

The first World Conference on Religion and Peace took place in the International Conference Hall in Kyoto, during the period of October 16 through 21, 1970. From thirty-nine nations, representatives of the leading religions of the world—Christianity, Buddhism, Shinto, Islam, Judaism, and so on—gathered in this ancient city during the splendid season of autumnal foliage to discuss three major issues: disarmament, development, and human rights. The conference was among the largest of the many held in Japan in recent years. But size was not its most distinguishing feature. It was of major significance for the whole world because it was a chance for religious men from many faiths to unite for the same purpose. In the meeting room, the saffron robes of Buddhists from Southeast Asia were seen side by side with the black cassocks of priests from Rome and the business suits of Protestants from Europe and America.

Evaluations of the importance of the conference were not unanimously favorable, for there were many who wondered what practical good could come of a gathering of people of religion and their discussions of peace. Perhaps there was some justification for skepticism about immediate results. But this does not invalidate the conference. Today mankind has arrived at the point at which nuclear war can destroy all life on the planet. In the face of this horrendous threat, the most cherished wish of the peoples of the earth is peace. The road to peace may be difficult, and conferences like the one held in Kyoto in 1970 may do little for the immediate solution of the problems of the world. But such conferences are steps on the way of achieving peace, and all steps—even half-steps—in that direction must be taken.

The land available may be small, and the climate may be harsh; but it is certain that if the seeds are kept locked in the granary no buds will sprout, no flowers will bloom, and no fruit will ripen. The only way to hope for results is to cultivate, fertilize, and sow whatever ground one has with the utmost diligence and care. This is the meaning of progress and development. And at the peace conference we sowed some of the first seeds ever planted with these aims in mind. But much preparation was needed before the conference could become an actuality. In connection with these preparations, I made several trips to America and Europe.

At the Japanese-American Inter-Religious Consultation on Peace, held in Kyoto, in 1968, Bishop John Wesley Lord of the United Methodists said that all war is war against God. Bishop John H. Burt of the Anglican Church said that respect must take first place in relations among individuals and that the teachings of God must take first place in relations among nations. I commented that the family of man is gradually becoming a reality.

From the time of this consultation, interest in a world religious conference began to pick up momentum. In Istanbul, in 1969, over twenty representatives from seven nations met to hold an interim advisory committee meeting to discuss the concrete issues related to when and where such a conference might be held.

Once Constantinople, the capital of the Eastern Roman Empire, Istanbul was and remains a flourishing city, though today few traces of the past remain. The city is still the juncture between Asia and Europe, between the East and the West. As I stood looking out at the Bosporus from a window in the Istanbul Hilton, "Look," someone said, "that's Asia on the other side. This is Europe. In the summertime, people swim the Bosporus. That means that they bring Asia and Europe together. It is our duty to use these two continents as the center of our operations in bringing the entire world together."

In discussing possible locations for the conference, we suggested a number of places. The non-Japanese members of the committee wanted to hold the meeting in Japan, whereas the Japanese members hesitated to accept the proposal. Finally the Japanese members were overruled, and Kyoto was selected as the site. At the Istanbul meetings, the general plan and scale of the world conference were set; and executive and preparatory committees were formed.

When our plane landed at Tokyo International Airport after the trip home, I was surprised and deeply moved to find the entire city covered with a silvery blanket of snow. I had been told that Istanbul, which is located on the same parallel as Hakodate on Japan's cold northern island of Hokkaido, could be a very frigid place. But its location between the Black and Mediterranean seas spares Turkey from most snowfall. The weather there had not prepared me for what I found in Tokyo; consequently, the snow made an especially vivid impression on me. Kinzō Takemura, who had become my secretary and was traveling with me, said, "Beautiful, isn't it? This snow looks like a sign of good things for the Kyoto conference next year." But I replied, "I don't know. Snow is beautiful, but it's cold too. To me, this snow suggests the need to be prepared to work very hard to win the good will of the Japanese religious world for this project."

When I held discussions with representatives of various Japanese religious sects and groups, I saw that my premonition had been justified. Still, I urged the great need for a bond that transcends considerations of sect and group. But the reaction to my pleas was decidedly cool. When I continued to press for cooperation, that cool reaction became downright unpleasant. And that was not the worst of it. Some people went so far as to say that my call for cooperation and unity among religious organizations was no more than an attempt to further my own ambitions. Other criticisms and gossip reached my ears. Though, in the light of the nature of much of the history of human religion, such accusations might seem deserved, they caused me intense unhappiness. But two things sustained me. One was my absolutely firm conviction that the world condition did not permit men of religion in Japan to remain idle bystanders in this movement and that it was our duty to devote sincere thought to ways of furthering our mission. As the chairman of the board of directors of the Japan Religions League, I felt it my responsibility to act as an envoy in this work. The second thing that gave me moral support was the knowledge that the entire membership of Risshō Kōsei-kai was behind my ideas and actions.

In thinking the situation over, I was reminded of what one of the non-Japanese delegates to the Istanbul meeting had said when a Japanese representative had expressed his conviction that the success of the world conference would depend on enthusiasm. On hearing this, the non-Japanese representative said that, of course, enthusiasm is important but that without knowledge and capital not only an international conference but almost any other human undertaking is impossible. I was painfully aware of the truth of this statement.

But gradually the people who had insisted on remaining bystanders at the outset began to react favorably to the idea, and a movement got under way. As this happened, taking humility and enthusiasm as my allies, I continued my efforts to build a basis for convincing negotiations. In this, the efforts of the other directors of the Japan Religions League were immensely important support.

In July, 1969, I attended two international conferences in Boston and its environs. The first was the twentieth World Congress of the International Association for Religious Freedom. The second was a series of meetings of the executive committee of the World Conference on Religion and Peace.

At the conclusion of the first conference, which was held at the Boston Hilton Hotel, I moved to Endicott House of the Massachusetts Institute of Technology for the executive committee meetings. Aside from myself, four representatives from Japan attended these meetings, which were to have an important effect on the concrete details of the planning for the Kyoto meeting. All the topics with which we dealt—theme, program, budget, representatives, and preparations—were too important to permit the least negligence. It was a trying experience because, as soon as representatives from other countries made pronouncements, those of us from Japan had to consult quickly and make our own opinions known. When the meetings were over, people often approached me to ask my opinions. Because of the language barrier, I was frequently unable to express myself as directly as I should have liked; and this added to my general sense of increasing fatigue.

On the morning of the second day after our move to Endicott House, after my usual morning devotionals, I went to the toilet and noticed black blood in my bowel movement. When I told the other members of my party about this, they agreed it was something that could not be ignored. Though they insisted that I rest, I hesitated, knowing that the conference scheduled for that day was of considerable importance. But after the other representatives promised to keep me well posted on the progress of the meeting, I agreed to rest.

One after another, people came to my room to tell me what was happening at the meeting and to consult with me when decisions had to be made. Many of the non-Japanese committee members paid visits to wish me well. The American representatives were especially solicitous. They told me that though the conference was important my own health was more important and that I ought to go back to Japan at once to consult a doctor. Failing that, they argued that I ought to allow them to call in a local doctor. But I would agree to neither proposal.

In May of the previous year, I had undergone surgery for a stomach ulcer. The case had not been considered serious; but I was told that, if I was going to continue carrying out a strenuous work schedule, I ought to have the operation performed. I did, and in two weeks I was out of the hospital, although the hospitalization for ordinary cases of such operations is from three to four weeks. I felt certain that the blood in my stool was related to the operation. A doctor would have told me at once if I had consulted one, but I refused to do so because I did not want to be sent to a hospital in Boston. After the meetings at Endicott House, I was to travel to England, Switzerland, and Rome on work for the world conference. This was my mission, but if I was to be hospitalized I would be unable to fulfill it.

From the following day, my diet was reduced to consommé and milk. Though I felt hungry all the time on this liquid nourishment, my spirits were high, as if in contradiction of my physical condition. The Reverend Kiyoshi Takizawa, a Christian minister who was with us, gave me *shiatsu* massage treatment morning and night. At last, it was definitely decided that the world conference would be held in Kyoto under the auspices of the Japan Religions League; and after three days of discussions, the meetings drew to a close. Then the Japanese representatives, together with Dr. Dana McLean Greeley, called on Edwin O. Reischauer, the noted scholar and former United States ambassador to Japan.

On the night following that visit, my party was scheduled to board a plane for London, where I hoped to talk with Dr. Michael Ramsey, who was archbishop of Canterbury at the time. I was to leave London later and proceed to Geneva for a meeting with Dr. Eugene Carson Blake. When the American representatives at the Endicott House meetings heard of my schedule, they immediately attempted to convince me of the folly of such trips. They insisted that even if I saw Dr. Blake there was no likelihood that he and the World Council of Churches, which he heads, would participate in the Kyoto conference. I admitted that I did not know whether I would be able to convince Dr. Blake to take part, but I insisted that making an attempt to convince him was my duty and that I felt compelled to carry it out. It later appeared that my American friends were deeply concerned about my health. They wanted me to return to Japan at once instead of taking the risk of aggravating my condition on what might turn out to be wasted traveling. But I would not listen and headed for Boston's Logan International Airport.

Our plane was so late that we were kept waiting at the airport for six hours. Boston, which faces the Atlantic Ocean, is a pleasant place. The climate is much less humid than that of Tokyo. Nonetheless, it is hot in the middle of the summer; and the heat told on a man who had been living for a few days on milk and consommé. My fellow travelers expressed concern over my condition and the pallor of my face. But I told myself that dying for the sake of my mission in the name of the Buddha ought to be my most cherished wish. I tried to smile as I reassured my companions that I was fine. The plane finally took off at midnight. We did not arrive in London until six o'clock in the morning. The all-night trip had tired us, but there was no time for rest, since, after checking into our hotel, we had to start at once for Canterbury. Members of the group asked if we might not rest and visit the archbishop on the following day. They said they were tired themselves, but I suspected that they were only worried about me and were claiming to be tired in order to force me to slow down. I reminded them that we were on a mission of great urgency. We ought to entrust our physical conditions to the Buddha. This was no time to complain of being tired, for we had to continue our work as long as our bodies continued to function. With this sense of mission, we all got into the car sent for us by the Japanese embassy and sped away along the roughly one hundred kilometers of road between London and Canterbury.

We were impressed with the dignity and grandeur of Canterbury Cathedral, which has a history of over a thousand years. We learned that the archbishop was away; but we had an hour's discussion with Canon R. J. Hammer, who had lived in Japan for a number of years and who was in complete sympathy with the idea of a world conference on religion and peace. We were told that the archbishop would like to see us in the afternoon two days later, but our plans to go directly to Geneva made an interview impossible on this occasion. Leaving further work on behalf of the conference in the hands of Canon Hammer, we started back along the road to London.

When we returned to our hotel, Reverend Takizawa remarked that I must be weary after so much unbroken traveling. I felt much better. There was no more blood in my bowel movements. The dull pain and the sluggishness I had experienced were gone. Still, I was afraid that the bleeding might start again if I was not careful. To prevent this, Reverend Takizawa gave me *shiatsu* treatments daily for the entire duration of the journey. In doing this, he encouraged and helped me a great deal.

Some time earlier, Takizawa had decided to learn *shiatsu* massage therapy in the hope of relieving the physical pain of the people to whom he explained the teachings of the Christian God. He has even made some original contributions to *shiatsu* therapy. I am convinced that the fervor with which he devoted himself to me increased the effectiveness of the therapy. I know that his concern moved me deeply.

A few years later, I had a chance to return a small degree of the kindness he had shown me. While undergoing *shiatsu* treatment at Takizawa's hands, I gradually learned how to give the same therapy. Once again in Japan, when I learned that Takizawa had suffered a slight stroke that had impaired his ability to move, forcing him to retire temporarily to a remote hot spring for treatment, I followed him and performed *shiatsu* on him. He remarked that I had become so proficient at the therapy that he was willing to call me his best student.

I had been unforgettably moved a few years earlier when Pope Paul VI told me that he felt Christians ought to pray for Buddhists and Buddhists for Christians. Then, as I moved along the path toward world religious cooperation, I found a chance for a Christian to help me, a Buddhist, and then for me to help a Christian by means of homely *shiatsu* treatment. This experience has remained in my mind, where it blooms like a small, important flower.

From London we flew to lovely, quiet Geneva, where we visited the hilltop headquarters of the World Council of Churches. Although Dr. Eugene C. Blake, Secretary-General of the council, was so busy that his schedule was filled for days in advance, when he discovered that a party of Buddhists had traveled all the way from Japan to see him, he immediately made time for us and welcomed us warmheartedly. Dr. Blake expressed interest in the conference and in what people of religion can do for the sake of world peace. He was eager to hear of the actions of Christians in Japan and other parts of Asia. His remarks were filled with consideration for travelers from a distant land and with the trust that men and women of religious faith feel for each other. I was happy and gratified that we had made the trip to Geneva after all.

In the evening of the same day we flew to Rome for our final call of the trip. On the following morning, we were informed that Paul Cardinal Marella was waiting to see us at the Vatican, the dome and towers of which were gleaming in the early light. This was my third trip to the Vatican; and I already felt a familiar warmness for the cardinal, who seemed to be extremely happy to see us as we entered his office. Immediately I broached the subject of the world conference and expressed our hope of inviting the pope. Cardinal Marella promised to cooperate in any way that we might see fit.

On the same day, in the Vatican, we met John Joseph Cardinal Wright, another person who was to prove to be of the greatest importance to the world conference. He had been an American representative to the meetings held in Istanbul. Suddenly thereafter he was elevated to cardinal and given a position that might be described as the minister of education of the Vatican.

Our prime goal in visiting the Vatican was an audience with Pope Paul VI, but his imminent departure on a trip to Africa seemed to make such a meeting impossible to arrange. From the Japanese embassy, however, we soon learned that despite his crowded schedule the pope would make time to grant us an audience the day before he was to leave the country. For this occasion, we traveled about twenty-four kilometers from Rome to the papal palace Castel Gandolfo. His Holiness was as warm and gracious in shaking my hand this time as he had been on the other occasions when we met. After our talk, in which I expressed our wish to invite him to Japan for the world conference, he gave a parting handshake and said the Japanese word *arigatō* ("thank you") by way of final greeting.

The seventeen days of the trip had been extremely busy. Falling sick on a journey, especially one to foreign countries, is a most unsettling blow. To be frank, I wondered if I would be able to complete my tasks safely when I was first stricken in Boston. My being able to live on milk and soup as I traveled from America to Europe to Japan was thanks entirely to the protection of the gods and buddhas.

The first World Conference on Religion and Peace was held with great success. Though my American friends in Boston had said that I could not expect him to come, Dr. Eugene Carson Blake of the World Council of Churches attended, as did representatives from the Vatican. Among the communist nations, the Soviet Union, Poland, East Germany, Romania, Bulgaria, and Outer Mongolia were represented.

Encounter is the essential starting point for all human relations. Only when encounters occur can discussions take place. And only from discussions can understanding, trust, and friendship be forthcoming. The road we must travel in the future is long, but meetings of people of religion from all over the world in the hope of achieving one great common goal are steps in the right direction.

34.
The Open Gate

PRAYERS for world peace were held in Kōsei-kai's Fumon Hall on October 23, 1970, only two days after the close of the peace conference in Kyoto. Ninety-four foreign representatives to the conference, joined by thirty-three Japanese representatives, attended the prayer services as guests.

At the beginning of the ceremony, the hall was darkened completely. Then a bell, like a clear note of courage and hope, sounded in the darkness. A red spotlight gradually shed warm light on the leaves of the bodhi tree in the center of the stage; and then a mystical blue light revealed the focus of devotion, a statue of Shakyamuni Buddha. To the sounds of music by the Kōsei Band and Chorus, a line of glowing lights formed across the stage and up the aisles of the auditorium. The lights were candles held in the hands of young girls of the Kōsei-kai Young Adults' Group. Some burning strong and bright, some flickering and pale, all of them moved steadily toward the figure of Shakyamuni. Reaching the stage, they first formed a circle of light; then they became a great glowing lotus. Standing among the lights, I thought that, though the power of each individual is small, by combining strengths, we can make a garden of this world, just as the girls with their candles, each only a small flame in itself, were able to come together to form a dazzling lotus of light.

The enthusiasm with which the members of Risshō Kōsei-kai joined in the prayers for world peace seemed to make a fresh and profound impression on the foreign guests. The members of our organization, for their parts, were eager to hear reports on the Kyoto conference from the foreign representatives. The first to make such a report was Archbishop Angelo Fernandes of India. In his remarks, he said that people of religious faith cannot stand by silent and do nothing about the poverty, injustice, and inequality that are already too prevalent in the world. He said that the first thing we must do is inform as many people as possible of the wretchedness that exists. Then we must provide assistance to the poor and oppressed. This aid must not be merely material: it must include spiritual support that will help the poverty-stricken and downtrodden to stand on their own. It made me very happy to hear how closely the words of Archbishop Fernandes agreed with my own thoughts and with the major aims of Kōsei-kai. Our mission is the opening of the hearts of all people and the planting in them of the desire to search for religious truth by following Shakyamuni Buddha's spirit of equality and great wisdom. And I have long insisted that, by means of individual religious practices and disciplines, each of us must strive to become a moving force in bringing peace to the world.

Other speakers on the platform at the services for world peace included Dr. Dana McLean Greeley, of the United States. Dr. Greeley, who had served as one of the chairmen at the peace meeting in Kyoto, said that those who live by the sword shall perish by the sword. He added the belief that, if the will of seekers of peace is strong, peace for the whole world can be achieved. He concluded by saying that all of us must strive together for the attainment of our goal. The next speaker was Metropolitan Galitsky Philaret, patriarch of Moscow, who commented on the distribution of the world's wealth as the cause of poverty. He said that the wealth of the world belongs to all peoples and that we ought to apply human wisdom to its development and more equitable distribution. But he insisted that the first thing to be done in the cause of global peace is the cessation of military preparations by all nations.

The building in which these speeches were made is called Fumon ("open gate") Hall. The spirit that built it and that it symbolizes by its very existence is the will to realize peace, equality, and justice on all levels of human society. In other words, the spirit of the open gate is the determination to guide all peoples to a way of life based on the Truth.

Kōsei-kai's Great Sacred Hall is a place for discussions and *hōza* counseling sessions, during which the members of the organization can deepen their religious faith, come into contact with others who share that faith, and refine and develop both faith and the individual personality. In other words, the Great Sacred Hall is a place primarily for the members of the organization. But as early as 1966, a proposal was made for the construction of another building, where the faith developed and strengthened within the membership can be directed outward to society in general. Agreement on the need for such a building was unanimous; and in the following year, ground-breaking ceremonies took place.

Buddhism is not for a specific group of people. It is for all humanity. We undertook the construction of this new hall in the hope of speeding up the process of bringing the true teachings to all the world and, in this way, of allowing all people to bathe in the compassion of the Buddha.

It was decided that the new building should be in the form of a double circle and that it should face the Great Sacred Hall. At first, there were people who argued that the building ought to be named Niwano Hall, but I opposed the suggestion. I felt that the use of the name of a single human being in connection with a building devoted to the development of all phases of culture and to the true Buddhist spirit would be presumptuous. I suggested that the building be known as Fumon Hall, or the Hall of the Open Gate. This name is a reference to the twenty-fifth chapter of the Lotus Sutra, "The All-Sidedness of the Bodhisattva Regarder of the Cries of the World," in which are described the ways in which this bodhisattva shows compassion for sentient beings and the myriad forms that he assumes to preach the Law.

In scale and equipment, Fumon Hall is one of the largest and most modern buildings in the Orient. It is outfitted with a revolving stage and with the latest acoustical and motion-picture equipment. The form of the building—two circles joined in one—is derived from the Seal of the Three Laws: "All things are impermanent"; "Nothing has an ego"; and "Nirvana is quiescence."

The twenty-eight columns on the exterior of the building symbolize the twenty-eight chapters of the Lotus Sutra. The statue of Kannon, the Bodhisattva Regarder of the Cries of the World, enshrined in the lobby on the second floor was created by Shinkan Nishikido, the artist who produced the statue of Shakyamuni in the auditorium of the Great Sacred Hall. The figure in Fumon Hall symbolizes the thirty-three forms that Kannon may assume in saving sentient beings from confusion and suffering.

Ceremonies to mark the completion of Fumon Hall had taken place on April 28, 1970. On that same day, roughly seven centuries earlier, at Asahigamori on Mount Kiyosumi, in Chiba Prefecture, Nichiren had chanted the *Daimoku—Namu Myōhō Renge-kyō*—for the first time. The day is, therefore, historic and memorable. To commemorate it and the completion of Fumon Hall, twenty thousand Kōsei-kai members from all over Japan gathered to attend ceremonies intended to mark the birth of what we call a "great palace of culture."

The prayers for world peace and the reports of foreign representatives to the Kyoto conference took place in Fumon Hall and in the Great Sacred Hall six months after the new building was finished. As I listened to the tumult of applause from twenty-five thousand people on that day, I thought, "How wonderful if Nichiren and Myōkō Sensei are observing this occasion now!" With the memory of Myōkō Sensei warm in my heart, I delivered the final message of the day. "The Kyoto conference had great significance because it was a chance for us to come together, discuss the issues at hand, and reach mutual understanding on them. But at present, we are at the stage where the program for peace has just been drawn up. The road ahead is long and will probably be rough. Nonetheless, all people of religious faith must join hands and walk toward our goal of peace."

To bring the ceremony to a close, the chorus sang a song entitled "The Road Lies Ahead." During the music, the foreign representatives to the conference all came to the stage and shook hands with members of the Kōsei-kai Young Adults' Group. The applause virtually rocked the auditorium; and the sight of many people from many lands, all wearing different kinds of clothes but all devoted to one aim, was deeply impressive. I felt life and hope glowing brightly in all faces. Everyone seemed to be experiencing a flame of friendship and trust that is impossible to describe in words.

Later we received letters of thanks for the prayer service from many of the foreign representatives who had already returned to their homelands. Mr. William P. Thompson, a Presbyterian in the

United States, wrote to say that the vitality and passionate religious faith of Kōsei-kai had made a deep impression on him and that he had reconfirmed his vow to work together with us for the sake of peace. Thich Nhat Hanh, a Vietnamese Buddhist monk, poet, and social worker, said that the activities of Kōsei-kai youth suggest the possibility of a Buddhist renaissance and that he lacked words to express his respect for our work. I was, of course, overjoyed to see that people were understanding Kōsei-kai's membership, its ideals, and its activities as they deserve to be understood.

At the executive committee meeting for the second World Conference on Religion and Peace, which took place in April, 1971, all the people who attended the prayers for world peace were unanimous in their praise for the activities of Kōsei-kai. They made the following kinds of comments.

"It was wonderful to see young people, children, and old people all working together in the hope of peace. It was especially beautiful to see many women whose eyes glowed with sincerity in the hope of peace. This is something very valuable. The meeting in Fumon Hall filled me with an awareness of the power of religion. This has all come about because of your strength as a leader."

"Your fervent but quiet passion for peace has bound the members of Kōsei-kai together. In the immense energy of your organization, I was able to see religion living today. None of us will forget how deeply moved we were by that day."

"Everyday activities are necessary in religion. Your activities as a leader in the everyday affairs of religion bore fruit at that meeting. Religious activities are founded on everyday affairs, and in the case of Kōsei-kai the foundation is firm. This proves that your leadership is reliable and strong. I have the greatest respect for this."

I listened to these remarks in silence. Though there may have been an amount of formal courtesy in what they said, these people from other lands were speaking the truth. The spiritual exchange that had taken place in Fumon Hall had refreshed the hearts of the representatives from abroad. What they said about me was unimportant. I travel throughout Japan and in many other lands on the work of the peace conference because I find the basis for such action in the Lotus Sutra. My efforts are in consonance with the wishes of the four million members of Kōsei-kai. In short, though we are distinct in body, Risshō Kōsei-kai and I are one in mind. And it was the recognition of this unity by the foreign committee members of the peace conference that made me happy.

Today in Japan there are people who misunderstand Kōsei-kai and who are very cold to the idea of the conference for world peace. There are others who try to throw cold water on Kōsei-kai efforts to help create a brighter society. But the remarks of these visitors from other lands showed that disinterested observers understand our aims as long as we are sincere. I resolved then and there to continue working in one mind with the members of Kōsei-kai.

In May, 1975, almost five thousand representatives from seventy-three nations gathered in Fumon Hall for the ninth meeting of the World Petroleum Congress. The theme of the meetings was "Petroleum for the Welfare of Mankind." Like the Olympic games, these conferences are held every four years. On this occasion, the conference began on May 11. In addition to the representatives from overseas, more than two thousand Japanese representatives attended the conference, which was of a mammoth scale and required tremendous backstage preparation. One of the main headaches of the planners was the selection of a hall. A number of buildings were considered, but for reasons of size or inadequacy of equipment, none of them proved suitable. The only choice left was Kōsei-kai's Fumon Hall. One Tokyo newspaper commented on the difficulties involved in finding a hall. The article went on to say that, because the meetings were to be held in the auditorium of a religious organization, agreement would have to be obtained from the various Islamic countries. As is known, the Islamic peoples are strict about other religions; and since much of the world's petroleum is from the Middle East, Islamic representatives at the conference would inevitably be numerous. The agreement was forthcoming, and the newspaper remarked that this revealed the authority of a newly risen religious organization.

Some of the people who spoke during the congress were F. D. Rossini, of the United States, president of the World Petroleum Congress; Manoutchehr Eghbal, managing director of the National Iranian Oil Company; Valentin Shashin, Soviet minister of the oil industry; and Rogers C. B. Morton, secretary of commerce of the United States. On opening day, I sat in the seats reserved for special guests because I was the head of the organization providing housing for the conference. The crown prince and crown princess of Japan, who attended the meeting that day, sat in the same part of the auditorium. When I greeted them, the crown prince complimented Kōsei-kai on the splendid building and expressed sympathy for the labor that preparations for the conference must have entailed.

The conference covered a wide field of subjects, including procurement, refining, and transport of petroleum, as well as other technological matters. Because of the crisis in oil supply that had arisen in 1973, the whole financial world was watching the proceedings.

Secretary Morton of the United States impressed me with the need for international cooperation in fields other than religion when he said that producer and consumer nations alike must work together to safeguard the world's petroleum supply.

The World Petroleum Congress meetings proved to me and others that Fumon Hall, built to carry Shakyamuni Buddha's spirit of equality and great wisdom to society in all cultural fields, had gotten off to a good start.

35. The Brighter Society Movement

WHEN I was invited to lecture at the Niigata prefectural general conference of the Brighter Society Movement, the local Kōsei-kai leaders took me to a shop specializing in the kind of buckwheat noodles called *soba,* which the Japanese love. People never forget the foods they enjoy during youth; and as one grows older, one experiences nostalgia for the plain fare of childhood. I am not especially particular about foods, but dishes made of rustic vegetables and herbs of the fields and mountains please my palate best. I remember with fondness bracken and osmund ferns and dishes made of yams and bamboo shoots, all of which were light and refreshing in flavor. Baked potatoes, too, were an important part of the diet of our family.

And I especially like *soba* noodles. We raised buckwheat on our land. As a child, I helped with the planting, fertilizing, weeding, and harvesting of the grain. Later I helped with the grinding in a stone mortar. To make noodles, buckwheat flour is mixed with water and kneaded well. It is then rolled thin and cut into slender noodles and boiled. *Soba* is best immediately after having been removed from the boiling water and drained slightly. For us, homemade noodles were an important staple; and I became rather proficient at their preparation.

The shop to which the Niigata Kōsei-kai leaders took me was a good one with a professional cook who knew his business. It might seem presumptuous of an amateur like me to offer advice to a professional cook. But from our conversation, he discovered that I had something interesting to impart and sincerely asked for my counsel.

I explained to him the way we had made *soba* noodles in the part of the country where I lived as a boy.

The direct, modest attitude of the cook struck me. People who are proud and arrogant about their abilities are unwilling to listen to the advice of others. But the cook in the *soba* shop had a spirit big enough to make him eager to learn from a person who knew even a little more than he. That is to say, he had the wholesome attitude that inspired him to want to learn the new and the unknown. This attitude is of the greatest importance for the person who seeks and wishes to master the way. All things are our teachers. As I ate the *soba* served in the Niigata shop, I became newly aware of the truth and weight of these words.

The Brighter Society conference, held in the Niigata Prefectural Auditorium, was larger than had been anticipated; over two thousand people attended. The members of Kōsei-kai sponsor this movement; and owing to their efforts, it has spread gradually into most of the rural areas of the nation.

Originally, in my travels about the country and in my meetings with local governors and mayors, I started the Spiritual Cultural Improvement Movement, which centered on the members of Kōsei-kai and which, though largely material in its orientation, strove to help people find a human way to live with each other and a way to put Buddhist teachings to maximum use in daily life. Though the title of the movement sounds somewhat formal, its aim was quite down-to-earth. It strove to instill in people the sense of responsibility to do such things as pick up broken bottles and empty cans carelessly left on beaches and in public places, to be kind to the handicapped, and to give consideration to the welfare of people living in homes for the elderly.

As the old maxim "Brighten the corner where you are" says, we ought to devote attention to the things that are close at hand. I always say that the person of religion is bound first to create a harmonious home. The feeling of stability and peace generated in such a home must then be spread to neighbors and gradually still farther outward to all of society. If there is trouble in the home, the Buddhist must do what he can to solve the problem. Similarly, if there is a conflict of egos in society, it is the responsibility of the Buddhist to soften the blows; resolve the conflict; and in this way, contribute to the development of a brighter society. The spreading of the spirit of peace and harmony was the meaning of the Spiritual Cultural Improvement Movement. Regional political bodies, welfare, educational, women's, and youth organizations all responded favorably to the movement. But it often happens that problems arise when Kōsei-kai assumes a leadership position.

Risshō Kōsei-kai originated the movement in keeping with the teachings of Buddhism. Since maximum participation by the largest segment of the population was a goal, it seemed advisable to make the organization of the movement flexible. We decided that we would ask welfare and educational groups to act as the major forces in the movement, while Kōsei-kai would remain active in the background. We felt that this would give the movement greater latitude for growth. In 1969, a new start was made under the name of the Brighter Society Movement.

The first meeting to take place under the new name was the Shikoku regional conference for the encouragement of the Brighter Society Movement, which was held in the Takamatsu Municipal Auditorium on the island of Shikoku. Later, nucleus organizations for the movement were established in Kyushu, central Honshu, Tokyo, northern Honshu, and many other parts of the nation. In my capacities as chairman of the Japan Religions League, chairman of the Japanese Committee of the World Conference on Religion and Peace, and a trustee of the International Association for Religious Freedom, I was invited to serve as a lecturer.

When asked the relation between the Brighter Society Movement and Kōsei-kai, I give the following explanation. The Brighter Society Movement is a civic undertaking; Risshō Kōsei-kai is only one of its sponsoring organizations. We are the kind of source of power that a relative might be. Acting as such is both our way of contributing to and serving society and a part of our mission. Our actions and service in relation to the movement reflect on the people around us and thus deepen their awareness of Kōsei-kai.

I often hear comments that the movement would like to invite me to its conferences but feels certain that I will be unable to attend because of my frequent overseas journeys. It is the mission of religion to bring peace to the heart of the individual. This peace in turn reaches from that individual to others and establishes harmonious relations between nation and nation and between mankind and nature. In other words, religion must be the power that generates peace and harmony in all aspects of life. But one religion working alone cannot achieve this goal. All religions must combine strengths to evolve true significance. Nor can such significance be found without religious cooperation, which is the reason for my travels all around the world. It is the support of the membership of Kōsei-kai that makes my journeys possible.

I continue to insist on supporting the Brighter Society Movement because the society in which we live in Japan gets worse with passing time. The cities are overcrowded; there are too many automobiles on the roads; wickedness is rife; and all kinds of unpleasant incidents occur. One of the most startling manifestations of our social ills is certainly the isolation and indifference that separate people from each other.

Five years ago, a leading newspaper carried an article stating that an unmarried man had died in his home and that it had been a week before anyone had found his body. Two years ago, a middle-aged woman died in her home; and it was eight days before anyone discovered her. Incidents of this kind show the extent to which members of society are indifferent to each other. But the worst that I have heard was this: in June, 1975, a corpse was discovered in a house; the person had been dead for two years.

People who remove themselves entirely from their neighbors and exchange words with them only when they play their television sets too loud or when their houses block the sunlight pay no attention to the elderly person who has not been seen recently or to the over-flowing mailbox suggesting that something is preventing the person from collecting his letters. I am deeply distressed to see that, while I continue my travels in the name of peace and international religious cooperation, society at home is becoming increasingly selfish and isolationist. I place hope in the Brighter Society Movement, whose members are striving to do something to alleviate the situation.

36.
Even a Small Lamp of Hope

IT WAS extremely hot and humid the night I stayed in a farmhouse in Hue, South Vietnam. Hue, an old city with a tradition of religious faith comparable to those of Kyoto and Nara, is located near the seventeenth parallel, which, at the time, divided North and South Vietnam. Many bloody battles were fought in this region. But when I was there, the war had bogged down. No automobile sirens were to be heard. At first, the only sounds were the small cries of the geckos on the walls and ceilings of the house. Stillness wrapped the town, the forest, and the fields like a thick blanket of fog. But later, we began to hear the distant thundering of artillery. Five or six shots, and the sound of the cannons stopped. Then, after a short lapse of time, the groan of the earth rumbling passed through the dark night sky. As I heard this ominous sound, I realized that the fighting was coming closer.

At the Kyoto conference, we resolved to strive for the peaceful conclusion of the Vietnam war; and as a step in that direction, each participating nation decided to send delegations representing the various religions to Vietnam on an observation mission. The delegation from the Japan Religions League arrived in Vietnam in December, 1970.

Our group of five people left Tokyo on December 18 and landed at Saigon airport at nine in the evening. I was the head of the delegation. Our plane had been three hours late, and some of the people who had come to welcome us had probably given up and gone home. Nonetheless, there was still a group from An-Quang Pagoda to greet us.

At our departure from Japan, friends had warned us to be careful and to take all necessary safety precautions to ensure that we could carry out our tasks without trouble. The people who gave us this advice were especially concerned because of the war going on in Vietnam; but when we arrived, Saigon was quiet.

Still, signs of war were plentiful. The national assembly building, located in front of the Caravel Hotel, where we were to stay, had a temporary roof because Viet Cong rockets had ripped the permanent one away. Sturdy barricades surrounded the presidential residence and the American embassy. Sentinels armed with machine guns patrolled the streets. Nonetheless, pedestrians and the people riding on Japanese-made motor bicycles did not seem to suffer under the threat they lived with. Worries about our safety seemed unfounded.

On the day after our arrival, we called at the Ministry of Foreign Affairs to explain the nature and purpose of our visit. We then went to An-Quang Pagoda, where we were greeted by the Venerable Thich Thien Hoa, chief priest; the Venerable Thich Thien Minh, the assistant chief priest; and hundreds of representatives of the Buddhist faith. Thich Thien Minh, who had represented the Vietnamese religious world at the Kyoto conference, was especially elated by our visit. In the afternoon, we called on the Venerable Thich Tam Giac of the temple Vinh Ngiem Tu and then visited the Buddhist youth center.

On December 20, we left Saigon for Hue. When our plane landed there, a large group of local Buddhists and members of the youth society and the Boy Scouts came to greet us. When our delegation drove away to go to the temple Dieu De Quoc Tu, we found ourselves accompanied by about forty automobiles and over one hundred motor bicycles driven by a protective escort of young people. On each vehicle fluttered a Buddhist flag. Along the way, hundreds of people, young and old, stood by the road shouting friendly greetings and waving Buddhist flags. Thich Thien Minh told us that the people at the airport and those beside the road had been awaiting our arrival since eight in the morning. We arrived at three forty in the afternoon.

We were told that eighty-five percent of the population of Vietnam is Buddhist. The enthusiastic welcome afforded by these representatives of that broad segment of the population gave us all the feeling of having touched the strong religious pulse of the people. About ten thousand people were waiting for us at Dieu De Quoc Tu.

On the following day, we visited Song My Pagoda, in the hamlet of My Xuyen, where we distributed relief packages to three hundred people. These parcels were part of ten tons of rice, clothing, and medical supplies donated by the various branches of Risshō Kōsei-kai and by other religious organizations. A group of people who had arrived in Vietnam somewhat earlier than our delegation had distributed the supplies in seven parts of the distressed Hue area. But these were not the first donations of the kind made in that part of the world: for a number of years, faithful Kōsei-kai members had been sending similar relief to Vietnam.

In the afternoon of the same day, we traveled to Quang Tri, which, located less than thirty kilometers from the seventeenth parallel, was the northernmost town in South Vietnam. Our way there was dangerous because the road was—or was said to be—mined. Nonetheless, over one hundred motor bicycles driven by members of the Buddhist youth center and decorated with Buddhist flags once again provided us with an escort. Watching these brave young people, I said to myself, "Even in a land aflame with war, the teachings of Shakyamuni are alive; and I am grateful."

Arriving at a small village temple in Quang Tri, we found ourselves surrounded by about five thousand people. As we gave out relief packages and shook hands, I made the following remarks.

"We have visited your country in the name of the World Conference on Religion and Peace. All of the participants of that conference—and especially Japan, a fellow Asian country—have vowed to work hard for peace. Of course, political methods and negotiations are important, but it is equally important for all people of religion to join hearts and hands and to stand up for the cause of peace."

I could feel the eyes of all the people on me. I wanted to talk with and to encourage each of them, but the exigencies of our schedule made this impossible. With regret, we moved on to the next village, where we saw deep traces of the kind of war fatigue we had not encountered in Saigon. At the small temple where we stopped, there were a thin old woman and some poverty-stricken farmers' wives and children. I saw a man limping, probably from a bullet wound received in the fighting. The faces of all these people were deeply shadowed by oppressive weariness.

War had been raging in Vietnam for twenty-five years. Someone estimated that the people killed in the war amounted to one in thirty-five of the entire population of Indochina and that the people wounded accounted for one in fifteen of the same population. The number of bombs dropped in Vietnam was three times the number dropped in World War II. The farther we went upland from Saigon, the more intense became the scars and signs of this horrendous war.

Not far from the second small village temple we visited was the Thai Lok Orphanage, operated by the Unified Buddhist Congregation of Vietnam. We called on the orphanage, where nuns were looking after the welfare of three hundred children ranging in age from tiny infants to young people sixteen years old.

At one point in the fighting between South Vietnamese government forces and the Viet Cong, the orphanage had been in the path of fire. Artillery shells burst around the frightened and screaming children, one of whom was killed by a stray bullet.

The fighting grew more intense, and the sounds of exploding cannon shells threatened to burst the eardrums of the nuns and the children. But there was no place to which they could escape in the constant rain of gunfire. Driven to desperation, the nuns decided to plead with the soldiers to halt fighting long enough for the children to find refuge. Both sides declared a one-hour cease-fire. The nuns and their charges fled to safety, but by that time three children had lost their lives.

Later, bombs dropped in raids by American forces destroyed the orphanage buildings. At the time of our visit, the nuns had managed to rebuild only a single one-story building. As I watched the children playing innocently without toys of any kind in a bare room, I had a painful feeling that I understood how the dying parents must have reacted to the sorrowful knowledge that they were about to leave defenseless young ones behind. It is estimated that there were five hundred thousand war orphans in Vietnam.

After leaving the orphanage, we passed through a village that had been occupied by the Viet Cong and then through a refugee camp on our way back to the farmhouse in Hue where we were staying. As we drove through devastated villages and places where fighting had occurred only a few hours earlier, I realized that the fears of our friends in Japan had some foundation in fact after all.

Our trip to Vietnam lasted only a brief week; but it produced rich results, for we had an opportunity to talk with many people in the war-torn regions and to discuss peace with them as we distributed relief packages. In addition, we were able to discuss peace and other matters with leaders of the Buddhist, Catholic, Cao Dai, and Hoa Hao faiths and with representatives of the universities, the press, and the peace movement.

On our return from upland to Saigon, we were told by the Japanese ambassador that the head of the Asian Department of the South Vietnam Ministry of Foreign Affairs was angry because, by not reporting our whereabouts to his office, we had caused grave concern about our safety. Our travels near the border had upset the southern government and had distressed the staff of the Japanese embassy. I apologized to the embassy and expressed my intention of going at once to apologize in turn to the Ministry of Foreign Affairs.

The head of the Asian Department was angry and sharp with me when he asked why we had traveled into a danger zone without permission. He added that had we done as the Ministry of Foreign Affairs told us a helicopter and cars would have been provided for us but that our going to such a place without approval was a source of great trouble to the government.

I said that I was sorry, but I did not actually care how much he scolded me. I knew that we had been able to light a small lamp of hope for peace in the hearts of people in the combat area. That was our real intention in going to Vietnam in the first place. I remembered the happy faces of the people who received the relief packages. I also remembered the courage of the members of the Buddhist youth center who accompanied us on motor bicycles decorated with fluttering Buddhist flags.

When I left the Ministry of Foreign Affairs, the powerful evening sun was casting long shadows on the ground. Though it was my first experience of a tart reprimand by the government of another country, I did not take it too seriously. My ears were too filled with the rumbling and the roaring of the cannons I had heard that night in the Hue farmhouse, and my heart was too full of the hope of bringing peace to the good people of the country with maximum speed for me to pay attention to a scolding.

37. Memorable Visitors

Both Michael Ramsey, then archbishop of Canterbury and primate of the Church of England, and Joseph Cardinal Höffner, archbishop of Cologne, visited Risshō Kōsei-kai's headquarters in Tokyo. Archbishop Ramsey was deeply interested in the movement to unify the Christian churches, in social problems rooted in religious and racial discrimination, in ethics, and in moral issues. He wrote many works on theological questions. As I mentioned earlier, I had tried to meet him during my trip to England following the executive committee meetings held near Boston, in 1970, in preparation for the first World Conference on Religion and Peace; however, our schedules had made a meeting impossible at that time.

But in 1973, he was invited by the Anglican Episcopal Church of Japan to spend three days in Japan meeting with church leaders and people in related fields to discuss religion and other matters. During his stay, he attended the general meeting of the National Christian Council of Japan and visited Saint Paul's University, Saint Luke's International Hospital, and Risshō Kōsei-kai.

I went to the entrance foyer of the Great Sacred Hall to greet the archbishop on the day of his visit. He was a spry man who did not look his eighty years. A soft light glowed in his clear blue eyes. As we shook hands, I noticed that his hand was large, soft, and warm. After our initial greetings, I conducted him to the sanctuary, where we stood in front of the image of Shakyamuni. I briefly explained to him the intentions of Kōsei-kai: "We are striving to bring peace to the world through the teachings of the Buddha. We feel that the basis of all religions is the belief that all human beings are the children of the Buddha or of God. Therefore we are convinced that all religions must transcend the limits of individual organizational differences in order to achieve the goal of religion itself. Since the time of the founding of Kōsei-kai we have attempted to achieve this goal by promoting cooperation among religious groups."

The look on the archbishop's face and the light in his eyes told me that he agreed with what I was saying. I continued, "That is why we always welcome visitors from other religious organizations. And we are especially honored to have you with us. It will make us extremely happy if you will observe the way we express our religious ideas and if you will take part in the next international peace conference."

The archbishop spoke in a quiet voice filled with sincerity when he said, "Among people of religion in all parts of the world, a movement is currently arising in the name of cooperation for peace. Kōsei-kai is one of the organizations working toward the realization of world peace. I think it is deeply significant that I have been given the opportunity to make this visit.

"It makes me happy," he went on to say, "to have a chance to learn of your fervent desire for world peace; to study your ideas, thoughts, aims, and the ways you practice them; and to engage in discussions with you. I have been especially impressed by the way in which the members of Kōsei-kai employ *hōza* for the sake of spiritual improvement."

Many people from religious organizations in other countries have visited Kōsei-kai, but Archbishop Ramsey particularly seemed to understand the true value of *hōza*. Several times, he said, "The steadfast study and the spirit of repentance I observe in your *hōza* counseling practices are truly wonderful." He added this comment: "The *hōza* helps you deepen mutual faith and develop a community of understanding and trust. In this sense, it reveals to me the vast energy that will help Kōsei-kai grow in the future."

Hōza provides us an opportunity to give active form to the spirit of our organization. In metaphorical terms, if the Brighter Society Movement and the movement for peace in which we take part are the body, *hōza* groups are the cells that constitute the body.

As might be expected of such a perceptive man, Archbishop Ramsey had detected the importance of *hōza* on his first visit. He was what might be called the representative of the national conscience of

Great Britain. During coronation ceremonies, his position made it necessary for him to remind the new monarch that he or she is a child of God. Archbishop Ramsey often expressed his opinions on various social issues on the British Broadcasting Corporation. Hearing his interpretation of Kōsei-kai and of *hōza,* I was deeply impressed by his personality and his role as the primate of the Church of England.

Cardinal Höffner of West Germany emphasizes social activities and is deeply interested in the development of religious sentiments in young people. Some religionists have said, "Young people today follow the impulses of the moment. Though intoxicated by the convenience of modern life, they are spiritually desolate. This state of affairs points to the present crisis of humanity." Cardinal Höffner made it clear that he deplores this situation.

I agree with him to an extent. But I feel that it is the duty of the person of religion to implant rich humanity in the hearts of people of all age groups. Indeed, I believe that people of religion ought to devote serious thought to the causes of their failure to save mankind thus far.

Cardinal Höffner went on to say, "The influence of the mass communication media—newspapers, television, motion pictures, and so on—is tremendously great. I believe that all people of religion in the world must join forces to exert a good influence on the mass communication media and, in this way, improve the effects these media have on young people." He added, "Buddhists must observe the social activities of the Christian religions, and Christians must study the spirituality of Buddhism. Both groups must learn from each other."

With this sentiment I am in full agreement. It is important to learn the good points of other religions. The willingness to learn reflects both recognition of the other party and respect for his beliefs. A sense of community and of cooperation is born of such an attitude.

I should like to take this opportunity to mention the support, both material and spiritual, that Cardinal Höffner gave the World Conference on Religion and Peace. He was good enough to ask us to hold the second conference in West Germany. When it was decided to hold the meeting in Belgium instead, he made substantial financial contributions.

In addition to Archbishop Ramsey and Cardinal Höffner, many other people from abroad have come to visit Kōsei-kai. Among them were Dr. Dana McLean Greeley, who had been extremely active in the World Conference on Religion and Peace and who was chairman of the International Association for Religious Freedom; Dr. Homer A. Jack; Alberto Moravia, the famous Italian novelist and former president of the international P.E.N. Club; Apostolic Pronuncio Bruno Wüestenberg, ambassador to Japan from Vatican City; Archbishop G. Hultgren, of Sweden; Bishop Juvenaly, of the Russian Orthodox Church; Metropolitan Galitsky Philaret, of Moscow; Thailand's Princess Poon Pismai Diskul, president of the World Fellowship of Buddhists; Thich Nhat Hanh, a Buddhist monk from Vietnam; Abraham Kaplan, professor at the University of Haifa; and Dr. Richard von Weizsäcker, an outstanding leader from West Germany.

When Bishop Juvenaly of the Russian Orthodox Church visited us, he was accompanied by people from the Soviet embassy in Tokyo. Viewed in a good light, this contingent of nonreligious people constituted a courteous formal visit. Viewed in a bad light, it was observation by government personnel. Under such circumstances, bland, amiable, noncontroversial conversation is the usually adopted policy. But I do not like bland conversation. I consider it rude to a visitor to put up a front by saying polite things that I do not mean. Consequently, I asked candidly, "I have read somewhere that Stalin graduated from a theological seminary. Is that true?"

"Yes," replied the bishop.

"If that is so," I pursued, "why did he change from a seminarian to a communist?"

Perplexity was clearly written on the face of the interpreter from the embassy.

I went on: "Marx said that religion is an opiate. I suspect Stalin found something rotten in the religion of his time that made him agree with Marx's opinion."

The interpreter was surprised. For a few minutes he and the bishop conversed together in Russian.

"Since I hadn't been born yet at the time—" the bishop said.

I thought I had asked no more than an ordinary question. But the people from the Soviet embassy obviously thought it was out of order. The confusion on their faces suggested that asking questions about the connection between Stalin and religion must be taboo. I realized this at once, but I could not see how true understanding could come of mutual concealment and hesitancy.

During our conversation, the bishop seemed to come to understand my feelings. At our parting handshake, I said, "Under the kind of system that prevails today in the Soviet Union, you are proving how true your religion is by constantly acting in such a way as to maintain the light of faith."

Under his stiff-looking beard, the bishop smiled and said, "Meeting you has encouraged me. When you have a conference of religious people, by all means invite me."

He understood and approved my wish to effect open exchanges of beliefs and opinions in a way that transcends national and ideological boundaries. Bishop Juvenaly looked directly in my eyes when he said, "You bear a heavy responsibility as a man of religion active throughout the entire world. Please take the best possible care of your health."

This made a lasting impression on me. Many people from at home and abroad have visited me at Kōsei-kai, but Bishop Juvenaly was the first to express concern about my health.

38. Steadiness

ONCE at a meeting of veteran politicians, as I was eating a tangerine, one of the men in the room asked me, "Mr. Niwano, you always look so healthy. Do you follow some special plan?"

I paused for a moment, then said, "Yes, I have a health plan." All the politicians in the room looked at me. Some of them even approached to hear what I was going to say. Laughing, I told them, "My health plan is never to tell lies."

First, they all looked thunderstruck. They had probably expected me to name something like golf as the secret to good health. Then laughter broke out all over the room.

I was not being sarcastic in saying to politicians that the way to stay healthy is to avoid lying. The mind of the person who lies is clouded and burdened. Lies are an obstruction to psychologically wholesome activity. And the person with an unhealthy mind cannot be physically sound.

My parents and my ancestors blessed me with health from my childhood. This enabled me to withstand the hardships and late hours of guidance and conferences during the founding years of Risshō Kōsei-kai and the strenuous schedule of domestic and international travel that I have kept up ever since then. My sound physical condition has made this possible, and for that condition I owe a debt of gratitude to my parents and to the gods and buddhas who have protected me.

Of course, with the passing of time, the human body ages and loses strength. This is a natural course that is beyond our control. It is not possible to prevent aging and physical deterioration, but it is possible to slow them down by adopting a safe health program that suits individual needs and conditions.

In some periods of my life, I have arisen each morning before dawn to perform the cold-water ritual. In the winter, the water seemed to cut my skin when I poured it over my entire body. But I felt psychologically fulfilled as a consequence of this discipline. I always went through this routine before any important ceremony.

The cold-water ritual became a long-established habit with me. Then one day I received divine instructions that it was no longer necessary. Still, I was so accustomed to it that I disobeyed the instructions. But when I poured the cold water over my body, for the first time in my life I received a powerful shock, as if someone had struck me with a stick. It was an uncanny thing that taught me the need to gauge regimens of this kind to one's physical condition. At that time, I was over fifty, an age in life when prudence is important.

In addition to the cold-water ritual, I have used yoga and golf as ways of keeping fit. Yoga requires patience and long training, but it has beneficial effects on the body.

I did not begin to play golf until I was fifty-eight. Until then, I had disliked the game for two reasons. First, as a farmer, I was convinced that turf would damage the soil of the golf courses. Second, I reacted against the idea of human beings' taking up large tracts of land to do no more than chase a small ball. But finally I gave in to my friends who had been trying to interest me in the game for the sake of the physical good it does.

Since, to complete a course, one must walk about eight kilometers, golf is one answer to the contemporary complaint of insufficient exercise. Looking at the distant green while walking on the turf, breathing the fresh air, and enjoying the blue sky are relaxing. As the result of the effects of golf, my legs and loins are still strong, and I can read for a long time without tiring my eyes.

In the past, I used to get a certain amount of exercise by walking my dog each morning. But the members of Kōsei-kai soon found out about this habit. Thereafter I often found people standing beside my path, hands raised in prayer and heads lowered. Since this was not conducive to carefree strolling, I soon abandoned the custom.

There is no special wonder-working health regimen, no secret method. The important thing is for the person to establish a suitable physical and mental rhythm in his daily life and to maintain that rhythm faithfully. I wake each morning the instant the radio emits the five-o'clock signal. After washing my face and doing some light calisthenics, I sit at my desk to write my diary entry for the previous day. I started keeping a diary in 1929, when I was discharged from the navy, and have kept one ever since. I have a bookshelf packed with diaries. After I have finished writing, I turn on the radio and listen to a program called the "Human-life Reader." If something in the program interests me, I make a note of it. Then I read the newspaper. Morning devotionals are conducted with the entire family. After breakfast, I watch television until the car from the headquarters building comes to pick me up.

Unless work is especially heavy, I get home at about six in the evening. After evening devotionals from the Lotus Sutra, we have dinner, which is usually enlivened by my grandchildren.

Sometimes I tease my friends by telling them how popular I am with ladies of all ages. "The young ones love to hug me," I say. Of course, the ladies to whom I refer are my family: my wife, my daughter-in-law, and my grandchildren, who greet me each evening on my return from work. The minute I sit down, the little girls climb up in my lap. The time I spend holding my granddaughters on my knees after dinner is the most restful in my day. I usually go to bed at ten or ten-thirty. This is the rhythm that, with very rare alterations, governs my days. It is the basis of my good health.

Although it has nothing direct to do with health, I am now studying calligraphy and ink painting. I started both in the spring of 1970. Ink paintings by famous Zen priests have distinctive characteristics. I am very much attracted to painting pictures of Bodhidharma (the twenty-eighth patriarch in line from Shakyamuni Buddha and the first Zen patriarch in China), who was born long ago in southern India. It is said that he was an unusual child from his early years. According to a traditional story, Bodhidharma's father once showed his sons a jewel and asked them what they thought of it. Bodhidharma's elder brothers commented on its beauty and luster. Bodhidharma, however, said, "Humanity is more precious than this jewel, and the greatest thing in the world is the Law." Bodhidharma's very name means "enlightenment to the Law." Later in his life, Bodhidharma traveled to China, where he meditated for nine years facing a wall. Because the greatness of the spirit of this man is something that we ought to learn from, I use him as a subject for my pictures.

On painting days, I do five or six pictures. Though the ink is called monochrome black, in fact it is said to have five different tonal qualities. Making each picture express what I want it to say is not a simple task. But I feel refreshed and composed after working on a picture when I have been able to enter the realm of total concentration known as *samadhi*. People suspect that my back must hurt after kneeling for a long time on the tatami to paint. Actually, however, I always feel physically and mentally better after a painting session. I intend to go on painting pictures of Bodhidharma because the remembrance of his nine years of meditation is both warning and encouragement for me in my work in the name of the World Conference on Religion and Peace.

39.
Duty Before Personal Feelings

THE executive-committee meetings of the World Conference on Religion and Peace were scheduled to take place in New York from November 2 through November 4, 1971. Discussions at the meetings were to deal with the second world conference. Representatives from eight nations plus observers were to attend. I was to represent Japan.

A large group of well-wishers gathered at Tokyo International Airport to see me off on the afternoon of October 27. At two fifty, not long before takeoff, the administrative director of Kōsei Hospital approached me. He had a pained look on his face as he whispered in my ear, "Mr. Izumida has just passed away."

"Kazuo? Dead?" I was unprepared. My voice trembled.

"Yes. About ten minutes ago. Doctors from Kōsei Hospital rushed to him. They did what they could, but it was too late."

The director of the hospital bit his lip and hung his head. At that moment, the loudspeaker announced the departure of my plane. The people who had accompanied me to the airport wished me well and urged me to take care of myself. None of them knew of the death of my son-in-law. I tried to keep my usual smile on my face as I bade them farewell, but my heart was heavy with the thought of my third daughter, Yoshiko, and the grief she must be suffering at the loss of her husband.

With a roar, the jet plane climbed into the late fall sky. Soon the streets and buildings of Tokyo receded into the distance. The capes and offshore islands became miniatures edged with narrow strips of white breakers.

"Excuse me, Mr. Niwano, but I'm a member of Kōsei-kai. Before

I joined I was scarcely worthy to be alive. But becoming a member has changed everything for me."

Quite by coincidence, the woman seated next to me on the plane was a Kōsei-kai member. She had married an American military man who had died. A widow, living in a foreign country, she had lost all incentive to go on. Fearing that death might be near, she began to be anxious. "But once I came into contact with the teachings of Kōsei-kai, I found courage and hope."

"No matter what the circumstances or environment," I said to her, "each human being has a mission to perform. Until spiritual enlightenment occurs, however, the person may not recognize his mission. The fundamental importance of the teachings of Kōsei-kai is to awaken the individual to his role in life and the road that he must travel to fulfill it."

The woman thanked me, brought her hands together in a prayerful attitude, and finally fell silent. As I looked at the cloudless blue sky, deep blue sea, and pale yellow horizon, my mind went back to my daughter Yoshiko.

She had married Kazuo Izumida in December, 1962. My two elder daughters had both been married in Niigata while my family and I were living apart. But Yoshiko was married in Tokyo. At the time, I was saving money to give her a wedding present. But I decided that I ought to donate the money to the building fund for the Great Sacred Hall. People from all over the country were sending in their contributions, and construction was rushing ahead in order to meet the target completion date of 1964.

When the family had been sent to Suganuma, in Niigata, my eldest son, Nichikō (whose name was changed from Kōichi in 1970), had been in the first year and Yoshiko in the third year of primary school. She was a sensitive girl who always made good grades. The virtual exile of living away from me in the country awakened simple, childish, but strong doubts in her mind.

Day by day, the family worked in the fields. There was no way of knowing how long this life would continue. Furthermore, there were few letters from me. "Father is a religious leader who saves other people. But why doesn't he live with us? Why does he inflict hardships on mother? Can religious leaders save the masses if they can't save their own families?"

These doubts, coupled with her concern for her mother, made Yoshiko distrustful of me and of Myōkō Sensei. Though some people might criticize her as narrow and selfish, actually she was merely unable at the time to understand Risshō Kōsei-kai's teachings and the Truth. Her distrust was born of her great sympathy for her mother's plight and of her belief that her father had been taken away from the family. I could not blame her.

When Yoshiko was in the second year of high school, she and her classmates went on a school trip to Kyoto and Nara. On the way back to Niigata, she and one of her friends called at the Kōsei-kai headquarters. Myōkō Sensei was sincerely happy to see them. She prepared food and went so far as to buy souvenirs. Some time later I received letters from Yoshiko and her friend thanking me, but no one wrote to Myōkō Sensei. I wrote the following letter to my daughter.

"I imagine that you are going ahead with your studies. I asked you to write a letter of thanks to Myōkō Sensei. Have you done it? I received a letter from your friend. Has she written to Myōkō Sensei?

"I know that you consider our way of life unreasonable and that you find emotional conditions extremely complicated. But as I have said to you often in the past, gratitude is gratitude; and you must try to view all issues from both sides.

"You graduate next year. If you are to go on to a women's college, you must prepare yourself by studying very hard. There is no point in discussing things with outsiders. Rely on what I have to say, on your own efforts and talents, and on fate.

"But since the gods and the buddhas determine fate, your true mental and spiritual state will depend on whether you are in harmony with them. I don't have to tell you that the proper attitude to have is to give each issue the significance it deserves and strive always for self-improvement. Everything taken into consideration, you probably are fated to be as happy as anyone else. The discipline you will have to undergo, however, may not be easy.

"You do not have to give thought to your school grades. The important thing is to develop what is good in yourself and gradually to correct what is bad. Reveal your own character, even to the extent of looking foolish if it is honest to do so. Listen to the criticisms of other people, and do the best you can to correct your faults as fast as possible. Always have the perfection of your own personality in mind. Self-perfection, not school grades, is the important thing. Be sincerely devoted. Live a life in which honest words are matched by honest deeds. Live a life of religious faith and good conscience. It doesn't matter if you follow others. Help people to go ahead first, then think of yourself. Always remember that what you do for the sake of others is more for your own sake than anything else can be. Work to make maximum spiritual progress without forgetting to be grateful to the gods and buddhas."

At about the time that I sent this letter, Yoshiko, who had no idea when our family would be reunited in Tokyo, made up her mind to become a schoolteacher and to care for her mother herself. The older girls were already mature. They had some understanding of the situation. The younger boys, Kinjirō and Hiroshi, were still too young to be concerned. The children who suffered most throughout the ten years in which we lived apart were Nichikō and Yoshiko. Nichikō kept his sorrows to himself. But Yoshiko did not fail to tell me how she felt. That, combined with the fact that she was my youngest daughter, made her especially conspicuous in my thoughts.

Years later, when she was dressed for her wedding, she knelt in the traditional fashion, putting both hands on the tatami in sign of humility, and lowered her head as she uttered the words that most Japanese brides say to their fathers: "In many ways, you have cared for me for a long time." I still recall the deep emotional feeling I experienced on hearing those words.

Kazuo Izumida, who had graduated from Keiō University, at first knew nothing about Kōsei-kai. There was something very pure about his personality, and he and my daughter Yoshiko were very close. When he visited my house, he made himself perfectly at home. He had no religious faith; but after a while, he came to study the Lotus Sutra and became a fervent member of Risshō Kōsei-kai. The married life of the young couple was perfectly harmonious; they had three sons. I felt completely at ease about their lives.

Two days before my departure for the executive committee meeting in New York, we held a small family party at my house. Kazuo politely poured sakè for all of our relatives. Before going home, lowering his head in a bow, he courteously wished me a safe journey.

I thought that it was strange that he should do so since I was certain that he would come to the airport on the twenty-seventh to see me off. Still, I smiled and nodded in response to his words. But those words were to be our final exchange in this life. The following day, Kazuo drove his car to work and collapsed when he arrived there.

When I heard the sad news of his death, just before I was to board my plane for New York, I could see Yoshiko's grieving, sorrowing face in my mind's eye. I wanted to cancel my trip and remain by her side. But then I realized that it would be impossible for me to do so. Although, as a father, I wanted to be with my stricken child, I was myself a child of the Buddha. As such I was embarking on a mission dedicated to the attainment of peace for the whole world. Carrying out my task was the best way for me to demonstrate love for my wife and children.

On the plane, I straightened up in my seat, looked for a moment at the distant sky, then closed my eyes and recited the *Daimoku*.

At the airport in San Francisco, local Kōsei-kai members greeted me; and I returned their greetings with a smiling face. One Japanese woman of about forty years of age turned to me with tears in her eyes and said, "My husband is a Negro. For years I have harbored a nagging feeling that I would be happier if he were not black. That feeling vanished when I first began studying the teachings of Kōsei-kai. Recently, my husband has begun telling me that he thinks we are a very happy couple."

I congratulated her on her happiness; and she went on to say, "In the past I have had experiences that were too bitter to describe. I had no one to whom I could talk about my troubles. I felt as if I stood alone in a deserted field extending all the way to the horizon. But after I came into contact with the Buddha's Law, everything changed. As my husband says, we are living a truly happy life. I flew all the way here to thank you."

The woman began sobbing again. She had flown to San Francisco from Chicago. I said to her, "The Buddha is protecting you. Make spiritual progress and treasure the happiness you now enjoy." Her face seemed to light up when she heard this. Although the Law of the Lotus Sutra knows no national boundaries, this Kōsei-kai member was isolated in a foreign country, in a place where she had few fellow believers and only rare opportunities to hear sermons on the sutras. Nonetheless, her faith was all the stronger. The tears in her eyes seemed very beautiful to me.

I smiled when I talked to this woman as I had smiled earlier in speaking with the Kōsei-kai member on the airplane. But when I was alone in my hotel room, a tremendous burden of grief settled on my heart. Although in this life it is impossible to predict the coming of the end, I felt my breast torn with grief over the sudden death of a man as young as Kazuo Izumida. On the following morning, I awakened earlier than usual.

No matter where I am, whether I am traveling in Japan or in foreign countries, I never fail to have incense and a small focus of devotion with me. On that morning, I lighted the incense and read from the Lotus Sutra. Usually I observe these small services with whoever is accompanying me on my journey. But on this occasion, I performed them before anyone could come to my room. They were prayers for the repose of Kazuo Izumida. I sent the following letter to my daughter.

"I am at a loss to know how to express my grief and sorrow at this sudden tragedy. Because it happened at the moment of my departure, I was unable to do anything but rely on the doctors and pray. All of this emphasizes the truth of the Buddhist belief that there is no constancy in this world. Nonetheless, your father was profoundly shocked. I was worried, of course, all the way to the airport; but when I heard the news from the hospital director, I was beside myself. I still seemed to hear Kazuo wishing me a safe journey, just as he had done at the party on the night of the twenty-fifth.

"Though I realize that there is no constancy in this world, I still regret what has happened. I feel that we might have taken better care of him earlier. But now it is too late. Your responsibility becomes very great. It is important that you brace yourself and try to grow spiritually stronger.

"In my hotel room in San Francisco, I read excerpts from the Lotus Sutra and the entire twentieth, twenty-first, twenty-fifth, and twenty-eighth chapters as a prayer for the repose of his spirit.

"Only a few days ago, in the *Bouquet of Life,* by Professor Daigaku Hanaoka, I read a passage about Ejō, the second patriarch of the temple Eihei-ji. While Ejō was studying under Dōgen, his mother fell gravely ill. According to the rules established by Dōgen, priests could visit their homes for a period of three days, twice a month. Apart from this visit, they were not allowed to absent themselves from the temple. Ejō's fifty colleagues urged him to obtain the head priest's permission and to return home, since it seemed his mother was about to depart this life. They argued that it would be highly unfilial of him not to be with her at such a time. Dōgen, who was listening to this, remained silent. After a while, Ejō shook his head and said, 'The precepts of Buddhism are more important. It would be more unfilial of me to break the ancient precepts in order to follow a personal inclination in connection with my suffering mother. If I broke the Buddhist precepts for a personal feeling, I would cause my mother to commit a final sin that would win eternal ruin for her.' After this, Ejō went unfalteringly about his religious study and training.

"I hope that this illustration will help you to understand my feelings and the way I had to force back my tears when I learned of the death of a son. I shall try to calm my heart while carrying out my duty before returning home. What I have said may seem clumsy, but please accept my deepest sympathies."

The executive committee meeting held in New York was highly eventful. First, we discussed the results of the first World Conference on Religion and Peace, heard reports from various participating nations, and then saw from the increasing effects of the conference that the seeds we had sown were taking root. But the major topic of interest was the second world conference.

Feeling that for the sake of maximum participation it would be wise to hold the conference in Europe, I made the following remarks: "Since Japan is a nation with a peace-oriented constitution, a nation that has forever renounced war, it was a suitable place for the first world conference. Happily, that first meeting has produced great results. But we must not stand still. For the next conference, we must make preparations for a policy that will stimulate greater participation on the parts of socialist nations."

Many of the members of the executive council saw eye to eye with my proposal. After debate and discussion, it was decided to hold the second world conference in 1973 in a suitable European country. Further, for the sake of greater harmonious cooperation between the United States and Japan, it was decided to hold a joint religious council meeting.

The Inter-Religious Consultation on Japanese-American Relations took place in June, 1972, in Honolulu. It was attended by forty representatives of the Christian, Buddhist, Shinto, and Jewish faiths and by specialists in the fields of politics and economics. Adopting the common stand that there should never be a recurrence of tragedies like Pearl Harbor, Nagasaki, and Hiroshima, those of us present exchanged thoughts and opinions fervently from early in the morning until late at night. At the time, the American government was adopting a protect-the-dollar policy that was breeding discord in economic relations with Japan. But for five days, we carried out our religious conference in a totally harmonious mood of affection and friendship.

This joint meeting promoted friendly relations among people of religion from both nations. Furthermore, it was an important step toward the realization of plans for the second World Conference on Religion and Peace. One of the important concrete results of the meeting was the massive "Honolulu Declaration," copies of which were sent to the governments of both countries. The keynote of the declaration and of the entire conference is contained in the following quotation: "A mutual interpenetration of the religious communities in many parts of the world is growing in intensity as communication becomes more readily available. We are compelled by various religious imperatives to work to make this encounter result in human helpfulness rather than competitive self-assertion."

At the conclusion of the executive-committee meetings in New York, we attended a meeting of the United Nations. Unfortunately, owing to his illness, we were unable to carry out our plans for a meeting with U Thant. We did see Adam Malik, however; and he listened eagerly to our explanations of the nature and purpose of the World Conference on Religion and Peace. He said that speaking from the standpoint of the entire United Nations he wanted to cooperate with us, especially since the activities of religious people were gaining in importance and were winning increasing confidence throughout the world. Listening to his words of intense interest, I had the feeling that we were truly on the way to the realization of the second conference.

The sky was dove gray when I arrived at Tokyo International Airport. I was stricken with a new pang of grief when I noticed the absence of Yoshiko Izumida among the group of people who came to greet me. Because of the tragic news I had received at my departure, the trip had been a gloomy one for me; but I could not let my personal suffering show. Fulfilling my duty with as good grace as possible seemed to be the least I could do in the way of a parting gift for the spirit of my son-in-law.

I am certain that other leaders of Kōsei-kai have suppressed personal feelings and family distress in order to fulfill their tasks. It is because it has leaders willing to make this kind of sacrifice that Kōsei-kai continues to flourish. I take this opportunity to express my gratitude to those leaders.

40. Louvain

THE SECOND World Conference on Religion and Peace was held in the city of Louvain, about thirty kilometers east of Brussels. The city, the name of which means "praise God," is surrounded by greenery. Of the sixty-four thousand people who live there, thirty-one thousand are students at the local university, which was founded in 1426 and is one of the world's leading Catholic institutes of higher learning. The large buildings of red brick that grace the town are for the most part university buildings or churches. The chimes of a clock tower announce each hour, and about fifteen minutes' walk from the center of the town are grassy fields and groves of chestnut trees.

The proprietor of a local shoe shop was very proud to announce to all comers that religious leaders from the whole world had come to hold a meeting in his beloved town. At the second world conference, fifty-three nations were represented. At the first conference, in Kyoto, there had been representatives from only thirty-nine nations. The second conference showed a heartening increase of fourteen nations.

That meeting marked an important turning point in the religious history of Europe and of the world. Although some of the increase in representation came from developing nations in Africa, a large percentage was from European nations. Europe has a long history of religious antagonism and warfare among the various branches of Christianity that have grown up there. The willingness of the leaders of those religious groups to abandon old prejudices and come together in one building for the sake of discussions of definite ways to promote peace suggests the initiation of an important new trend.

Many people contributed time and effort for the sake of the success of the meeting. Queen Fabiola of Belgium acted as head advisor. Leon Cardinal Suenens, also of Belgium, was chairman of the committee. Representatives of the Christian, Judaic, and Muslim faiths, as well as Jean Rey, former chairman of the European Economic Community; Pierre Harmel, of the French government; and Edward Massaux and Pieter De Somer, representatives selected by the president of the Catholic University of Louvain, formed the committee for the management of the conference. At the opening meeting, as the chairman of the Japanese Committee and the chairman of the first conference, I made the following remarks.

"I am deeply honored and privileged to be given this opportunity to speak to you at the very beginning of our second World Conference on Religion and Peace. As chairman of the Japanese Host Committee for the first world conference, I know the problems—and opportunities—involved and so I am glad to speak as we inaugurate this second conference.

"I remember with strong affection the historic first World Conference on Religion and Peace held in October, 1970, at Kyoto, Japan. We transcended our national boundaries and our religious boundaries. It was, I think, a great achievement in the history of world religions. At that conference, we discussed earnestly the problems that prevented peace and we talked with each other about what leaders of religion can and should do to ensure world peace with world justice. Through the conference, we deepened our mutual understanding, promoted friendship, and pledged to make further efforts for world peace by our continued cooperation.

"Time flies fast. It is already four years since we held the first world conference. During these years we, as members of the continuing World Conference on Religion and Peace, continued our works for peace. However, conflicts and regional wars have still occurred in some areas of the world and many of the difficult issues remain. Indeed, some of the issues have become more acute since last we met, especially such problems as pollution, population, and the shortage of such resources as oil and food. These are global issues demanding global solutions.

"We must, to face these fast-accumulating problems, reform our political and economic systems and structures. It is the mission of us leaders of religion to make people realize fully that we all belong to the human family and that we must all practice inner restraint to prevent social greediness.

"It seems to me that we should repent here that we have not been strong enough to realize the love of God and to practice the deeds of benevolence of the Buddha for the solution of various agonies that are facing mankind. Further, we should reconfirm and pledge to God and the Buddha our determination to make our best efforts at this conference."

As I spoke, I was aware of burning gazes and of a powerful tension in the air resulting from the passionate longing for peace and the deep sense of mission of the members of the audience.

In an article about our conference, one of the Japanese newspapers said: "Because they feel that religion and people of religious faith are powerless to do anything about the problems facing the world, the journalistic media have paid no attention to the announcement that at the end of this month the second World Conference on Religion and Peace will be held at Louvain, in the suburbs of Brussels.

"While speaking of the crisis of civilization and the end of the world, people continue to devote themselves to faith in reason and in the almighty material things of life. They insist that man must use his powers of reason to solve the problems that he has created. Controls must be applied to solve the population explosion; controls must be applied to consumption in order to prevent the exhaustion of the world's physical resources; limitations must be applied to nuclear weapons to prevent the threat of a nuclear war; social welfare policies must be adopted to ensure human happiness. At any rate, there is still time before the final cataclysm.

"People who argue in this way ask, 'What good can gods and buddhas do for the mind of man?' 'What value to practical politics is a meeting of people of religion who discuss peace?' This general view of the journalistic media toward our efforts indicates the powerful hold faith in scientific technology and reason still have on the minds of contemporary human beings.

"But it is the very faith in science and reason that has caused the current world crisis. In the relentless drive to satisfy human greed—mistakenly considered a good in its own right—man has come to regard everything other than himself as an object for his use. In a vehicle with the engine of greed open full, he is speeding down a highway called material progress. But he has not yet realized that the brake of reason is broken.

"Give no thought to death or tomorrow. Trust only in historical progress. This kind of Western rationalistic thought has guided the world until the present. But the man driving the vehicle is beginning to do odd and disturbing things with the steering wheel. At last, the person of religion, who until this point has remained asleep, has awakened. Religious people from the whole world have decided to overcome their differences and to come together in Louvain.

"Oppressed by material civilization, representatives of the established religions—Christianity, Buddhism, Shinto, Islam, Hinduism, Judaism, Sikhism, Zoroastrianism, Jainism, and others—find in this meeting a chance to begin programs of reviving their teachings and of restoring their faith."

I have made this lengthy quotation because I think it is a comparatively accurate view of the conference. Believing firmly in technology and reason, man is racing along in a vehicle with the engine of instinctive greed open full. What can be at the end of the road? Even those people who realize that the destination is destruction rarely rise to take action. The World Conference on Religion and Peace serves as a stern warning bell.

Not all of the journalistic reactions to the Kyoto conference were positive. But the conference in Brussels could not be overlooked because of the topics it covered. The basic theme was "Religion and the Quality of Life." Four workshops were formed to deal with the subtopics: "Disarmament and Security," "Economic Development and Human Liberation," "Human Rights and Fundamental Freedoms," and "Environment and Survival." Further energetic and passionate debates and discussions were held in five commission sessions.

Although the conference was to an extent covered by Japanese journalists, in Europe the proceedings of each day's meetings were carried in full in the newspapers. The proper evaluation of the significance of the conference as reflected in the articles in European journals made me happy. We had progressed a long way from the conditions that had prevailed at Kyoto. And as I read the daily articles, many scenes that had taken place during the four years of preparation for the conference flashed into my mind.

In April, 1972, the Japanese Committee of the World Conference on Religion and Peace was set up; until that time, activities in connection with the conference had been carried out by the Commission on International Affairs of the Japan Religions League. But as the conference developed, a separate organization became essential. That committee was referred to as a domestic Japanese ecumenical movement, in comparison with the ecumenical movement that was playing an important role in world Christianity at the time. When selected as the first chairman of the committee, I vowed we should perform our duties in a spirit of sincerity and respect and reverence for truth, humanity, and harmony. "Minimum peace means the absence of war. Maximum peace means a world in which all people respect each other and live in a spirit of harmonious mutual love and compassion. Although we have not yet succeeded in achieving even minimum peace, we must realize that our mission as people of religion is to define maximum peace." These words were spoken by Professor Yoshiaki Iisaka of Gakushūin University, in Tokyo, but they represent the goal toward which the Japanese Committee of the World Conference on Religion and Peace must strive.

The decision to hold the second conference in a "suitable" country in Europe was taken at an executive-committee meeting in New York, in 1971. Thereafter, no further progress was made. My trip to West Germany and three other European countries in the summer of 1972 was for the sake of preliminary preparations for the conference, the scheduled date for which was 1973. I felt that if the meeting was to take place in Europe, West Germany was the best place.

At Bonn, I discussed West German religious affairs with Dr. Maria Lücker, who had been a member of the executive committee for the Kyoto conference, and with the Reverend Norbert Hans Klein. I learned that there are important leaders of Protestant, Catholic, and Eastern Orthodox groups in West Germany and that President Gustav Heinemann of West Germany had served as an officer in a Protestant organization.

The question of selecting a meeting place demanded careful consideration, but promptness too was important. My next step was to travel to Cologne for a discussion with Joseph Cardinal Höffner, to whom I expressed my hope of holding the conference in West Germany. As the cardinal shook my hand and looked directly at me with his impressive, clear blue eyes, he expressed agreement with my wish. (As I mentioned earlier, Cardinal Höffner visited Kōsei-kai headquarters in Tokyo.) Then I and other representatives of the executive committee called on President Gustav Heinemann in the official residence. Together with me were Dr. Lücker, Dr. Greeley, and the Reverend Toshio Miyake of the Konkō-kyō Church of Izuo. We explained the nature of the Kyoto conference and expressed our hope of holding the second one in West Germany. The president was enthusiastic and offered full cooperation because he felt that a peace movement on the part of people of religion was of the greatest importance. He added, "This is only a personal opinion, but it would be most meaningful if the second World Conference on Religion and Peace could be held in Berlin."

I was in full agreement with his sentiments. At the end of World War II, Berlin was divided into east and west zones. The scars of war remain in the city, and I hoped that a world conference for peace there would help heal them. Our interview with the president was scheduled for only twenty minutes, but the discussion was so vitally interesting that the time was extended until it had consumed a full hour. Even when it finally became necessary to leave the official residence, we still had many topics left to discuss.

In addition to meeting the president of West Germany, I had an interview with Metropolit Irenäus, the highest leader of the Greek Orthodox Church in Western Europe. I attended a meeting of the Catholic Committee for Justice and Peace, where I made a report on the Kyoto conference and explained the purpose of my visit to West Germany. At a dinner meeting of the West German Catholic Central Committee, I discussed many things with religious leaders. Later I met Bishop D. Hermann Kunst, who represented the Evangelische Kirche to the West German government, and Dr. Metz, executive secretary of MISEREOR, the Catholic organization for development and self-help. Both of these men promised to cooperate in plans for the conference.

Later I visited Switzerland and Holland. In both countries I was very busy listening to and sharing opinions about the conference with such people as Bernard Cardinal Alfrink, the top Catholic leader in all Europe, whom I met in Holland; and Dr. Joseph J. Spae, general secretary of SODEPAX (the Committee on Society, Development and Peace of the World Council of Churches together with the Pontifical Commission on Justice and Peace), whom I met in Switzerland. When I returned to Japan, I felt as if a great burden had been lifted from my shoulders, since we had advanced beyond the executive committee's vague "suitable" country to a definite location: Berlin.

But somewhat later, the tragic events at the Munich Olympics occurred. Understandably, the West German authorities were nervous about holding a large international conference, and it became necessary to seek another European location.

I traveled to Europe again, this time visiting religious leaders in Hungary and Romania. I called on a monastery in the outskirts of Cluj, in Romania. The monastery was located in much more remote mountains than I had expected; we still had not arrived after thirty minutes' driving. As I looked at the early summer landscape of Eastern Europe from the car window, I suddenly remembered that I had brought no gift. I make a custom of taking small presents to places that I visit for the first time. The gift itself is of no importance; it might be anything. It is only that offering something expresses the spirit in which I come. I consider it a matter of courtesy.

We arrived at the hilltop monastery just before noon, and the abbot kindly invited me to lunch. After the meal, I removed my pocket watch and offered it to the abbot as a token of my appreciation for the warm hospitality of his monastery. After I explained the meaning of the ideogram *wa* ("peace") engraved on the watch, the abbot, with wide-open eyes, said that he was happy to accept the gift and that he would preserve it as one of the treasures of the monastery.

Finally, at the conclusion of this third trip to Europe, we decided definitely to hold the second World Conference on Religion and Peace in Belgium. My own part in the decision was small. It was the cooperation of many coworkers and the support of the more than four million members of Kōsei-kai that made it possible for our discussions to prove convincing and to bear fruit. With the determination of a site for the conference, my mission was nearly accomplished. I suspect that I may be better suited to preliminary preparations of this kind than to appearing in the limelight.

The second World Conference on Religion and Peace was held during the week between August 28 and September 3, 1974. Debates, plenary sessions, commission sessions, executive committee meetings, and group councils took place day and night. It was not unusual for the day's proceedings to continue until ten in the evening. On one occasion, when discussions had lasted until one thirty in the morning, a delegate jokingly said, "Well, everyone, see you tomorrow—I mean today!"

For me, the conferences were only part of the schedule. There were meetings with the Japanese delegates, discussions with religious scholars, press conferences, and other meetings with people in the communications field. At the conclusion of a busy day, often someone would come unexpectedly and ask, "May I have a word with Mr. Niwano?" One German student who had been impressed with my book *Heiwa e no Michi* (*A Buddhist Approach to Peace*) followed me about and, whenever I had a moment's leisure, asked me to explain the teachings of Kōsei-kai, about which she intended to write a paper. I was much busier at that conference than I had been at Kyoto.

The Kyoto conference had been held in the cool autumn, not in the summer. Moreover, I am accustomed to the Japanese climate and conditions. Further, Belgium is on a time schedule nine hours different from that of Japan. Brussels' day is Tokyo's night, and it was two or three days before my body adjusted to the difference. But I had no time to worry about such things. And in fact, I was so healthy and vigorous that I surprised myself.

Four months before the second world conference, at the invitation of the China-Japan Friendship Association and the Buddhist Association of China, I visited Peking, arriving on April 20. By an odd coincidence, that was the day on which China and Japan signed an agreement relative to air travel. Liao Cheng-chih, president of the China-Japan Friendship Association, and Chao Pu-chu, president of the Buddhist Association of China, greeted me with a remark about the strange fateful connections of such coincidences.

Much information is available on the industry and the people's communes of China, but the world of Chinese religion is virtually unknown. At the time of the Kyoto conference, I had wanted to invite representatives from China but had known no way to make contacts. My hope to learn more of the religious situation there and to invite representatives to the second conference was the major purpose of my visit.

At my request to be introduced to as many religious leaders as possible, Chao Pu-chu convened a meeting of more than twenty people at the temple Guang Ji Si, in Peking. At the meeting I discussed the Chinese religious situation with representatives of the Buddhist, Moslem, Catholic, and Protestant faiths and learned that there are 800,000 Protestants and 10,000,000 Moslems in China. Religious freedom is guaranteed, and there are no restrictions on missionary activities. But the Chinese believe that Western Christianity is a tool of imperialistic aggression. Chinese Protestants have no connections with Protestants in other nations; they operate on the basis of what is called the three "selves": self-propagation, self-development, and self-regulation. All of the religious groups hold that the religions of the past were used for the benefit of imperialism and the exploitation of the people and feel that it will be some time before China is ready to take part in an international religious conference. Nonetheless, I am convinced that the way is being opened and that religious exchanges between China and Japan are the first step.

"In the West it is believed that daily life is a matter for the individual human being isolated from others. The Buddhist belief, however, is that all things are intimately related in that they all partake of the universal life-force. This surprises us but offers important suggestions for the way we ought to live in the future." This, of course, was embarrassing to us Japanese, who, after the end of World War II, have tended to abandon our tradition as old-fashioned and outmoded and to adopt wholesale Western rationalism and materialism. I am made especially aware of the rashness of the Japanese people when I see that people of the West are now beginning to assimilate as valuable many of the ideas that we have abandoned. Among these ideas is that the buddha-nature pervades all.

Another thing that impressed me about the Louvain conference was the lack of polarization into groups believing that we ought to act boldly to promote peace and groups feeling that, for such matters as development and disarmament, we must rely on specialists. In the second conference, the general attitude was that in connection with peace there must be no specialists and that everyone must do his part. Our actions must take the form of aid and compassion; but in addition, we must all remember the basic nature of religion and engage in prayers, spiritual purification, and other activities dedicated to spiritual improvement.

The belief that "dogma separates whereas service unites" symbolized another mood prevailing at the conference. In the history of man, perhaps nothing has tended to fall into exclusivism and self-righteousness as often as religion. At the second conference, we were all striving to concentrate on things we have in common and to deemphasize our differences. We wanted to break the barriers among us and to fill in the gaps separating us because we felt that this was the only way for man to survive and protect the limited resources of the earth.

The issue of violence or nonviolence sparked a heated debate in a commission on human rights and fundamental freedoms. Attending this meeting as a representative of Ghana was Bishop Peter Sarpong, who initiated a series of lively exchanges when he asked whether resistance to oppression was to be considered violence. He was speaking of the oppression suffered by the black peoples of Africa. American and European representatives stated that oppression is wicked but that to resist by means of violence is not the way of the person of religion.

Indignant at this, Bishop Sarpong lashed out: "Nonviolence means death to us!"

Silence fell on the room. When he regained composure and resumed his talk, Bishop Sarpong was being closely observed by everyone in the place.

"Who took away Africa? Not only have the black people been robbed of their land, they are now being subjected to racial discrimination. To abolish discrimination and oppression and to win back their lands, the black people have no recourse but violence. Did you call it violence when you fought Nazi Germany? Must Christians deny violence to the black people?"

It is true that peace without justice is no peace; on the other hand, employing violence for the sake of justice constitutes a threat to peace. The pronouncement of Bishop Sarpong and his attitude toward political oppression reveal the gravity of the dilemma we face in connection with peace and violence.

The remarks of the Vietnamese representative provided topics for active discussion. He said, "A year and a half have passed since peace was supposedly established in Vietnam, but foreign nations continue to supply arms. Consequently, fighting has not ceased; and during this time, ten thousand people have lost their lives." He added his wish that foreign nations would discontinue supplies of arms, for, as long as they refused to do this, warfare would go on. His comments amounted to a severe criticism of the Vietnam peace pact. The issue aroused sharp debate between the representatives of the Soviet Union, which supported the pact, and the representatives of the United States, which maintained that the pact was only a deception. As I listened to them, I recalled the poem written and delivered at the opening plenary session of the conference by Thich Nhat Hanh, monk, poet, and representative of the Unified Buddhist Congregation of Vietnam:

"I walk on thorns,
but firmly,
as among flowers."

In discussions on "Disarmament and Security," a Japanese representative asked the Indian delegation what the people of India thought of the nuclear tests recently conducted by their government. To this, an Indian representative replied, "It is only natural for a nation like India, where development is still retarded, to conduct nuclear experiments for the sake of the peaceful application of nuclear power. Ninety-eight percent of the population of India was in favor of the experiments."

Another Japanese representative, astonished at this attitude, objected: "Japan was the first nation in the world to experience the horror and misery of an atomic attack. A nuclear tragedy of that kind must never again be permitted to occur."

In a stern tone of voice, Philip J. Noel-Baker, an English recipient of the Nobel Peace Prize, replied, "Precisely. No nation should conduct nuclear experiments, no matter what the reason."

Ours was a religious meeting unrelated to political policies and national interests. As people of religion, we were all expected to express our thoughts openly, even if they ran counter to the policies of our nations. But I realized that, in cases like that of the Indian representative, speaking only as a religious leader, without consideration of national interest, is sometimes very difficult. This is a serious problem that remains to be solved.

On the final evening of the conference, we held a meeting at Saint Peter's Church in the heart of Louvain. We invited five hundred local citizens to join us and to hear a report on the conference and to listen to the "Louvain Declaration," concerning disarmament, development, human rights, and conservation of the environment. During the seven days of the conference, we had experienced spirited debates of a kind that did not occur at the conference in Kyoto. I believe that this is a sign that the religious movement is moving from a static to a dynamic phase and that the debates indicate the enthusiasm of the representatives. I was deeply impressed by the beauty of the figures of the Israeli and Arab representatives, who, at the end of the conference, shook hands and walked quietly away, side by side.

A follow-up committee solidified plans to hold the third World Conference on Religion and Peace four years later in New York. At the same time, a European Committee was established. I regard this as one of the most important outcomes of the Louvain conference, since it meant the broadening of the movement by the addition of a European axis to an effort that had earlier centered on the United States and Japan.

One morning during the course of the week of meetings, all the representatives boarded five buses and drove to the Breendonk Concentration Camp, located in the suburbs of Antwerp. Said to be the only camp of its kind preserved in its former condition, Breendonk was used by the Nazis from 1940 to 1944 to contain four thousand citizens, many of them Jews. More than four hundred people were shot or strangled there. Silent and dust-covered, the massive concrete walls, iron bars, torture rooms, banks of narrow bunks, blankets, and sunless solitary cells are just as they were during the war. Merely imagining the hellish things that must have happened there chills the blood.

In the courtyard are the remains of the execution sites: the stakes to which were tied the heads of people to be strangled and the dirt embankments that prevented the ricocheting of bullets fired at prisoners being shot. Visitors to this place stand in silence in one corner of the yard and make offerings of flowers and prayers for the repose of the souls of the people who died there. Archbishop Angelo Fernandes quietly said, "We have all been profoundly shocked by the sight of this place. Let us pray for the sakes of both the oppressed and the oppressors." Listening to him, I held my prayer beads in my hand and prayed that all the spirits of those who had been in the concentration camp would attain perfect enlightenment.

Though people have different religions and speak different languages, they all mourn the dead with the same kind of sorrow. Standing in Breendonk, I was deeply impressed with the truth that the worldwide spreading of the Lotus Sutra would do more good than hundreds of symbolic words.

On the way home from the Louvain conference, we visited Rome to make a report to the pope on the proceedings. He touched me deeply when he said that he had prayed for the success of the conference throughout its duration.

Our party arrived in Tokyo on the afternoon of September 9. The following day was the eighteenth annual memorial observance of Myōkō Sensei's death. The services were held in the Great Sacred Hall, where I made my report and a vow before the spirit of Myōkō Sensei for continued spiritual growth. As I looked at the photograph of her displayed for the ceremony, I seemed to hear her say, "Congratulations; I am watching as faith in the Lotus Sutra spreads throughout the nations of the world."

41. Better than Treasures or Traditions

ON A DAY when I had traveled to Nara to see patriarch Zen'ei Nakayama at the headquarters of the religious organization Tenri-kyō, I finished my business early and had time left to visit Tsubosaka-yama Minami Hokke-ji, one of the important temples for the Buzan branch of the Shingon sect of Esoteric Buddhism. The temple, which is popularly called Tsubosaka-dera, venerates a statue of the Thousand-armed, Thousand-eyed Kannon, Bodhisattva Regarder of the Cries of the World. It is famous throughout Japan for its associations with a story about a blind man miraculously cured by the powers of this Kannon. The story had been given dramatic form in the *Bunraku* puppet theater and in Kabuki. Many people today continue to revere the Tsubosaka-dera Kannon and to believe that it can cure eye illnesses.

At the top of a sloping path leading through groves of cedar and cypress is a gate housing statues of two fierce-looking guardian deities. Inside the gate, on the left, are four one-story houses for elderly blind people and a two-story, reinforced concrete sound library. The head priest maintains these facilities and takes part in a movement to help lepers in India, as well. Because his efforts to realize the mercy of the Bodhisattva Kannon on earth make me very happy, I proceeded at once to the temple office to make a monetary contribution.

A priest named Benki, from the temple Gankō-ji, is said to have founded the Tsubosaka-dera in the year 700. He sat in Zen meditation, holding in his hand a crystal jar (*tsubo*), considered a secret treasure of the temple, until he had a vision of the Bodhisattva Kannon. He left the jar on the top of the slope (*saka*) and carved the statue of the Bodhisattva that is now the main image of the temple. The jar and the slope give the temple its name.

At the top of a gentle incline planted with cedars that are about three hundred years old is the vermilion-painted, three-story pagoda. Beyond this is the worship hall, a deep-eaved building erected in about the fourteenth century. Still farther along stands the octagonal main hall, which houses the statue of Kannon carved by Benki. In the temple precincts, I saw young married couples with their children, middle-aged women on tours of sacred places, and groups of other visitors.

With the help of a handrail installed there for the benefit of the handicapped, a blind man was making his way up the slope to a place from which there is a sweeping view of the surrounding plain. Of course, for the blind, the view has no meaning. But for their sakes, the temple has planted flowers with rich fragrances—roses, gardenias, magnolias, sweet daphne, daffodils, and dozens of other varieties. The blind can enjoy the fragrances and the singing of the birds as they sit on the chairs arranged around concrete tables. The chairs are devised in such a way that when someone sits on one of them music flows from speakers installed under the tables. The garden becomes a place of fragrances and sounds for people who have lost the ability to see. Here and there, placards in Braille provide various kinds of information about the place.

Suddenly I heard an announcement over a loudspeaker: "Would Mr. Nikkyō Niwano of Risshō Kōsei-kai please come to the priests' quarters. The head priest of the temple would like to speak with you."

Though young, the head priest is serene and modest. He thanked me for making a contribution to the work for lepers in India; and I congratulated him on the excellent home for the elderly blind, the assistance he is offering the handicapped, and the splendid garden of fragrances and sounds. He said that in doing these things he and his fellow priests are only carrying out the duties of followers of the Bodhisattva Kannon.

Perhaps this is true; but in the present world, just this kind of work and the kind of spiritual growth it represents are in danger of being overlooked.

The head priest said, "No matter how excellent the teachings left by Shakyamuni, unless we priests put them into practice and attempt to carry them to others, they will perish. And it will be we priests who have killed the words and heart of Shakyamuni."

His comment is a stern criticism of the present state of Buddhism. A rebuke of this kind is a living thing only when uttered by a person who, like this head priest, puts his beliefs into practice. I agreed with him completely when he said, "The days of monastery Buddhism have passed. Buddhist statues of the highest aesthetic merit are only cold curiosities when they are used as objects to be shown for admission fees."

I too have often felt that many priests are very much like guides waiting for tourists. The positive activities of this head priest and his magnificent work for the help of others refreshed me. Contact with Tsubosaka-dera, which is popular with the people because it is a living realization of the compassion of the Bodhisattva Kannon, produced in me a spiritual cleanliness that I had not experienced for a long time. I decided then to make a pilgrimage to the thirty-three revered temples in the Osaka-Kyoto area.

In the past, Japanese priests traveled to China to study. While there, they made pilgrimages to famous Chinese temples. After World War II, priests visited the sacred places of India. But these priestly journeys are somewhat different from the kind of lay pilgrimages made by Moslems to Mecca, Christians to Jerusalem, and many Japanese to various holy places in Japan.

Today pilgrimages are much more comfortable than they were in the past. It is possible to board trains or planes and travel quickly anywhere one wishes. There is no specified garb for such trips. But in the past, high and low alike put on all white, including white arm coverings; donned large straw hats; and carried staffs. This costume indicated the equality of all people before the Buddha and the determination of the pilgrims to overcome all difficulties in their path.

My family preserves the memory of one of our ancestors who, for an unclear reason, decided to make a pilgrimage to the thirty-three revered temples around Osaka and Kyoto. It took four or five years to complete the journey, and when he returned home safely, he was extremely happy that he had gone. In his old age, he decided to repeat the pilgrimage. The family objected. They argued that he ought to be satisfied to have made the trip once and told him that he must be prepared for the possibility of never returning home alive. He paid no attention and, with a ceremonial farewell drink of water, departed. Everyone worried about him; and indeed, he died somewhere along the way.

I wanted to follow in his steps, to stand before a waterfall in the precincts of a temple and try to recapture the thoughts he had thought long ago, and to feel the rain in a temple courtyard while I wondered how similar rain had inspired him.

My procedure in visiting temples was first to pray before the main hall and then to examine the main image and other treasures before adding my seal to the others in the temple-office register. Sometimes, head priests who knew of me asked that I talk with them for a while. Such talks usually took place in temple offices.

In the past, I believed, and said publicly, that going from one temple or shrine to another and putting money in collection boxes does not constitute religious faith. But as I made my own pilgrimages, I found that such activities have a significance of their own. In the chapter of the Lotus Sutra entitled "Tactfulness," it is said that one may attain buddhahood by merely bowing one's head in passing a shrine or Buddhist temple.

Certainly in visits to temples it is possible to meet people whom one had not expected to meet and to hear many interesting things. The true significance of pilgrimages is not the monetary contributions, but the many different encounters that help the individual grow, refine his religious faith, and come closer to enlightenment. I found such experiences so meaningful in the first part of my pilgrimage that I decided to extend my tour to include the thirty-three revered temples in the Tokyo area, as well as those in the Osaka-Kyoto area.

In my tour of sixty-six temples, I was greeted in a variety of ways. In some temples, the priests were cold to me as a representative of an upstart religious organization. In others, they were friendly and often demonstrated interest in the work of the World Conference on Religion and Peace. The head priest at the temple Hōraku-ji, in a remote part of Ibaraki Prefecture, was especially interested in this aspect of my activities. I told him as much as I could about the peace conferences, religious circumstances in China and Vietnam, the ecumenical movement in the Christian faith, and the Brighter Society Movement.

Of all the things I observed during my travels, the most impressive was the ability of temples that make living contributions to religious activities to capture the hearts of large numbers of people. This is true of such places as the Tsubosaka-dera, in Nara, and the Kiyomizu-dera, in Kyoto. The possession of famous works of art or of a venerable tradition is not enough. For the temple to live in the minds of the people, the head priest must teach in an inspiring way, and the whole staff must attempt to put the mission of their faith into practical work. Seeing this was the most valuable experience of my pilgrimage.

42.
The Echo of "Excellent, Excellent"

On February 9, 1975, after a lecture to members of the Brighter Society Movement, held in Shiga Prefecture (northeast of Kyoto), I had an opportunity to visit the temple Mii-dera, lying at the foot of Mount Nagara, close to the shore of Lake Biwa. The main image of the temple, a figure of the Six-armed Nyoirin Kannon, is the first statue of Kannon brought to Japan by the great priest Kūkai (774–835). During the middle ages, it was kept in the palace as a guardian of the imperial family. As might be expected of a statue with such a background, it has solemn dignity and seems to radiate a light of compassionate love.

From an observation pavilion not far from the precincts of the temple, I stood and looked at the dully gleaming, lead-colored waters of the lake, which, on that cold, windy day, produced in me a mood of gentle gloom and travel weariness.

Mii-dera has been the largest temple in its immediate region since the eighth century. For centuries, the sound of its bell, cast in 1603, has brought comfort to people daily, morning and evening—especially in the evening when workers are returning tired from their day's labor. As I stood looking out over the gray waters, I seemed to hear the tolling of that ancient bell. The imaginary sound brought to my mind the hundreds of years of faith in Buddhism of the countless people who have lived within the range of its sound.

Later on the same day, I visited the great monastery Enryaku-ji, on Mount Hiei, where I made a report on the second World Conference on Religion and Peace to the supreme patriarch, Etai Yamada.

On my return home, I found a letter informing me that the Meadville/Lombard Theological School, a graduate school affiliated with the University of Chicago, wanted to confer on me an honorary Doctor of Laws degree. The sudden announcement caused me some perplexity because my life has been one of faith, not of searching for fame and glory. The person leading such a life has no need of titles and degrees. Ever since the founding of Kōsei-kai, I have lived in the Buddha's Law, especially the Lotus Sutra. In the early days, my efforts to save people from suffering and, later, my work for the peace conferences all have found their basis in the Lotus Sutra. And as long as I live, I intend to follow the same course. It is the only one for me.

But my secretary urged me to accept the degree, since doing so would mean great happiness for the members of Risshō Kōsei-kai. The reason for conferring the degree was given as my efforts for religious cooperation and worldwide peace, but this work was made possible by the support and encouragement of the entire membership. In other words, the degree would be tantamount to recognition for the work of the whole of Kōsei-kai. Ultimately, since the happiness of the organization is both my happiness and my reason for living, I came to the conclusion that I ought to accept the honor.

The awarding of the degree took place on March 5, during ceremonies to commemorate the thirty-seventh anniversary of the founding of Kōsei-kai. Thirty-five thousand people were gathered for the occasion; and the congratulatory applause as I accepted the degree from Dr. Malcolm R. Sutherland, president of the Meadville/Lombard Theological School, thundered through the Great Sacred Hall. Until that moment, I had been uneasy about the acceptance; but as I looked at the radiantly happy faces of all the people present, my doubt vanished. I was left with only joy in my heart.

That evening, after devotional services, my wife said in a somewhat unusual tone of voice, "I seem to hear a voice calling 'Excellent, excellent.' "

Wondering what she could mean by such an odd thing, I looked at her in silence. She went on, "I don't hear the voice from the sky. But the pope has sent you invitations to see him, and now you have received this honorary degree. I hear 'Excellent, excellent' because the Law you teach is true."

"That's an interesting thing to say," I remarked, lightly bringing my hands together in the thankful and prayerful *gasshō* attitude.

In chapter eleven of the Lotus Sutra, "Beholding the Precious Stupa," there is the following passage:

"Then from the midst of the Precious Stupa there came a loud voice, praising and saying: 'Excellent! Excellent! World-honored Shakyamuni! Thou art able to preach to the great assembly the Wonderful Law-Flower Sutra of universal and great wisdom, by which bodhisattvas are instructed and which the buddhas guard and mind. So is it, so is it, World-honored Shakyamuni! All that thou sayest is true.' " My wife's remark had referred to this passage.

At the time of the founding of Kōsei-kai, I spent the bulk of each day in serving the Law and was unable to devote myself wholeheartedly to the work of my small milk store. As a result, our income decreased. That was a time when our growing children had large appetites. It was only natural that my wife, on whom the entire burden of the household fell, should sometimes complain. Although she felt that religion is a good thing, she wondered about our daily needs and wanted to know how long I was going to persevere in my life of faith. But I could not abandon the affairs of the members of Risshō Kōsei-kai. Since I could not lie to my wife and give her a spurious deadline for my return to full-time devotion to business and the family, I quoted a line from the Lotus Sutra: "I shall continue my faith until I hear the voice of the Buddha calling from the sky, 'Excellent, excellent.' "

My answer to my wife was visionary; she had nothing to say to it. Usually her complaints tapered off after I made it. Naturally, she was not satisfied; and in my heart, I felt apologetic. But in those days my greatest wish was to revere the teachings and to spend even a little more time bringing them to the widest possible audience. This was the only answer I could give her.

When she suddenly made the comment about "Excellent, excellent," I recalled, as vividly as if it had been yesterday, the way my wife had been thirty years earlier. Over that long period, she has had her own feelings and impressions of the things that have happened. And as I reflected on what they might have been, I felt my heart grow full.

I must admit that "Excellent, excellent" is justified in the light of the international spreading of Kōsei-kai, the yearly increases in membership at home, the success of the Brighter Society Movement, and the vigorous activities of the Young Adults' Group. In my own family, my wife has been actively engaged in daily religious training for the past thirteen years. My sons Nichikō and Kinjirō are devoting themselves to spreading the faith. And my youngest daughter, Yoshiko, who lost her husband nearly seven years ago, has recovered from her grief and is now deeply devoted to the Buddha's Law.

On that March evening, I turned to my wife and said, "But we've only started." And she replied, "I think so, too." Being alive and having religious faith filled my heart with profound joy.

On the following morning, when the car came to take me to work, we had our usual bustling scene at the door, my grandchildren in the forefront and other members of the family behind them, wishing me a good day. As I started to get into the car, my little granddaughter Katsue, who is three years and six months old, rushed to me and asked, "Grandfather, are you going to join Kōsei-kai again today?"

"Yes, I'm going to join again today," I answered, looking into her upturned face.

I am beginning today; I am a lifetime beginner. My little granddaughter has no deep understanding of Risshō Kōsei-kai, but her words brought clearly to my mind the importance of preserving, always, the freshness of the emotional impact I experienced when I first encountered the Lotus Sutra. I stroked my granddaughter's hair for a moment then, getting into the car, closed the door. We pulled slowly out into the street.

We traveled the same road as usual. Soon the green roof of the Great Sacred Hall drew into sight. The weather was bright. I knew I would be busy again that day, but my heart was full of morning.